Autism from the Inside Out

A Handbook for Parents, Early Childhood, Primary, Post-Primary and Special School Settings

Emer Ring, Patricia Daly
and Eugene Wall (eds)

PETER LANG

Oxford • Bern • Berlin • Bruxelles • New York • Wien

Bibliographic information published by Die Deutsche Nationalbibliothek. Die Deutsche Nationalbibliothek lists this publication in the Deutsche National-bibliografie; detailed bibliographic data is available on the Internet at http://dnb.d-nb.de.

A catalogue record for this book is available from the British Library.
Library of Congress Cataloging-in-Publication Data
Names: Ring, Emer, 1960- editor. | Daly, Patricia, editor. | Wall, Eugene, 1954- editor.
Title: Autism from the inside out : a handbook for parents, early years, primary, post-primary and special school settings / Emer Ring, Patricia Daly, Eugene Wall.
Description: Oxford ; New York : Peter Lang, 2018. | Includes bibliographical references and index.
Identifiers: LCCN 2018005665 | ISBN 9781906165826 (alk. paper)
Subjects: LCSH: Autism in children--Ireland. | Parents of autistic children--Ireland. | Autistic youth--Education--Ireland.
Classification: LCC RJ506.A9 A8699 2018 | DDC 618.92/85882--dc23 LC record available at https://lccn.loc.gov/2018005665

Cover image: drawing by an anonymous eleven-year-old child with autism spectrum difference attending a mainstream primary school, reproduced with permission.

Cover design by Brian Melville.

ISBN 978-1-906165-82-6 (print) • ISBN 978-1-78707-838-3 (ePDF)
ISBN 978-1-78707-839-0 (ePub) • ISBN 978-1-78707-840-6 (mobi)

© Peter Lang AG 2018

Published by Peter Lang Ltd, International Academic Publishers,
52 St Giles, Oxford, OX1 3LU, United Kingdom
oxford@peterlang.com, www.peterlang.com

This publication has been peer reviewed.

Printed in Germany

Autism from the Inside Out

Contents

Figures and Tables

Cover image: This drawing was completed by an eleven-year old child attending a mainstream primary school. A core principle of the research on which this book is based was to capture and include children's voices. Children were invited to draw a picture of their school experience and subsequently describe the drawing to the researcher. The child described his drawing as depicting himself and his friend inside the classroom window looking out at the school yard. In this drawing, the child challenges the assumption that children with ASD prefer social isolation to engaging both with each other and their peers. Critically, the child communicates the responsibility for us as educators to create enabling and inclusive environments for all children.

ADAM HARRIS

Foreword

Since I was a very young child, Ireland has been on a journey in terms of how it understands, supports and includes children with 'special' or 'additional' educational needs. We have moved, relatively quickly, from a model in which virtually no children who thought differently were educated in their local community to a point in which the vast majority are today. Indeed, this shift in policy and thought played out directly in my own life – as someone on the autism spectrum.

When I was first diagnosed with Asperger's Syndrome as a young child, my parents faced a stark choice. Should they send me to mainstream school, where they knew I would be able for the curriculum but would receive little or no support in accessing it and could well be labelled 'the bold boy' as a result? Or should they send me to a special school, where they knew I would receive lots of support but wouldn't have the same academic opportunities or get to know my local peer group? On balance, my parents opted for the latter and I spent the first three years of my education in a special school setting. I really benefited from my time there but policy and thought began to shift too and so, shortly before my eighth birthday, I moved to a local mainstream school with a real commitment to inclusion but also supports to help me thrive such as a Special Needs Assistant (SNA) and access to resource teaching hours. This certainly changed the trajectory of my life, and the broader policy and thought underpinning educational journeys like mine has doubtless changed the lives of countless other people and, dare I say, the education system itself.

Whereas once schools and teachers may rarely have heard words like 'autism' or 'Asperger's', now you would be hard pushed to find a school or teacher anywhere in Ireland who does not have direct experience of teaching a member of the autism community. Whilst once autism might have sounded like an exotic or rare condition, it is now something that children and young people encounter as part of day to day life in their community. Indeed, the education system has become 'autism aware'.

However, there is a distinct difference between awareness and understanding. Awareness is about knowing something exists; understanding is about stepping into a person's shoes and validating their perspective. Awareness is a vital first step in any journey towards inclusion; however, it is only the first step. I am aware that Mandarin Chinese is a language; however, I don't understand it. As a result, I can't meaningfully include a person who only speaks that language. In the same sense, we must ensure that all who work in our education system truly understand autism and the unique way in which autistic people communicate, understand and experience the world around us. 'Mainstreaming' has been something of a buzzword for some time – we have mainstreamed people, but we now must mainstream knowledge if we are to ensure inclusive education is not about legal access to buildings or educational institutions but rather about unlocking a person's potential and respecting and celebrating diversity.

That is what excites me about *Autism from the Inside Out: A Handbook for Parents, Early Childhood, Primary, Post-Primary and Special School Settings*, edited by Professor Eugene Wall, Dr Patricia Daly and my friend Dr Emer Ring, with contributions from a broad range of academics from Mary Immaculate College. This book is an important tool in bridging the gap between awareness and understanding – providing all who support autistic students with accessible knowledge and practical methodologies, which can be employed both at home and in the classroom. This book builds on the proud history of Mary Immaculate College in relation to autism research and early childhood and teacher education, which has not only been extensive but has also recognized the unique needs of autistic students. Too often excellent research never converts to any real practical purpose from the point of view of families on the ground; this text harnesses a number of years of hard work into something we can all learn from. In the course of my own work as an autism advocate I have the opportunity to visit many schools and so often see excellent examples of inclusion that you would love to 'bottle' and bring to every school. This book, which is built on data from the research carried out by Mary Immaculate College staff as part of the National Council for Special Education's Autism Policy

Advice, does just that, highlighting examples of good practice which can be employed in any early years setting or school.

It is important that this book takes a long view of autism, from the early years setting through to post-primary education. I am very often asked questions by parents and teachers which look for a 'eureka' moment for me. What helped me make friends? What allowed me to cope with the transition to mainstream school? How do I manage my sensory system? The answer is never one thing or one moment. It is always the culmination of work by a variety of key people in my life, at a number of key junctures, which, over time, has enabled me to learn and to overcome some key challenges. I socialize today because my parents pushed me to join extra-curricular activities from when I was around five years old, but also because I did transition year when I was sixteen years old. I managed the move to mainstream school because I had an excellent principal and SNA in the school I moved to, but also because the special school I was in worked to support my transition for many months prior to my move. In autism, there are no quick solutions, but you reap what you sow. The work of a teacher in second class may appear to change little, but it may be cashed in ten years later for all to see! For that reason, it is important that there is better joined up thinking between educators and the sectors that make up the system. It is welcome to see a publication which very much advocates team work in terms of supporting a child. I know that an important aspect of my educational journey was the positive relationship Mum and Dad had with my school and the active role my SNA played in the Individual Education Plan planning process. Too often, titles, egos and mutual unease can lead to disjointed and even dysfunctional approaches. This book not only advocates teamwork but backs up its benefits with evidence.

It is also useful to have a distinctly Irish resource. Many parents and teachers spend their evenings trawling the web (and I hope AsIAm.ie!) or reading books with a British or American perspective. There are lots of fantastic international resources; however, there are too few Irish insights sensitive to our own system. This book will help parents, early childhood, primary, post-primary and special school teachers to understand the supports on offer to students with autism in an Irish context, the research underpinning those supports and how they can be best utilized. Due to

the Irish character of the text it should also be compulsory reading for all
policymakers with an interest in the area of inclusive education. The book
provides a balanced view of our system, examining what works well and
where we need to further develop and improve.

Most importantly for me, this book is respectful of the autism community and seeks to promote a positive discourse on the condition and how
autistic people can be best supported. This comes across clearly through
the bold decision of the editors to drop the word 'disorder', which you will
find nowhere in this book. This is most important in moving away from
a dated medical model but also in being accurate – indeed, it has always
amused me that a group of people known for being disordered and emotive
(neurotypical or non-autistic people) would call those of us who think in
definite terms and are analytical in our approach 'disordered'! However,
this handbook goes further than just language in terms of challenging our
understanding; at its core is a constant reminder about the need to take a
strengths-based approach, to recognize and affirm the different ways autistic
people think and to highlight the many 'man made' barriers autistic people
contend with daily, particularly the challenging sensory environments of
so many of our early years settings and schools.

In conclusion, this book should not sit on every shelf of every early
years, primary, post-primary or special school setting – it should be in the
hands of every educator and parent supporting autistic students!

Adam Harris
Founder-CEO, AsIAm

EMER RING, PATRICIA DALY AND EUGENE WALL

Introduction: Autism from the Inside Out: Context, Background, Rationale and Structure

Context

Education provision for children with autism spectrum difference (ASD) has developed significantly on a global basis, since Hans Asperger in Vienna and Leo Kanner in the US began their pioneering work in the 1930s (Kanner 1943; Asperger 1979). We now know that learners with ASD experience the world in a fundamentally different and diverse way than those who do not have ASD (Grandin 1995; Barton 2012; 2014; Silberman 2015). Consequently, teachers must be in a position to adapt their teaching in a manner that has been described as non-intuitive in order to provide effectively for learners with ASD (Ring and Prunty 2012; Ring 2015a). While research has contributed to our understanding of providing effectively for children in early years settings, primary, post-primary and special schools, children with ASDs are commonly exposed to dubious intervention programmes and strategies that lack efficacy and which have not been objectively verified (Simpson 2005). The focus of the research on which this book is based was to empirically evaluate education provision for children in Ireland based on a framework developed by Middletown Centre for Autism (MCA) and the NCSE (MCA and NCSE 2013), with reference to best practice internationally in the area. This research was conducted by a team of nationally and internationally renowned experts in education and psychology at Mary Immaculate College (MIC). A specific aim of the research was to identify and disseminate best practice across the education system in relation to providing enriched educational experiences for children with ASD and to assist government departments to develop policy with reference to this best practice. A number of these researchers have now collaborated with colleagues at MIC for this publication, *Autism from the Inside Out: A Handbook for Parents, Early Childhood, Primary, Post-Primary and Special School Settings*. This chapter provides a background to the research and the rationale and structure for the book.

Situating the Research: Difference or Disorder?

Up until the recent publication of *The Diagnostic and Statistical Manual of Mental Disorders*, 5th edition (DSM-V) (American Psychiatric Association (APA), 2013), autism or autistic spectrum disorder (ASD) was described as a triad of impairments in social interaction, patterns of communication and flexibility of thought and behaviour (Ring, McKenna and Wall 2015). While the current classification system also includes these areas, a further dimension refers to a child's hyper/hypo reactivity to sensory input or an unusual interest in sensory-related aspects of the environment. This dimension, which had been advocated for a long period of time, is a welcome addition to the classification system and gives due recognition to the sensory challenges experienced by children with autism and the importance of addressing these challenges (Bogdashina 2006; Ring 2015a).

The concept of 'disorder' as a defining feature of autism has been challenged by both individuals with autism and their parents/carers, who describe their experiences in terms of 'difference' (Claiborne Park 1982; Grandin 1995; Greene 2006). The research adopted a position of 'difference' rather than 'disorder' and conceptualized the features associated with autism as differences to be acknowledged, understood, celebrated and accommodated. Therefore throughout the book, the term 'autism spectrum difference' (ASD) is purposefully adopted to reflect the differences experienced individually by children with ASD. The terminology of difference is intended to convey a positive value reflective of the wealth of different individual potential, which as educators we have a responsibility to cultivate and foster (Parrini 2014).

Background to the Research

In 2013, the Minister for Education and Skills in Ireland requested that the NCSE prepare policy advice on education provision for children with ASD. The NCSE is an independent body that was established in 2003, under the Education for Persons with Special Educational Needs (EPSEN) Act, 2004 (Government of Ireland 2004). The NCSE has a range of statutory functions in relation to developing and improving education provision and support services for children with special educational needs, including the commissioning and disseminating of research and advising the Minister for Education. In response to the minister's request, the NCSE commissioned an overview and empirical evaluation of education provision for children with ASD in Ireland based on the Evaluation Framework developed in collaboration with MCA (MCA and NCSE 2013). A range of evaluations, policy and best-practice guidelines from Ireland, Northern Ireland, the wider United Kingdom, the USA, Canada and Australia was consulted and informs this Evaluation Framework. The report on which the research is based has been published by the NCSE (Daly et al. 2016).

Education Provision for Children with Autism Spectrum Difference in Ireland

In Ireland, a legislative presumption in favour of including all children with special educational needs in mainstream schools is enshrined in legislation (Government of Ireland 1998; 2004). This is further augmented by the availability of targeted provision for children aged four to eighteen years in the school system. Education provision for children with ASD includes nineteen dedicated autism special schools, ninety-five special classes at pre-primary level, 378 special classes at primary and 152 special classes at post-primary (Daly et al. 2016). There are currently 3,137 mainstream primary schools, 141 special schools and 732 post-primary schools in Ireland, with recent research suggesting that one in every sixty-five children, or 1.5 per cent of the school population, has an assessment of ASD (NCSE 2016). A school-based July Education programme (JEP) is also available for children with ASD and/or a severe or profound general learning disability. Home-based JEP provision is available if the school in which the child is enrolled is not providing the school-based JEP (Department of Education and Skills (DES) 2013). Home Tuition funding is also available where children are unable to attend school for reasons such as chronic illness, for children with special educational needs seeking an educational placement and for children with ASD in the context of early educational intervention (DES 2014). Additional supports, including an allocation of additional teaching, assistive technology and/ or special needs assistant (SNA) support, are provided to support the inclusion of children with ASD in mainstream primary and post-primary schools (NCSE 2016). Special classes and special schools are established with a staffing ratio of one teacher and a minimum of two special SNAs for every six children (Daly et al. 2016). The role of the SNA is to assist children with special educational needs who also have additional and significant care needs and additional SNAs may be allocated in accordance with the care needs of individual children. In Ireland, SNAs do not have a teaching role.

In contrast to other countries, where the provision of early childhood care and education (ECCE) at preschool level has long been a feature of children's experiences, Ireland has only recently begun to focus specifically on providing free universal access for all children to ECCE (Ring 2015b). All children in Ireland can access free preschool education from the age of three for a period of two years (Healy 2016). In June 2016, the Better Start Access and Inclusion Model (AIM) was introduced to support the inclusion of children with additional needs, including ASD, at preschool level (Rogers 2016). The model, which is based on national and international research evidence, was developed following extensive consultation with a wide range of stakeholders, including the parents of children with additional needs. In accordance with best practice, the seven-level model (which can be viewed at <http://aim.gov.ie>) adopts a child-centred approach through focusing on identifying and responding to each individual child's developmental level, abilities and needs rather than relying exclusively on formal diagnoses.

While early intervention classes were included in the evaluation on which this book is based, ECCE provision was not specifically included. However, in the belief that education provision for children with ASD should be viewed as a seamless continuum from preschool to post-primary level, the signposts provided in this book are designed to provide advice for parents, early childhood, primary, post-primary and special school settings.

An Evaluation of Education Provision for Children with Autism Spectrum Difference in Ireland

The research evaluation framework developed by MCA and the NCSE was designed for use in all education settings (MCA and NCSE 2013). It comprises four structured themes, referred to as 'statements', relating to education provision for children with ASD: Teaching and Learning, Inclusive School Culture, School Management and Staff Development. Each theme has a number of linked criteria and associated performance indicators. Within the four statements, there are nineteen criteria and eighty-four performance indicators. Figure 1 provides a summary of the four statements and associated nineteen criteria.

While the criteria of the Evaluation Framework were isolated and addressed individually for the purpose of evaluating provision in this research context, education provision for children with ASD was conceptualized as a dynamic, interlinked process comprising all of the criteria and performance indicators. Similarly, while the book is structured with reference to these four structured themes, individual chapters are inextricably linked and intertwined with each other and reflect both the potential and complexity of difference inherent in ASD.

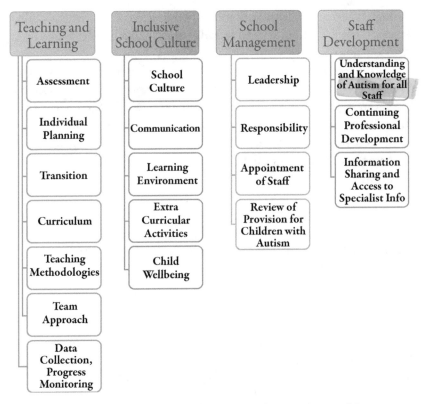

Figure 1: Middletown Centre for Autism and National Council for
Special Education Evaluation Framework

Evaluation Research Methodology

A rigorous, multi-faceted methodological approach was adopted for the
research, concerned with capturing the voices of all stakeholders and incorporating both an individual-focused and environmental lens. A summary
of the multiple-case study research approach and the wide range of data
sources collected and analysed is detailed in Table 1. A range of research
strategies was adopted and included semi-structured interviews conducted
with principals, teachers, special needs assistants (SNAs) and parents;
observation of practice; a review of documentation related to education
provision for children with ASD and child conversations.

Table 1: Summary of the Multiple-Case Study Research Approach and Data Sources

Principal Interview	Teacher Interview	Classroom Assistant Interview	Student Conversation	Student Drawing	Parent Interview (Telephone)	Document Review	Observation of Practice
21	48	33	29	41	60	24	35

Data were collected from twenty-four sites. In order to ensure that school-based sites reflected the range of state-funded provision in Ireland, a stratified sampling process was employed based on the following dimensions: urban/rural; gender; socio-economic grouping; language medium (Irish-/English-medium schools); early intervention; provision type (mainstream provision, special class provision in mainstream schools and special schools (ASD-specific and generic special schools). Within these categories, sites were selected randomly from the available databases. The selection of JEP Home Sites and Home Tuition was based on a self-selection process as parents were initially contacted by the DES and invited to participate. Sites were then selected pragmatically based on geographical proximity to the researchers. The research sites are detailed in Table 2.

Table 2: Research Sites

Site Details	Number of Sites
Autism-Specific Early Intervention Classes	2
Children included in Mainstream Primary Schools	3
Children included in Mainstream Post-Primary Schools	3
Special Classes in Mainstream Primary Schools	2
Special Classes in Mainstream Post-Primary Schools	2
Special School for Children with Mild General Learning Disability	1
Special School for Children with Moderate General Learning Disability	1
Special School for Children with Severe or Profound General Learning Disability	1
Autism-Specific Special School	3
Children availing of Home Tuition	3
Children availing of the July Education Programme	3

The role of observation in both understanding professional practice and improving its quality was central to the research methodology (Wragg 1999; National Council for Curriculum and Assessment (NCCA) 2009). A Documentary and Classroom Analysis Schedule was developed and linked to the four statements, nineteen criteria and eighty-four performance indicators included in the Evaluation Framework (MCA and NCSE 2015). Eleven key sections were delineated in the schedule and comprised: School Culture and Leadership; Learning Environment; Assessment; Individualized Planning; Transition Planning; Curriculum; Teaching Methodologies; Data Collection/Monitoring of Progress/Outcomes; Team Approach; Parental and Children's Involvement and Staff Development. Individualized Education Planning, sections of the School Plan, classroom displays and samples of children's work were examined in the context of the documentary analysis.

In the belief that the voice of the child should be at the centre of education provision for children with ASD, the researchers were particularly concerned to capture the voice of the child as envisaged in Article 12 of the United Nations (UN) Convention on the Rights of the Child (UN 1989). Combining the child conference approach developed by Clark and Moss (2011) with the draw-a-picture approach implemented by Lambert and Coad et al. (2014), children were invited to illustrate how they experienced their education settings and engage in conversations related to these experiences. Child conversations were conducted in groups and twenty-nine conversations were conducted with forty-one children. The drawing element was designed to accommodate the challenges children with ASD encounter in communicating verbally, with children's responses indicating that when supported in a dialogic manner, children with ASD communicate their experiences in a coherent, meaningful and informative manner (Ring 2016). Table 3 demonstrates the manner in which children's responses corroborated the positive findings of the research in relation to the development of inclusive practice in education settings and children's sense of 'belonging' which emerged from the research.

Table 3: Exemplars of Children's Drawings

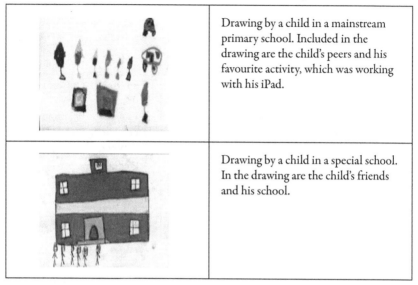

	Drawing by a child in a mainstream primary school. Included in the drawing are the child's peers and his favourite activity, which was working with his iPad.
	Drawing by a child in a special school. In the drawing are the child's friends and his school.

Data Analysis

Data were uploaded electronically using Nvivo software (QSR International) and analysis was conducted with reference to the Evaluation Framework (MCA and NCSE 2015). As summarized in Table 4, a quantitative recording mechanism from 1–5 was applied to the data collected in each subsection of the Document Review and Observation of Practice and equated with a scale of unacceptable to excellent, which was in turn equated with the percentage of data sources confirming the relevant findings. A specific suite of language linked to this scale was used consistently in reporting the research findings.

Validity and reliability measures were adopted through methodological triangulation using multiple sources of evidence; the development of the quantitative analysis and reporting element detailed in Table 4 and the calculation of an inter-rater agreement score between one of the principal

Table 4: Measurement and Weighting Criteria for Evaluation Data

1	2	3	4	5
never/almost never	rarely	sometimes	often	always/ almost always
Confirmed by Findings from 10% of Data Sources including Document Review/ Classroom Observation	Confirmed by Findings from 20% of Data Sources including Document Review/ Classroom Observation	Confirmed by Findings from 50% of Data Sources including Document Review/ Classroom Observation	Confirmed by Findings from 90% of Data Sources including Document Review/ Classroom Observation	Confirmed by Findings from All Data Sources
Unacceptable	Acceptable	Good	Very Good	Excellent

investigators and the researcher for each subsection of the Documentary and Classroom Observation Schedule. It is important to note, however, that the research findings are limited by the small sample size and the possibility that the findings represent the individual responses of the research participants only, which has implications for the generalization of the research findings.

Notwithstanding these limitations, the research fulfilled its aim in producing evidence-based findings related to the exploration of specific contexts and individuals and provides a robust foundation for the signposts for practice suggested in this book.

Rationale

The research identified a wide range of positive practice in relation to teaching and learning, creating inclusive school cultures, the key role of leadership and management and staff development. Assessment, planning, the inclusion of the child's voice, curriculum access, the availability of external support services and parental involvement were among the areas identified for further improvement.

Critically the research findings clearly identified a need for additional guidance, advice and support for parents, early years teachers, primary, post-primary and special school teachers to support them in enabling all children with ASD to achieve their full potential in appropriately responsive education settings. This publication therefore focuses on highlighting best practice in the education of children with ASD identified during the research project and provides guidance, advice and effective strategies for supporting children with ASD at home and across education settings from preschool to post-primary settings. As the title of the book suggests, ASD is examined from the inside out through a theoretical lens from which practical practice-based strategies are identified.

The Structure of the Book

The book is divided into three sections and structured to reflect the Evaluation Framework developed by MCA and the NCSE (MCA and NCSE, 2013). Part I, 'Teaching and Learning', comprises six chapters, Part II, 'Creating an Inclusive Culture', is made up of three chapters and Part III, 'Management and Staff Development', contains three chapters.

Part I: Teaching and Learning

The first six chapters of the book address the key components necessary to create an enriched, responsive and appropriate teaching and learning environment for children with ASD. Egan suggests that in order to promote successful learning, teaching must be rooted in a knowledge and understanding of the nature and educational implications of ASD for teaching and learning. Effective teaching strategies and pedagogical approaches underpinned by a robust evidence-based theoretical framework are presented and described. The value of including play in the curriculum for children with ASD is explored by O'Sullivan, who argues that children with ASD can engage in and benefit from all types of play, provided specific support is provided to enable them to participate more fully in the broad range of play experiences. Feeney highlights the pervasive impact sensory differences have for children with ASD in terms of their wellbeing and ability to engage with the environment and education experiences. The sensory differences of children with ASD are examined and strategies are suggested for parents, teachers and others working with, and supporting, children with ASD. The exponential growth of the SNA scheme in recent years is considered by Griffin and examples of positive practice are juxtaposed with discrete areas for development in relation to the evolving role of the SNA/ Inclusion Support Assistant; the promotion of the child's independence and the need for a continuing professional development framework for SNAs. Dunleavy-Lavin, Heaney and Skehill interrogate the role of individualized planning for children with ASD and query its status as either a bureaucratic requirement or critical for effective practice. The contribution of individualized education plans (IEPs) to providing a structure for the systematic planning and evaluation of teaching and learning for children with ASD is discussed. Finally, Ryan argues that inclusive assessment approaches require flexibility and a deep appreciation of the distinct characteristics of ASD. Specific guidance is provided to ensure that assessment approaches are sensitive in uncovering high-quality evidence of children's achievements and optimizing their ongoing learning for the future.

Part II: Creating an Inclusive Culture

Part II of the book begins with O'Byrne reflecting on how the research data from the ASD evaluation can support schools in developing positive communication with parents and supporting the development of inclusive school cultures. Communication, decision-making and the role of fathers are examined and an invitation is extended to teachers to create their own personal philosophy of parental involvement. Based on the concept that physical, temporal and interactional environments impact significantly on the education experiences of children with ASD, Ring harnesses the Reggio Emilia experience and introduces a model of conceptualizing the environment as the 'third teacher' for children with ASD. It is suggested that recruiting the environment as a 'third teacher' has the potential to impact positively on children's wellbeing, level of engagement and belonging and provide a potential solution to the oft-cited 'behaviour' problem associated with ASD. Daly presents the current interpretations of wellbeing evidenced in the research evaluation and details the implications for parents, early childhood, primary and post-primary teachers in supporting the wellbeing of children with ASD at home and across educational settings.

Part III: Management and Staff Development

The final three chapters in the book are concerned with the critical role and impact of management on ensuring quality education provision for children with ASD. Long highlights the responsibility of management to ensure that a focus is maintained on developing an awareness, knowledge and understanding of the implications of ASD for children's learning, with particular reference to the provision of focused continuing professional development opportunities. Fitzgerald describes the centrality of leadership in providing for effective education provision for children with ASD and weaves together findings related to effective leadership derived from data collected for this particular research with current international research related to educational leadership. Finally, Tynan presents self-evaluation as a key process for ongoing improvement of educational provision for children with ASD across early childhood, primary, post-primary and special school settings.

Conclusion

The inclusion of children with ASD in education systems continues to challenge governments and school systems globally. Inclusion has been described as a process involving a programme, curriculum or educational environment where all children are welcomed and included on equal terms, feel they belong and can progress to achieving their full potential in all areas of development (Department of Children and Youth Affairs (DCYA) 2016). Through purposefully adopting a terminology of difference, the book advocates for the creation of an environment that acknowledges, embraces, celebrates and accommodates children's diversity. This book aims to provide parents, early years, primary, post-primary and special school teachers with advice, guidance and support in ensuring that children with ASD are welcomed and included on equal terms in enriched, responsive and inclusive education environments. As suggested by Adam Harris in the Foreword, the book will also be a valuable reference for a range of other stakeholders, including multi-disciplinary teams; SNAs; individuals with ASD and policymakers.

In this book, the term 'early childhood teacher' is used to refer to those professionals responsible for the education and care of pre-school children. The terminology is consonant with the work of the great American Educator John Dewey (1859–1952), in which he described the role of the teacher as, interalia, an interpreter and guide who supports the child to re-enact, rediscover and reconstruct experience on a daily basis (Ring and O'Sullivan 2018).

Bibliography

American Psychiatric Association (2013). *Diagnostic and Statistical Manual of Mental Disorders* (5th edn) (DSM-V). Washington: American Psychiatric Association.

Asperger, H. (1979). 'Problems of Infantile Autism', *Communication*, 13, 45–52.

Barton, M. (2012). *It's Raining Cats and Dogs: An Autism Spectrum Guide to the Confusing World of Idioms, Metaphors and Everyday Expressions*. London: Jessica Kingsley Publishers.

Barton, M. (2014). *A Different Kettle of Fish*. London: Jessica Kingsley Publishers.

Bogdashina, O. (2006). 'Autistic Accounts of Sensory-Perceptual Experiences: Should we Listen', *Good Autism Practice*, 7(1), 1–12.

Claiborne Park, C. (1982). *The Siege: A Family's Journey into the World of an Autistic Child*. Boston, MA: Back Bay Books.

Clark, A., and Moss, P. (2011). *Listening to Young Children: The Mosaic Approach* (2nd edn). London: National Children's Bureau.

Daly, P., Ring, E., Egan, M., Fitzgerald, J., Griffin, C., Long, S., McCarthy, E., Moloney, M., O'Brien, T., O'Byrne, A., O'Sullivan, S., Ryan, M., Wall, E., Madden, R., and Gibbons, S. (2016). *An Evaluation of Education Provision for Students with Autism Spectrum Disorder in Ireland.* Trim: National Council for Special Education.

Department of Children and Youth Affairs (2016). *Diversity, Equality and Inclusion Charter and Guidelines for Early Childhood Care and Education.* Dublin: Department of Children and Youth Affairs.

Department of Education and Skills (2013). *July Education Programme 2013. Frequently Asked Questions – Revised April 2013.* Athlone: Department of Education and Skills.

Department of Education and Skills (2014). Circular 0048/2014: *Home Tuition Scheme 2014/2015 – Special Education Component.* Athlone: Department of Education and Skills.

Government of Ireland (1998). *Education Act, 1998.* Dublin: The Stationery Office.

Government of Ireland (2004). *Education for Persons with Special Educational Needs (EPSEN) Act (2004).* Dublin: The Stationery Office.

Grandin, T. (1995). *Thinking in Pictures and Other Reports from my Life with Autism.* New York: Vintage Books.

Greene, C. (2006). 'I Should have Listened to My Mother. A Mother's Account of her Journey towards Understanding her Young Child with Autism', *Good Autism Practice*, 7(1), 13–17.

Healy, F. (2016). 'Expansion of the Early Childhood Care and Education Programme', *Education Matters*, 119–121.

Inter-Departmental Group (2015). Supporting Access to the Early Childhood Care and Education (ECCE) Programme for Children with a Disability. Accessed online on 11 December 2017 at <http://nda.ie/nda-files/Supporting-Access-to-the-Early-Childhood-Care-and-Education-for-Children-with-a-Disability.pdf>.

Kanner, L. (1943). 'Autistic Disturbances of Affective Contact', *Nervous Child*, 2, 217–250.

Lambert, V., Coad, J., Hicks, P., and Glacken, M. (2014). 'Young Children's Perspectives of Ideal Physical Design Features for Hospital Built Environments', *Journal Of Child Health Care*, 18(1), 57–71.

Middletown Centre for Autism and National Council for Special Education (2013). *Evaluation Framework to underpin the Evaluation of Educational Provision for Students with ASD.* Trim: National Council for Special Education.

National Council for Curriculum and Assessment (2009). *Aistear: The Early Childhood Curriculum Framework*. Dublin: NCCA.

National Council for Special Education (2016). NCSE Press Release 15 July 2016. 'Major Education Report finds 14,000 Students have an Autism Diagnosis.' Accessed online on 11 December 2017 at <http://ncse.ie/wp-content/uploads/2016/07/6_Press_release_ASD.pdf>.

QSR International (2013). *NVivo 10*. Melbourne, Australia.

Parrini, C. (2014). 'Recognising Identities to Embrace Diversity'. In A. Fortunati (ed.), *San Miniato's Approach to the Education of Children*, pp. 79–89. Pisa: Edizioni ETS.

Ring, E. (2015a). 'Autism: considerations for the future of education of children with autism in mainstream schools: Experiences from research in Ireland'. In *Conference Proceedings* (5th edn), pp. 349–457. Padova: Libreria Universitaria.

Ring, E. (2015b). 'Early Years Education-Focused Inspections: A Reason to Celebrate', *Children's Research Digest*, 2(2), 42–46.

Ring, E. (2016). 'Why the Voice of the Child Matters for Education in the 21st Century'. In *Conference Proceedings* (6th edn), pp. 667–672. Padova: Libreria Universitaria.

Ring, E., and Prunty, A. (2012). 'Adapting the Curriculum to Include Learners with Autistic Spectrum Disorders in Irish schools'. In T. Day and J. Travers (eds), *Special and Inclusive Education: A Research Perspective*, pp. 289–302. Oxford: Peter Lang.

Ring, E., McKenna, M., with Wall, E. (2014). 'Ensuring Quality Educational Experiences for Children with Autistic Spectrum Differences: Perspectives for the classroom'. In P. M. Rabensteiner and G. Rabensteiner (eds), *Internationalisation in Teacher Education*, pp. 207–229. Batlmannsweiler, Schneider Verlag Hohengehren GmbH.

Ring, E. and O'Sullivan, L. (2018).'The Question is 'What has School-Readiness Got to Do with Anything? The Answer is 'Nothing Whatsoever' – Why Early Childhood Education Must Find a New Word to Replace 'School Readiness' and Start a Play Revolution', *Early Times Magazine*, Autumn 18, 8–9.

Rogers, M. (2016). 'The Better Start Access and Inclusion Model (AIM)', *Education Matters*, 125–129.

Silberman, S. (2015). *Neurotribes. The Legacy of Autism and How to Think Smarter about People who Think Differently*. London: Allen and Unwin.

Simpson, R. L. (2005). 'Evidence-Based Practices and Students with Autism Spectrum Disorders', *Focus on Autism and Other Developmental Disabilities*, 20(3), 140–149.

United Nations (1989) *United Nations Convention on the Rights of the Child*. Accessed online on 16 December 2017 at <http://www.ohchr.org/EN/ProfessionalInterest/Pages/CRC.aspx>.

Wragg, E. C. (1999). *An Introduction to Classroom Observation* (2nd edn). London: Routledge.

PART I

Teaching and Learning

MARGARET EGAN

1 Effective Teaching Strategies to Promote Successful Learning

ABSTRACT

In order to engage in effective teaching to promote successful learning, intervention to meet the needs of children with autism spectrum difference (ASD) must be rooted in a knowledge and understanding of the nature and educational implications of ASD for all teaching and learning. Therefore, while the chapter reminds its audience that all children are individuals with unique strengths and learning needs, it provides a theoretical framework for understanding children with ASD, which underpins the strategies and pedagogical approaches that participants in the study, conducted by Daly et al. (2016), nominated as being effective, in their lived experience.

Introduction

Autism spectrum difference is considered to be a neurodevelopmental difference in thinking and perceiving the social world. The term embraces a wide spectrum of differences, in social interaction, social communication, social imagination and sensory processing (American Psychiatric Association (APA) 2013). What Wing, in 1996, described as a triad of impairments, the author suggests has evolved into a tetrad of differences.

While such categorization is essential to diagnosis, it is important to acknowledge that children with ASD are individuals and may present as more 'idiosyncratic' (Ripley 2015: 9) than their neurotypically developing peers who may conform more readily and easily to social norms. Therefore, if a teacher has experience of working with one child with ASD in early years, primary, post-primary or special school settings, it may, or may not inform future practice. Each child with ASD will present his/her own unique learning profile of strengths and needs. Effective teaching strategies to promote successful learning 'require an understanding of how people with autism think and feel' (Grandin 1995a: 33). Such an understanding is critical from early years to post-primary level, because 'without a coherent working model of the processes that may be at work to produce the behaviours typical of autism we are reduced as educators to a piecemeal approach, ... or following 'recipes' for successful teaching' (Cumine, Dunlop and Stevenson 2010: 24). International literature concurs that educators can make a real difference (Jordan 2005; Attwood 2007; Nelson 2012; 2015; Notbohm 2012; Grandin and Panek 2013; Perner and Delano 2013). Early childhood, primary and post-primary teachers are flexible practitioners, adjusting teaching on an ongoing basis to meet the needs of all learners. Therefore, some teaching and learning strategies are best practice for *all* children and some may need to be adjusted, to be more discrete and explicit for successful learning.

This chapter adopts a multifactorial explanation of how children with ASD think, feel and learn, which has evolved in the research literature over more recent decades (Cumine et al. 2010; Ripley 2015), to understand the characteristics which have implications for all teaching and learning. The neuropsychological framework provides a theoretical rationale and underpinning for the teaching strategies and pedagogical approaches that participants in the study nominated as being effective, in their lived experience working with children in early years, primary, post-primary and special school settings.

Key Signposts: Introduction

- Autism spectrum difference embraces a tetrad of differences in social interaction, social communication, social imagination and sensory processing.
- Each child presents his/her own unique learning profile of strengths and needs and an experience of working with one child with ASD cannot be equated with an experience of working with every child with ASD.
- Effective teaching strategies to promote successful learning across early years, primary, post-primary and special school settings require an understanding of how children with ASD think and feel.

Theoretical Framework

The neuropsychological theoretical framework (Cumine et al. 2010; Ripley 2015), embraces theories of understanding/explanation and relate to three distinct fields: Theory of Mind: Central Coherence and Executive Functioning.

Theory of Mind

Theory of Mind (ToM) (Leslie and Firth 1985; Baron-Cohen 1995) is one such explanation and refers to the understanding that others have thoughts, feelings and motivation that impact on behaviour. It is the human ability to mind read and is based on the widely known 'Sally – Anne' experiment (Leslie and Firth 1985; Baron-Cohen 1995). The fourteen-month-old toddler who throws the toy from the cot, which is then rescued by the caregiver and returned, already knows that this is a strategy to engage joint attention. Baron-Cohen (1995) asserts that joint attention is a prerequisite for the development of ToM. For children with ASD, this ability is severely impaired, the implication of which is that some children find it difficult to make sense of the social behaviour of others and the social world generally, which consequently causes anxiety and exacerbates responses that may not be conducive to successful learning. Understanding the emotions of others and self is a characteristic difficulty and addressing this need involves a wide use of visuals of self and others, video role play, real artefacts from the child's own experiences. The requirement of such an approach is succinctly surmised by Grandin (1995a: 34) who points out that 'I think totally in pictures'. The creation of what she calls 'mental videos' insists on the real participation of self, which leads to learning that can be recalled when necessary. Pedagogical strategies can be directly informed by Grandin's experience, in relation to which she notes that 'this method of thinking is slower than verbal thinking. It takes time to play the videotape in my imagination' (p. 35), which has implication for 'wait-time', allowing the child to self-process at his/her own pace. Such advice, in relation to mental

processing, is relevant to all learners and relates to Central Coherence and
Executive Functioning.

Central Coherence

Central Coherence (CC) is described by Frith (2003) as the ability to form
coherence over a wide range of stimuli. Vermeulen (2012), expands this
theory to suggest that it is not the focus on detail that distinguishes the
child with ASD but rather, the ability to focus on the detail that is context
relevant. Frith (1989) suggests that neurotypical thinking is characterized
by a bias towards thinking of the whole to understand the detail. Those
with ASD, on the contrary, she theorizes, have a bias towards the processing of detail. Detail processing can lead to sensory overload, which has
implications for sensory rich classrooms. Furthermore, Vygotsky (1978)
insists that meaning is mediated through language, stating that language
functioning is implicated in the comprehension of overall meaning where
irrelevant detail is ignored. For many with ASD, however, 'a situation, a
performance, a sentence is not regarded as complete if it is not made up
of exactly the same elements that were present at the time the child first
confronted it' (Kanner 1943, cited in Cumine et al. 2010: 28). Weak CC,
therefore, may account for the characteristic resistance to change and
rigid thinking patterns, which can also be explained by this bias towards
detail processing. Daly et al. (2016), consistently acknowledge the anxiety experienced and displayed by children during transitions to differing
tasks or contexts. Furthermore, children with ASD are not context sensitive, finding it challenging to read social situations with the automaticity
of their peers, which relates to impaired ToM. Such characteristics have
implications for the necessary provision of structured, predictable classrooms, where routines are clearly indicated and visually supported. The
criticality of directing attention to the environment for children with ASD
is discussed further in Chapter 8. Clear instruction and expectation are
critical and benefit all children. Central Coherence theory also suggests
that children with ASD can attend to tasks for extended periods when
motivated, an appreciation of which is foundational to planning effective

teaching to support time on task and greater self-directed learning, which relates to Executive Functioning.

Executive Functioning

Executive Functioning (EF) is defined by Ozonoff (1995), citing Luria's (1966) definition as the ability to maintain an appropriate problem-solving set for the attainment of a future goal. Such functioning is responsible for behaviour mediated in the frontal lobes and is often discussed in relation to children with attention deficit hyperactivity disorder (ADHD) (Barkley 1998; 2014) as it relates to planning and organization, attention, inhibition control and self-regulation that is context sensitive (Ozonoff, South and Provencal 2005; Robinson, Goddard, Dritchel, Wisley and Howin 2009). It is also associated with working memory, the impairment of which is highlighted by Grandin (1995b: 145): 'I cannot hold one piece of information in my mind while I manipulate the next step in the sequence'. Grandin (1995a; 1995b; 1995c) reminds teachers of the importance of clear teacher instruction and engagement in task analysis, in order to present tasks in a structured sequence, which will need to be visually supported. Forward and backward chaining refer to the scaffolding of such steps, for task completion. Structure and routine are critical in developing a safe environment where engagement is guided by a significant other, using visual supports to scaffold other-regulated engagement to more self-regulated engagement reducing anxiety for the child, overall. Interestingly, it has been suggested in recent literature that development of ToM and EF, in relation to self-regulation, can motivate social interaction and language development, which has implications for teaching and learning in the social milieu of the early years and school settings.

In summary, ToM provides an understanding of the challenges children with ASD experience in relation to reading and interpreting people in social contexts, which manifests in social skills' differences generally. Theories, related to CC, suggest a unique style of processing. Differing EF can explain characteristic challenges associated with working memory, planning and self-regulation. Each of these theories has contributed to current understanding of how children with ASD think, feel and learn. However, in isolation, no single paradigm of explanation is adequate in the conceptualization of such a spectrum of abilities and needs, but together they provide a window for clearer understanding as well as a theoretical framework to inform intervention.

Key Signposts: Theoretical Framework

- The neuropsychological theoretical framework, adopted for this chapter, embraces three theories to understand autism spectrum difference.
- *Theory of Mind* (ToM) explains that children with ASD find it challenging to mind read. They may find is difficult to make sense of the social behaviour of others and the social world generally. Some will need to access mental images of themselves in such situations. Teachers need to note that this thinking in pictures is slower and therefore, may need greater 'wait-time', allowing the child to self-process at his/her own pace.
- *Central Coherence* (CC) is the ability to form coherence over a wide range of stimuli. It is theorized that children with ASD have a bias towards the processing of detail as opposed to the whole. Detail processing can lead to sensory overload, which has implications for sensory rich classrooms.
- *Executive Functioning* (EF) is responsible for behaviour mediated in the frontal lobes; it relates to planning and organization, attention, inhibition control and self-regulation that is context sensitive. It is also associated with working memory. The implication for effective teaching and learning is that teacher instruction must be clear, engagement by the teacher in task analysis is necessary in order to present tasks in a structured, visual sequence.

Teaching Strategies for Children with Autism Spectrum Difference

The range of evidence-based strategies, highlighted by teachers in the study Daly et al. (2016), are discussed in this section. Figure 1.1 provides a summary. The theoretical framework, set out in this chapter, provides a lens for such discussion.

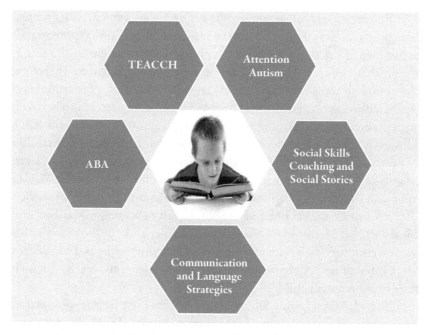

Figure 1.1: Teaching Strategies Selected by Teachers in the Irish Study

The Treatment and Education of Autistic and related Communication-handicapped CHildren (TEACCH)

The Treatment and Education of Autistic and related Communication-handicapped CHildren (TEACCH) was one approach that was consistently nominated by teachers, as the following quote illustrates: 'Elements of the Treatment and Education of Autistic and related Communication-handicapped CHildren (TEACCH) approach were used in an excellent manner by almost all schools' (Daly et al. 2016: 79). While the centrality of the role of environment for children with ASD will be discussed more fully in Chapter 8, it is critical, at the outset, to understand the implications of the theoretical framework presented in this chapter, for creating appropriate teaching and learning environments. A TEACCH approach constructs a particularly structured environment. Therefore, it is foundational to all intervention presented in this section.

Research literature recognizes the TEACCH approach as a whole-life approach, to scaffold children to realize their functional potential. It recommends key adaptations to the physical environment in the recognition that children with ASD are primarily, visual learners. Therefore, the approach sets out to provide visual information in a structured and predictable manner, as research suggests a significant correlation between such predictability and reduced anxiety levels among learners with ASD. However, the social world is unpredictable and therefore, it is vital that children are exposed to change from an early stage, so that they can learn how to negotiate social situations, efficiently and effectively. The TEACCH approach insists that adaptations must occur in three areas of the child's life; the home; the school and the community (Schopler, Mesibov and Hearsey 1995; Mesibov and Shea 2010; Schopler and Mesibov 2013). This section concerns itself primarily with the education setting and considers a set of interconnected elements, which relate to structured teaching which have benefits for all children.

The TEACCH approach recommends that there be clear boundaries segmenting the classroom space into discrete stations. This makes the physical environment more predictable as children are clear on where to go and what to do when they get there. For example, in the area set out for on-task engagement, or task completion, distractions are kept to a minimum. A visual schedule forecasts and reminds the child of the sequence of the day (part of day), the activities that will occur and the order in which they will occur. Daly et al. (2016: 52) note that in all settings 'visual schedules were individualized, determined by the needs of individual children and used appropriately and discretely'. Visual schedules, incorporating task analysis present each step of a task visually and sequentially. First/next visuals indicate for the child 'what I have to do now', 'how much do I have to do', 'when will I be finished' and 'what will I have to do next'. Table 1.1 outlines the examples of visuals, cited in the research literature (Cohen and Sloan, 2007; Goldstein, Naglier; 2013; Meadan, Michaelene, Oskrosku, Triplett and Michna 2011), that are being used in settings, according to data. The table also indicates the purpose of these visuals.

Table 1.1: Visual Supports

Example of Visual	Purpose of Visual
Visual Schedule: Visual of Whole Day Activities/Morning Session/Next Activity	Make the day predictable/prompt transitions.
First/Next Visual	Make the day predictable/prompt transitions. Prompt what to do now, which may be followed by a more preferred activity.
Task (Analysis) Visual	Indicating the steps to be taken to begin and complete task.
Cue Card	Non-verbal, visual instruction, for example, STOP sign to indicate the end of a session on the computer.
Reward Card/Token Economy Visual	Support appropriate behaviour.
Choice Board	Encourage self-directed action and scaffold choice-making skills.

Teachers in the study noted that visual cues were used effectively to support teaching and learning for all children as illustrated in this quote: 'it's not just Rory that it's benefitting – it's for everyone' (Daly et al., 2016: 79). Structured teaching that maximizes visual presentation and minimizes verbal instruction benefits many children in classrooms but such an approach maximizes the strengths of children with ASD, in order to minimize the potential difficulties, highlighted in the theoretical framework. A TEACCH approach utilizes the child's visual skills, their preference for predictability and adherence to routine, to scaffold successful learning. Its structure scaffolds their sensitivity to context and reduces anxiety, which, if not appropriately addressed, can manifest in disengagement and disequilibrium for the child as explained previously in the theoretical framework. It is an approach that is suited to all age groups, those in early years, primary, post-primary, special school settings and beyond. Overall, a TEACCH approach seeks to promote functional independence, which is key for children with ASD.

> *Key Signposts: The TEACCH Approach*
>
> - *TEACCH* is recognized as a whole-life approach to scaffold children/persons to realize their functional potential.
> - It recommends key adaptations to the physical environment and aims to provide visual information in a structured and predictable manner, in the recognition that children with ASD are primarily, visual learners.
> - Structured teaching that maximizes visual presentation and minimizes verbal instruction benefits many children in classrooms, but such an approach maximizes the strengths of children with ASD in order to minimize the potential difficulties.

Structure is a characteristic that TEACCH shares with other educational programmes (Boucher 2009; 2013) and while it is important for successful outcomes, it is also critical to consider child-led interactions, which, by implication, may be less structured, transferring greater autonomy from adult to the child with ASD. Theoretically, the need to encourage *joint attention*, to develop *ToM*, insists on approaches and activities that may be less structured but are appealing to the senses and use the child's special interest(s). A special class teacher noted the importance of finding out about children's interest, which is key to unlocking their learning potential. One current approach, that systematically embraces activities described by many teachers in the study, to capitalize on the child's interest in order to gain attention, is *Attention Autism*.

Attention Autism

Attention Autism (AA) is an approach based on an understanding of present levels of performance in relation to attention and communication development and focuses on where to go next. It capitalizes on the rigid thinking patterns, visual learning style, sensory sensitivity and the interests of the child with ASD, in particular. Gina Davis, a specialist speech and language therapist, developed *Attention Autism*, and emphasizes that teachers, parents and professionals must offer what she describes as an irresistible invitation to learn (Davis 2017). The aim of the programme, according to the website, is to develop natural and spontaneous communication with visually based and highly motivating activities (Davis 2017), which is best practice for all teaching and learning. Such an approach to interactions links nicely to the Standards and Components of *Síolta*, the National Quality Framework for Early Childhood Education (Centre for Early Childhood Development and Education (CECDE) 2006) and *Aistear*, the National Curriculum Framework National Council for Curriculum and Assessment (NCCA) 2009) in Ireland. Also, the NCCA's Guidelines for Good Practice (NCCA 2009) describes how the adult can support children's learning and development across four themes, one of these themes is *Interactions*. Such guidance appreciates that *all* children learn and develop by interacting with others. The adults, in this case, are those who are

> respectful listeners and keen observers, who are prepared to negotiate, who change their practice, and who make meaning with children are those who are most responsive to them. They know the children well, are sensitive to their current level of understanding, know their interests and intentions, and pitch activities and experiences which are just beyond what they can currently do and understand so that they can extend their learning. (NCCA 2009: 51)

Engaging with AA means that adult and child advance through a series of four stages, each stage building on the previous one to expand the skill repertoire of the child with ASD. The approach advocates that joint attention be led by the child initially, before guiding the child to share the interest of the adult. Stage One uses a bucket, filled with visually stimulating and engaging objects/toys to focus attention. Stage Two involves the adult leader modelling a simple activity, which aims to sustain the child's attention and is known as the 'Attention Builder' stage. Stage Three expects the child to engage with the adult and focuses on the development of joint attention, specifically. This stage also seeks to develop turn taking and important emotional regulation as children have to wait to engage with another. Stage Four builds on these significant skills in social communication and aims to develop the child's engagement in activity with another also and to shift attention. The latter involves the child taking an individual task to their own station to work on and complete independently, after which, they return to the group to share their individual work. Such activities and skill development can then be generalized to curriculum-based activities to facilitate classroom-based teaching and learning.

Davis (2017) and Middletown Centre for Autism (2017) note that it is essential to attend training in the AA model, before incorporating it into classroom practice. Together, they have also developed a model, which is appropriate for post-primary children. The format is adapted to ensure it is age appropriate, for example, each session begins with a 'Getting in the Zone' stimulated by a 'toolbox' containing items of interest. *Attention Autism* is now one of the main interventions used by Middletown Centre to develop social skills in post-primary schools.

Key Signposts: Attention Autism

- *Attention Autism* aims to develop communication through the use of visually based, highly motivating activities, which offer motivation to the child with ASD.
- The approach acknowledges that joint attention must be led by the child initially, before guiding the child to share the interest of the adult.
- *Attention Autism* is in keeping with Síolta (CECDE 2006) and *Aistear* (NCCA 2009) in Ireland.
- *Attention Autism* is now one of the main interventions used by Middletown Centre to develop social skills in post-primary schools.

Social Skills Coaching and Social Stories

Appropriate social engagement is defined throughout the literature as demonstrating competent behaviour in the particular social context (Spense 2003; Westwood 2015; Brusnahan 2017). Social activity involves two or more people. A lack of understanding of the complexity of reciprocal social interaction has been identified as is one of the main characteristics of ASD (Wing 1996). Social differences, according to Gray (2015) and Baker (2001; 2003), can be defined as both a skill/performance deficit for the child and a problem of social acceptance by peers and society, generally. Therefore, social skills' groups should include peers who do not have ASD as well as those with ASD. Research literature (Westwood 2015; Quill and Stansberry Brusnahan 2017) suggests that in order for social skills coaching to be effective one needs to:

- Assess to identify present levels of performance;
- Define and target the precise skills to be taught;
- Plan intervention that is intensive and long-term in nature to teach the skill(s);
- Promote maintenance and generalization and transfer of new skills into functional daily living;
- Monitor progress of such maintenance and generalization.

Small group coaching involves appropriate modelling; role-playing; rehearsing and practice; feedback on skill performance; positive reinforcement and counselling. Teachers are in a key position to provide the three conditions that Westwood (2015) considers critical for social interaction and skill development, generally, and include opportunity; continuity and consistency of social milieu and support and safety from others. Sometimes, children with ASD, need more explicit coaching (Quill and Stansberry Brusnahan 2017). Data from the study also indicates that many teachers in Irish classrooms use *Social Stories*.

A *Social Story* (Gray 1994; 2000; 2015) is a short, simple story written from the perspective of the child that provides instruction on positive, appropriate social behaviour (Crozier and Sileo 2005; Gray 2015). Social stories are used by parents, teachers, special needs assistants (SNAs), and therapists to teach social and conceptual understanding. The story is written in a predictable style and may be supported visually to accurately describe a context, skill, achievement or concept (Gray and Leigh 2001; Gray 2015). A key feature of a Social Story is that it is permanent. It can provide the child with reassurance and much needed structure, which reduces anxiety

(Baker 2015). These stories are written from the child's own perspective; involve much information gathering to ensure that they are both factual and relevant to the child's needs. The stories make socially appropriate behaviour explicit and thereby provide information on the perspectives of others, their thoughts and feelings, an area of significant challenge for the child; the latter having been outlined within this chapter's theoretical framework. According to Nelson (2013: 28), 'the rewards are twofold': they are helpful for the child and allow the teacher or significant other, who is writing the story, to develop a deeper insight into the child's world and the different ways of thinking experienced by the child. There are Irish publications based on the concept of the Social Story that clarify social situations through the use of story and attractive visuals. Valerie Sheehan is creator of 'Tony the Turtle' (Sheehan 2014), a series of picture story books designed for children with ASD and their parents. Children can sit and look at the pictures, illustrated by Susan Meaney, which tell their own story, while parents can sit and read to their child. Adopting a similar approach to USA-based Siobhan Timmins who adopted and adapted Social Stories for her son Mark, Avril Webster, an Irish mother, created the 'Off We Go' series of books to help Stephen manage everyday activities. These books (Webster 2008; Timmins 2016) can prepare the child for an upcoming outing and/or as visual prompts to explain what comes next in a particular activity or task. Some of Webster's (2008) books are also available in APP format.

In summary, a *Social Story* is individualized for the child and its presentation will depend on the child's strengths, needs, interests and stage of development, using personal photographs, photographs of particular social situations and/or objects, signs or symbols. Del Valle, Mc Eachern, A. and Chambers (2001) note that *Social Stories* are most useful for children who have basic language. Difficulties in language and communication cover a wide range, from the functional communication of basic needs to problems with social communication such as conversation skills, and/or acknowledging the needs of others (Owens 2014). Therefore, communication and language development, discussed in the next section, is a priority learning need for many children with ASD.

Key Signposts: Social Skills Coaching and Social Stories

- Effective social skills coaching
  - defines and targets the precise skills to be taught;
  - is intensive and long-term in nature;
  - promotes maintenance and generalization and transfer of new skills into functional daily living. (Westwood 2015)
- Sometimes, children with ASD, need more explicit coaching. Many teachers use *Social Stories* to teach such skills.
- *Social Stories* are individualized and consider the child's strengths, needs and interests.
- There are Irish publications based on the concept of the social story that clarify social situations using story and attractive visuals.

Communication and Language Strategies

The theoretical framework highlights many of the challenges that children with ASD encounter in relation to communication and language, generally. There are varying modalities that people use to communicate. Most can speak, and therefore, speech is recognized as a universal mode. There are other communication modes used for those who experience challenges. A multifactorial approach to understanding children's needs, outlined in the theoretical framework, in accordance with the DSM-V (APA 2013), recognizes that communication differences affect a whole skill range, from poorly integrated verbal and nonverbal communication, through to differences in understanding and use of nonverbal communication, to total lack of facial expression or gestures. Verbal skills may or may not be delayed but can often be disordered, affecting language meaning, which impacts on central coherence. These differences may present as showing no communicative intent, not understanding other people's communication, or, not having a verbal means to communicate, through to subtle differences, which may manifest in literal interpretation of language, including idioms (Owens 2014). Children with ASD often have difficulty with complex, abstract language and may misinterpret metaphors, slang terms, and colloquialisms. It is increasingly recognized, for example, that the language of teaching and learning is quite often idiomatic, which contributes to the child's confusion in the social context of school, thus raising anxiety levels, with associated high levels of disengagement. Teachers in the study emphasized that all verbal exchange in the teaching and learning environment needs to be presented clearly, avoiding any unnecessary complicated instruction. They highlighted that task analysis, to break instruction and tasks, generally, into small steps, is critical and visual supports to scaffold each step can provide a valuable overview of the task at hand. Figure 1.2 outlines some strategies evidenced in the data.

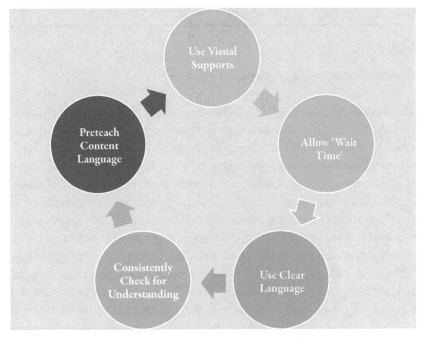

Figure 1.2: Strategies to Support Language Understanding

Supporting children who are significantly challenged to understand the language of others and/or who are non-verbal, or whose communicative intent is difficult to interpret, or who communicate their needs, desires, emotions and/or knowledge through a range of behaviours, can be challenging. It is important to appreciate the child's frustration and to understand that this behaviour is communicative. It is critical to indicate, respectfully, such a desire to understand the child's message. It is also crucial to introduce the child to an alternative/augmentative means of communication. Many teachers in the study used 'picture exchange', and more specifically, *Picture Exchange Communication System* (PECS) to facilitate and develop communication for students with ASD. The PECS is an augmentative/alternative communication (AAC) system developed by Bondy and Frost in 1985 and it was used, initially, for children with ASD at the Delware Autistic Programme in the USA (Bondy and Frost (1994; 2011). The intervention teaches the child to give a picture to a 'communication partner' who immediately reinforces this behaviour with a reward of significance to the student. It is underpinned, theoretically, by applied behaviour analysis (ABA), more specifically, Skinner's (1957) work on Verbal Behaviour. Functional verbal operants are systematically taught in six phases. The aim is that such an intervention will lead to independent communication for the child with ASD. 'How to Communicate' is the title given to Phase One, which teaches the child to exchange one picture for an item he/she desires or to request an activity. Phase Two is known as 'Distance and Persistence' and involves the generalization of Phase One into different settings with different 'communication partners'. This phase also aims to make the communicator more persistent to use this single picture to initiate communication. 'Picture Discrimination' is involved in Phase Three. During this phase, the child will need to discriminate between numbers of pictures to make a request for the object. These pictures are placed on a communication board or book where pictures are velcroed for ease of storage and removal for communication purposes. Sentence Construction is the goal of Phase Four, where children construct simple sentences such as 'I want ...'; 'I like ...'; 'I need ...'; and exchange the picture for the item requested. Phase Five teaches children to answer questions with pictures and Phase Six teaches the skill of responding to questions, such as, 'What do you see?' to which the child will select their picture in response.

While PECS was originally developed for work with young children, it is internationally recognized that the intervention can be used with adolescents and adults who have a full spectrum of abilities and needs in relation to communication, cognition, socio-emotional and physical development. As evidenced in the report: 'PECS was used to very good effect … to foster and encourage children's communication' (Daly et al. 2016: 79). Teachers were using some High Tech. augmentative/alternative communication systems (AAC), also. In relation to AAC devices, High Tech. describes all electronic communication devices from single message switches to highly sophisticated, computer-based communication devices and include, voice output communication aids to facilitate speech and mobile devices, which include a range of portable devices such as tablets and mobile phones. One programme developed for this latter technology is Proloquo2Go (Assistiveware 2017).

Proloquo2Go, according to its website, is a symbol-supported communication app 'to promote language development and grow communication skills, from beginning to advanced communicators' (Assistiveware 2017). It is an app that can be used on itechnology. The app focuses on 'core words', 80 per cent of common vocabulary. It offers what its website describes as three vocabulary levels, that is, Basic Communication, Intermediate Core and Advanced Core Vocabulary. It is more flexible and user friendly than a PECS folder. The student using his/her iPad or iPhone does not present as 'different'. One parent in the Irish study emphasized that 'technology has been huge … we have a little app on her phone … the 'tablet' and everything like that has helped hugely' (Daly et al. 2016: 105). This comment reminds teachers that collaboration with parents and the multidisciplinary team working with the child is critical to monitor the use of such technologies, to ensure that the device and/or software is being appropriately accessed by the child and that he/she is benefitting from its use in a multi-functional and socially communicative manner. Teachers must also be aware of children's sensitivity and tolerance to sensory stimulation in the environment, which could influence learning and levels of anxiety. Such sensory considerations are discussed further in Chapter 3.

It is critical that a child feels well in order to learn well. Behaviour for learning is critical according to current research literature. As earlier indicated, behaviour often communicates that the student is not able to learn for one reason or other. Applied Behaviour Analysis (ABA) was recognized in the study as an effective analytical approach to better inform effective teaching to promote successful learning at all levels.

Key Signposts: Communication and Language Strategies

- Communication differences affect a whole range of skills.
- The *Picture Exchange Communication System* is an augmentative/alternative communication (AAC) system that teaches the child to give a picture to a 'communication partner' who immediately reinforces this behaviour with a reward of significance to the student.
- PECS is internationally recognized as an intervention that can be used with adolescents and adults who have a full spectrum of abilities and needs in relation to communication, cognition, socio-emotional and physical development.
- Proloquo2Go is a symbol-supported communication app to promote language development and communication skills.
- Collaboration with parents and the multidisciplinary team working with the child is critical to monitor the use of such technologies, to ensure that the device and/or software is being appropriately accessed by the child and that he/she is benefitting from its use in a multi-functional and socially communicative manner.

Applied Behaviour Analysis (ABA)

It has been recognized for decades that Applied Behaviour Analysis (ABA) is an effective approach that can be used with children of all ages and abilities. It is a systematic approach to observing behaviour, measuring it, analysing the target behaviour and the function the behaviour serves. It is based on behaviourism and more specifically, behaviour modification (Skinner 1957) and its goal is to replace inappropriate behaviour with more appropriate behaviour that will serve the same function. Some teachers in the study took some aspects of ABA and used them in conjunction with other approaches. Others were purists and used only a strict behavioural model. A one-to-one approach was commonly used with younger children, but the aim of any effective programme is to establish 'normal' conditions and naturally occurring reinforcers, which holds implications for fading rewards.

A Functional Behaviour Assessment (FBA) is central to the overall process and it involves systematic analysis of the antecedents (A), or what comes before this Behaviour (B) and its reinforcer, recorded as the Consequence (C), of the B. Interventions, which may involve direct teaching of a key skill, should then be based on analysis of the *ABC*. Progress monitoring is an integral part of intervention and the instructional approach is adapted, based on continuous observational assessment and its recording. The Ministry of Education in Ontario (2007) succinctly states that ABA methods can be used to:

- increase positive behaviours;
- teach new skills;
- maintain behaviours;
- generalize or transfer behaviour from one situation to another;
- restrict or narrow conditions under which interfering behaviour occurs.

It is not possible to detail the full range of ABA strategies and techniques in this chapter. A fuller explanation is provided in much of the international literature, including, Alberto and Troutman's (2013) text, which is specifically for teachers. Table 1.2 provides a brief overview of the key steps involved in conducting a six-step approach to FBA-based intervention (Bambara, Janney and Snell 2015).

Table 1.2: Six-Step Approach to Functional Behaviour Assessment (FBA)-based Intervention

Step 1	Define the 'problem' behaviour Define level of priority • Destructive (this is a health and safety issue and warrants priority) • Disruptive • Distracting
Step 2	Information gathering • Interviews with key stakeholders • Case history and student profile • Target behaviour analysis – time interval sampling/ABC recording
Step 3	Develop an hypothesis of the function of the behaviour
Step 4	Design a plan for positive behaviour support (PBS)
Step 5	Implement the PBS plan
Step 6	Evaluate the plan by consistently recording observation data and reviewing it and adapting and adjusting the intervention plan

Functional Behaviour Analysis is not simple, because 'human behaviour will always be determined by many factors and by different factors at different times' (Cumine et al. 2010: 80). These authors agree, however, that 'careful detective work by practitioners and parents using the 'autism lens' can suggest some useful hypotheses and a range of useful strategies' (p. 80). Such a systematic approach to intervention monitors children's progress efficiently and effectively, which was acknowledged in the study.

Key Signposts: Applied Behaviour Analysis

- Applied Behaviour Analysis is a systematic approach to observing behaviour, measuring it, analysing the target behaviour and the function that it serves.
- A Functional Behaviour Assessment is central to ABA and it involves systematic analysis of the antecedents (A), or what comes before this Behaviour (B) and its reinforcer, recorded as the Consequence (C), of the B.
- Specific initial and continuous professional development in such an approach.

Conclusion

This chapter adopts a neuropsychological theoretical framework as a coherent working model for the selection and application of effective teaching strategies to promote successful learning for children with ASD. The study by Daly and colleagues (2016) acknowledges that teachers' repertoire of ASD specific teaching methodologies was excellent, and included those discussed in this chapter. It was noted that 'classroom and school environments were well-structured and students navigated the environment comfortably and confidently' with particular attention 'directed towards visual approaches to learning and accommodating students' sensory differences' (Daly et al. 2016: 10). Mainstream approaches were used instinctively and were 'second nature' to teachers' practice. Table 1.3 outlines the critical ingredients, cited in an increasing body of international evidence

(Attwood 2006; Boroson 2016; Morling and O'Connell 2015), in relation to effective teaching strategies to promote successful learning for *all* students, including those with ASD. The majority of teachers in the report cited these six approaches to intervention, as being effective teaching strategies to promote successful learning.

Table 1.3: The Six 'Musts' for Effective Teaching and Learning

• Intervention programmes must be of sufficient duration and intensity to ensure maintenance and generalization.
• Intervention must begin from where the child is at and must be cumulative in nature building and reviewing concepts and skills.
• Instructional language must be clear, sequential and visually supported.
• Teaching must make explicit links with previous teaching and learning and that which is current. Such teaching and learning must be of functional value to the child and real life connections must be made to this teaching and learning.
• The teacher must scaffold the child through the learning process, in keeping with Vygotsky's theory on guiding students to their ZPD.
• Teaching and learning must integrate foundation skills, such as attention, with higher order processes of a more metacognitive nature concurrently, to ensure that children reach this ZPD and be able to apply and generalize such teaching and learning.

When we consider the six 'Musts' in Table 1.3, it becomes increasingly evident that what is being highlighted by data is how teachers *differentiate* (Sousa and Tomlinson 2011) the curriculum from the perspective of universal design for learning (UDL), that is, implementing effective teaching strategies to promote successful learning for *all* children. Data, presented in the study also recognize teachers' knowledge that 'these children think differently and experience the world differently and they have to be taught differently (Daly, 2016: 134). In accordance with Ordetx (2012), professional experience has led those who educate and nurture children with ASD to realize, that grouping cannot be based solely on diagnosis. Throughout this chapter, it has been emphasized that the uniqueness of each child requires careful planning to celebrate strengths, 'we capitalize on their strengths by using what motivates them to provide optimal learning' (Daly, 2016: 135). These strengths are then used to inform effective teaching to address priority learning needs (PLNs), leading to successful learning. One teacher describes effective teaching methodologies much more succinctly as a 'whole variety of what's appropriate for that child at that particular time' (Daly, 2016: 55).

Finally, the voice of teachers concludes this chapter with a critical statement: 'the core bit is "good teaching" ... build[ing] on what's gone before' (Daly 2016: 55). Professional practice insists that '"good teaching" starts by "taking the lead from the child", as one teacher succinctly explained' (Daly, 2016: 53) and more concur, '[we are] starting where they are at because otherwise it just does not work really' (Daly, 2016: 78).

Bibliography

Alberto, P. A., and Troutman, A. (2013). *Applied Behaviour Analysis for Teachers* (9th edn). New York: Pearson.

American Psychiatric Association (2013). *Diagnostic and Statistical Manual of Mental Disorders* (5th edn) (DSM-V). Washington: American Psychiatric Association.

Assistiveware (2017). Proloquo2go. Accessed online on 11 December 2017 at <http://www.assistiveware.com/product/proloquo2go>.

Attwood, T. (2007). *The Complete Guide to Asperger's Syndrome*. London: Jessica Kingsley.

Baker, J. (2001). *Social Skills Picture Book*. Arlington, TX: Future Horizons.

Baker, J. (2003). *Social Skills Training*. Arlington, TX: Future Horizons.

Baker, J. (2015). *Overcoming Anxiety in Children and Teens*. Arlington, TX: Future Horizons.

Bambara, L. M., Janney, R., and Snell, M. E. (2015). *Behavior Support: Teachers' Guides to Inclusive Practices*. Baltimore, MD: Paul H. Brookes.

Barkley R. A. (1998). *Attention Deficit Hyperactivity Disorder: A Handbook for Diagnosis and Treatment*. New York: Guilford.

Barkley R. A. (2014). *Attention Deficit Hyperactivity Disorder: A Handbook for Diagnosis and Treatment* (4th edn). New York: Guilford.

Baron-Cohen, S. (1995). *Mindblindness: An Essay on Autism and Theory of Mind*. Cambridge, MA: MIT Press.

Baron-Cohen, S., Leslie, A. M., and Frith, U. (1985). 'Does the Autistic Child have a Theory of Mind?'. *Cognition 21*, 37–46.

Bondy, A., and Frost, L. (1994). 'The Picture Exchange Communication System'. *Focus on Autistic Behavior*, 9(3), 1–19.

Bondy, A., and Frost, L. (2011). *A Picture's Worth and Other Visual Communication Strategies in Autism*. Bethesda, MD: Woodbine House.

Boroson, B. (2016). *Autism Spectrum Disorder in the Inclusive Classroom*. New York: Scholastics.

Boucher, J. (2009). *The Autistic Spectrum: Characteristics, Causes and practical Issues*. Los Angeles, CA: SAGE.

Boucher, J. (2013). *The Autistic Spectrum: Characteristics, Causes and practical Issues* (3rd edn). Los Angeles, CA: SAGE.

Centre for Early Childhood Development and Education (2006). *National Quality Framework for Early Childhood Education*. Dublin: Centre for Early Childhood Development and Education.

Cohen, M. J., and Sloan, D. L. (2007). *Visual Supports for People with Autism*. Bethesda, MD: Woodbine House.

Crozier, S., and Sileo, N. M. (2005). 'Encouraging Positive Behavior With Social Stories: An Intervention for Children With Autism Spectrum Disorders', *TEACHING Exceptional Children*, 37 (6), 26–31.

Cumine, V., Dunlop, J., and Stevenson, G. (2010). *Asperger Syndrome: A Practical Guide for Teachers*. London Routledge.

Daly, P., Ring, E., Egan, M., Fitzgerald, J., Griffin, C., Long, S., McCarthy, E., Moloney, M., O'Brien, T., O'Byrne, A., O'Sullivan, S., Ryan, M., Wall, E., Madden, R., and Gibbons, S. (2016). *An Evaluation of Education Provision for Students with Autism Spectrum Disorder in Ireland*. Trim: National Council for Special Education.

Davis, G. (2017.) *Attention Autism*. Accessed online on 25 November2018 at <http://ginadavies.co.uk/>.

Del Valle, P., Mc Eachern, A., and Chambers, H. (2001). 'Using Social Stories with Autistic Children, Journal *of Poetry Therapy*, 14 (4), 187–97.

Frith, U. (1989). *Autism: Explaining the Enigma*. Oxford: Blackwell.

Frith, U. (2003). *Autism: Explaining the Enigma* (2nd edn). Oxford: Blackwell.

Goldstein, S., and Naglier, J. A. (2013). *Interventions for Autistic Spectrum Disorder: Translating Science into Practice*. New York: Springer.

Grandin, T. (1995a). 'The Learning Style of People with Autism: An Autobiography'. In K. A. Quill, *Teaching Children with Autism: Strategies to Enhance Communication and Socialization*, pp. 33–52. New York: DELMAR.

Grandin, T. (1995b). 'How People with Autism Think'. In E. Schopler and G. B. Mesibov (eds), *Learning and Cognition in Autism*, pp. 137–156. New York: Plenum Press.

Grandin, T. (1995c). *Thinking in Pictures*. New York: Bloomsbury.

Grandin, T., and Panek, R. (2013). *The Autistic Brain: Thinking Across the Spectrum*. New York: Houghton Mifflin Harcourt Publishing Company.

Gray, C. (1994). *The New Social Story Book*. Arlington, TX: Future Horizons.

Gray, C. A. (2000). *The New Social Stories Book*. Arlington, TX: Future Horizons Inc.

Gray, C. (2015). *The New Social Story Book, Revised and Expanded 10th Anniversary Edition*: Arlington, TX: New Horizons.

Gray, C., and Leigh, A. (2001). *My Social Stories Book*. Cheshire: Jessica Kingsley.

Jordan, R. (2005). 'Autistic spectrum disorders'. In A. Lewis and B. Norwich (eds), *Special Teaching for Special Children: Pedagogies for Inclusion*, pp. 110–121. Maidenhead: Open University Press.

Meadan, H., Michaelene, M., Oskrosku, B., Triplett, A, Michna, A. F. (2011). 'Using Visual Supports with Young Children with Autism Spectrum Disorder'. *TEACHING Exceptional Children*, 43(6), 28–35.

Mesibov, G. B., and Shea, V. (2010). 'The TEACCH Program in the Era of Evidence-Based Practice'. *Journal of Autism and Developmental Disorders*, 40(5), 570–579.

Middletown Centre for Autism (MCA) (2017). *Attention Autism*. Accessed online on 11 December 2017 at <https://www.middletownautism.com/>.

Ministry of Education Ontario (2007). *Effective Educational Practices for Students with Autism Spectrum Disorders: A Resource Guide*. Ontario: Ministry of Education.

Morling, E., and O'Connell, C. (2015). *Supporting Children with Autistic Spectrum Disorders*. London: Routledge.

National Council for Curriculum and Assessment (2009). *Aistear: The Early Childhood Curriculum Framework*. Dublin: National Council for Curriculum and Assessment.

Nelson, L. (2013). *Autistic Spectrum: Target Ladders*. Cheshire: LDA.

Nelson, L. (2015). *Autistic Spectrum: Target Ladders* (2nd edn). UK: LDA.

Notbohn, E. (2012). *Ten Things Every Child with Autism Wishes You Knew*. Texas: Future Horizons.

Ordetx, K. (2012). *Teaching Theory of Mind: A Curriculum for Children with High Functioning Autism, Asperger's Syndrome, and Related Social Challenges*. London: Jessica Kingsley Publishers.

Owens, R. E. (2014). *Language Disorders: A Functional Approach to Assessment and Intervention* (6th edn). USA: The Allyn and Bacon Communication Sciences and Disorders.

Ozonoff, S. (1995). 'Executive Functions in Autism'. In E. Schopler and G. B. Mesibov (eds), *Learning and Cognition in Autism*, pp. 199–222. New York: Plenum Press.

Ozonoff, S., South, M., and Provencal, S. (2005). 'Executive functions'. In F. R. Volkmar, R. Paul, A. Klin, and D. Cohen (eds), *Handbook of autism and pervasive developmental disorders* (3rd edn), Vol. 1: *Diagnosis, development, neurobiology, and behaviour*, pp. 606–627. Hoboken, NJ: Wiley.

Perner, D. E., and Delano, M. E. (2013). *A Guide to Teaching Students with Autistic Spectrum Disorder*. Arlington, VA: Division on Autism and Developmental Disabilities of the Council for Exceptional Children.

Quill, K. A., and Stansberry Brusnahan, L. L. (2017). *Do-Watch-Listen-Say: Social and Communication Intervention for ASD*. Baltimore, MD: Paul H Brookes.

Ripley, K. (2015). *Autism from Diagnostic Pathway to Intervention*. London: Jessica Kingsley Publishers.

Robinson, S., Goddard, L., Dritchel, B., Wisley, M., and Howlin, P. (2009). 'Executive functions in children with Autism Spectrum Disorders'. *Brain and Cognition* 71, 362–368.

Schopler, E., Mesibov, G. B., and Hearsey, K. (1995). 'Structured teaching in the TEACCH system'. In E. Schopler and G. B. Mesibov (eds), *Learning and Cognition in Autism*, pp. 243–268. New York: Plenum Press.

Schopler, E., and Mesibov, G. B. (eds) (2013). *Learning and Cognition in Autism*. New York: Springer Science & Business Media.

Sheehan, V. (2014). *Tony the Turtle Series*. Cork: Valerie Sheehan.

Skinner, B. F. (1957). *Verbal Behaviour*. New York: Appleton-Century-Crofts.

Sousa, D. A., and Tomlinson, C. A. (2011). *Differentiation and The Brain*. Bloomington, IN: Solution Press.

Spence, S. (2003). 'Social Skills Social Skills Training with Children and Young People: Theory, Evidence and Practice'. *Child and Adolescent Mental Health*, 8(2), 84–96.

Timmons, S. (2016). *Successful Social Stories for Young Children with Autism*. London: Jessica Kingsley.

Vermeulen, P. (2012). *Autism as Context Blindness*. Kansas, KY: AAPC.

Vygotosky, L. (1978). 'Interaction between learning and development'. In L. Vygotsky, *Mind in Society*, pp. 79–91. Cambridge, MA: Harvard University Press.

Webster, A. (2008). *Off-We Go Series*. Annacoty: Off We Go Publishing.

Westwood, P. S. (2015). *Commonsense Methods for Children with Special Educational Needs*. London: Taylor and Francis.

Wing, L. (1996). *Autistic Spectrum: A Guide for Parents and Professionals*. London: Constable.

LISHA O'SULLIVAN

2 A Right to Play: Our Responsibility to Include Play in the Curriculum for Children with Autism Spectrum Difference

ABSTRACT

This chapter explores the value of including play in the curriculum for children with autism spectrum difference (ASD). The research conducted by Daly and colleagues (2016), suggests that play may be underutilized as a pedagogical approach in the education of children with ASD. This is consistent with earlier research, which suggests that integrating play within the curriculum is challenging in early years and primary contexts, more generally (Ring et al. 2016). In response to findings in the report *Evaluating Educational Provision for Students with Autism Spectrum Disorder in Schools* (Daly et al. 2016), this chapter contemplates the capacity of children with ASD to learn through play. Here it will be argued that children with ASD, can engage in, and benefit from, all types of play, but they may need specific support to participate more fully in the broad range of play experiences available in educational contexts. Given the social nature of learning, the facilitation of children's participation in social play with peers is also considered.

Introduction

Learning is maximized when the curriculum provides opportunities for independent play, which can involve peers and adults naturally scaffolding learning, as well as during adult-led learning experiences which retain an element of play (O'Sullivan and Ring 2016). For children with ASD, direct instruction is often emphasized in an effort to compensate for emotional, cognitive and social differences (Mastrangelo 2009). While approaches

grounded in behaviourist principles are associated with reductions in ritualistic behaviours and gains in skill development, there is less confidence
in the capacity of these approaches to promote skill generalization and
maintenance (Owens, Granader, Humphry, and Baron-Cohen 2008; Paul
2008). Moreover, a playful pedagogical approach may have an edge in areas
such as joint attention, self-regulation, play skills and social skills (Josefi
and Ryan 2004; Kasari, Chang and Patterson 2013). At a minimum, a
playful pedagogical approach should be included alongside more direct
instruction in programmes for children with ASD (Wolfberg 2003; Paul
2008; Kasari et al. 2013).

In Ireland, *Aistear*, the early childhood curriculum framework, has
been developed for children from birth to six years, including children in
the early primary grades. *Aistear* identifies play as a key context through
which all children develop as competent and confident learners (National
Council for Curriculum and Assessment (NCCA) 2009). Children with
ASD, therefore, are entitled to learn in a child-centred way that builds on
individual interests and celebrates diverse ways of exploring, meaning-
making and knowing. Daly and colleagues (2016) suggest that there is
scope to use *Aistear* more comprehensively to support the learning of children with ASD. Through looking at how certain play experiences support
learning, and through identifying the support children with ASD may
require in order to learn through different types of play, adults will be
better equipped to develop a curriculum that is more closely aligned with
the principles of *Aistear*.

Key Signposts: Introduction

- For children with ASD, direct instruction is often emphasized to the detriment
  of more playful pedagogical approaches.
- Playful pedagogical approaches potentially impact on joint attention, self-
  regulation, play skills and social skills.
- Including a playful pedagogical approach alongside more direct instruction supports children with ASD to learn in a child-centred way that builds on individual
  interests and celebrates diverse ways of exploring, meaning making and knowing.

The Capacity of Children with Autism Spectrum Difference to Learn through Play

A lack of spontaneous play, social play and pretend play are generally associated with an assessment of ASD (Kasari et al. 2013). While these social and cognitive differences in the play of children with ASD are empirically grounded, there is a possibility that children's capacity for play is underestimated (Mastrangelo 2009). Play can be conceptualized as a motive or attitude characterized by choice, a focus on means over ends, imagination, self-chosen rules and an active non-stressed mind-set. It is this motive or attitude that gives play an advantage over other pedagogical approaches in the education of young children (Gray 2013).

Play being self-chosen, fosters autonomy, which is an important aspect of self-motivated learning (Gray 2013). Developing autonomy can be difficult for children with ASD, and overly directive adult interactions can further inhibit children's opportunities to become autonomous (Josefi and Ryan 2004). Supporting children engaging in self-directed activity is a valid educational goal in itself and has the added benefit of increasing motivation, concentration and perseverance (Whitebread 2012). Play involves a focus on *means over ends* with the motivation being the activity itself, rather than some goal external to the activity (Gray 2013). When children build a sandcastle, for example, it is the building of the castle rather than having the castle that is the foremost motivation. Pedagogical approaches for children with ASD often favour discrete outcomes and tangible reward systems (Mastrnagelo 2009). Such practices cultivate *a means to ends* rather than *means over ends* attitude. While opportunities for free-play ensure that children with ASD can pursue activities which are intrinsically rewarding to them, fostering a *means over ends* focus during adult-led activities can facilitate a more integrated and holistic learning experience. Play is also characterized by an imaginative element. All types of play can involve imagination as children assign their own meanings to objects, materials, people and behaviours (Barnett and Owens 2015). While children with ASD demonstrate differences with imagination, they are capable of thinking imaginatively (Scott 2013). They may, however, use their imagination differently and need more support to translate imagined ideas into form.

When children play, their activity is guided by self-chosen rules, which requires considerable self-control (Gray 2013). Children adhere to self-chosen rules when deciding how roles will be enacted or how something will be constructed. Children with ASD can experience difficulties with self-regulation (Bieberich and Morgan 2004). Play is important for supporting this aspect of development as children are more inclined to practise self-control when adhering to self-chosen, rather than other imposed, rules. Finally, play involves an active, non-stressed mind-set (Gray 2013). During this type of active learning, children demonstrate engagement, concentration and persistence (Moylett 2013). The emphasis on outcomes, coupled with a tight schedule of therapeutic interventions, can often contribute to a stressed mind-set for children with ASD (Mastrangelo 2009). In addition to space and time, children's sensitivity to various sensory stimuli, which are discussed in Chapter 3, also influences the extent to which the environment supports this type of active learning (Ring, McKenna and Wall 2014).

Children with ASD demonstrate the capacity to direct their own activity, to focus on means over ends, to think imaginatively, to abide by self-chosen rules and to engage in active learning. While the differences they demonstrate in terms of imagination are significant, these differences should not be equated with an absence of play. Play is not all or nothing and is best conceived as a continuum whereby the attitude is more or less playful (Pellegrini 2009). Pedagogically, it is important that we distinguish between teaching children with ASD to play, per se, and teaching them to engage in more cognitively and socially advanced forms of play. Children with ASD, like all children, are motivated to engage in play, albeit in their own unique ways. When learning activities retain elements of play, we avoid making sharp work-play distinctions and children will come to see learning as playful (Howard and McInnes 2013).

> ### Key Signposts: The Capacity of Children with Autism Spectrum Difference to Learn through Play
>
> - Play can be conceptualized as a motive or attitude characterized by choice, a focus on means over ends, imagination, self-chosen rules and an active non-stressed mind-set.
> - The differences children with ASD demonstrate in terms of imagination should not be equated with a lack of motivation to play.
> - Children with ASD, like all children, demonstrate the capacity to play.
> - It is important that we distinguish between teaching children with ASD to play and teaching them to engage in more cognitively and socially advanced forms of play.

The Five Types of Play

Research continues to demonstrate that children benefit from a broad range of play experiences, including physical play, object play, pretend play, symbolic play and games with rules (Whitebread, Basilio, Kuvalja and Verma 2012). These five types of play can be solitary or social and can occur indoors or outdoors. It is through these five types of play that children explore, make meaning of experiences, and learn. The play opportunities of children with ASD can be more limited, given their narrower repertoire of play interests. Furthermore, their unpredictable reaction to new experiences can become a source of anxiety for adults who may, as a consequence, inadvertently restrict certain play experiences (Josefi and Ryan 2004).

Physical Play

Physical play involves active exercise play, rough and tumble play and fine-motor practice (Whitebread et al. 2012). During active exercise play, children engage in physical movement for its own sake. As children with ASD can find participating in structured physical education activities challenging, it is important that they have opportunities to pursue active exercise play (Memari et al. 2015). As described in Chapter 3, some children with ASD will seek out experiences that stimulate their proprioceptive and vestibular systems (Tomchek and Dunn 2007). Running, jumping, climbing, spinning and swinging all activate these systems and provide an appropriate way for children to satisfy their needs for sensory and physically exhilarating input (Wolfberg 2003). Moreover, incorporating playful active exercise breaks during the day through rhymes or songs can support children with ASD engaging in more sedentary and cognitively demanding tasks.

Rough and tumble play involves physically vigorous behaviours, such as chasing and play-fighting (Pellegrini 2011). Despite adult concerns around safety, children are highly attracted to this type of play. Rough and tumble play can contribute to self-regulation as it requires reciprocal role-taking in alternating between the dominator and the dominated and self-handi-capping through, for example, controlling one's own strength so as not to cause real harm (Pellegrini 2009). While rough and tumble play might be overwhelming for some children with ASD, others will be attracted to the tactile and physical input it provides. Moreover, the reciprocal nature of the activity offers a predictable structure within which to engage with peers, which is why this type of play has been associated with positive social inter-action for children with ASD (El-Ghoroury and Romanczyk 1999). Adults can support rough and tumble play through identifying places for play (e.g. outdoors rather than indoors) and agreeing rules (e.g. co-players need to be asked to play/no real hitting). If it is not feasible to facilitate rough and tumble play within the education setting, parents and siblings might be in a position to facilitate it at home (El-Ghoroury and Romanczyk 1999).

Fine motor practice includes activities such as colouring, cutting and manipulating materials and supports strength and control in the finer muscles in the wrists, hands and fingers, while also contributing to self-regulation (Whitebread et al. 2012). Some children with ASD engage in sensori-motor-based activities in ritualistic and stereotypical ways, such as repeated colouring or stringing beads (Tomchek and Dunn 2007). Although it remains difficult to infer what children's main motivation for engaging in such activities is, in some instances the motivation might be the mastery of fine-motor skills or alternatively this may be a sensory response to an internal or external stimulus. Crucially as educators and parents, freely chosen engagement provides us with an avenue to progress the child's learning and development across the curriculum from early years to post-primary school. If a child displays an interest in an activity such as cutting, this preference could be embedded in activities such as collage, which have greater potential to encourage creativity, problem-solving and social interaction.

Key Signposts: Physical Play

- Children with ASD can find participating in structured physical activities challenging, so it is important that they have opportunities for active exercise play.
- Rough and tumble play can be attractive to children with ASD as it provides tactile and physical input.
- The sensori-motor based activities in which children with ASD engage can provide opportunities for fine-motor practice.

Object Play

Object play involves children's exploration with objects and the use of objects to construct or make something (Whitebread et al. 2012). It can involve a broad range of objects, including natural and everyday materials, malleables such as play dough, in addition to constructive play objects, for example, bricks, blocks and building systems. Objects can be highly interesting to children with ASD, with these children often being described as more object than people orientated in their play (Kasari et al. 2013).

Exploratory play provides opportunities for children to learn about their physical world and the objects in it. The sensory profile of children with

ASD can make certain objects more, or less, attractive to them. While malleable materials may appeal to children who seek out a particular tactile sensory input, other children may be oversensitive to such materials (Tomchek and Dunn 2007). Some children may find everyday objects more satisfying than commercially manufactured toys (Holmes and Willoughby 2005). Treasure baskets and heuristic play activities (Goldschmeid and Jackson 1994), which include a wide range of every-day and natural objects, present opportunities to align play more closely with children's observed interests. Children with ASD may need support moving from stereotypical manipulation of objects to more exploratory style interactions (Mastrangelo 2009). For a child who primarily explores objects through mouthing, the adult has a key role in modelling how the object could be explored using other senses, for example using the object to make noise. Adults can also model how objects can be combined in novel ways, such as extending purely tactile exploration with water through modelling how containers can be used to fill and empty water.

Children with ASD can demonstrate difficulties with joint attention where this involves 'the ability to share attention with another person while both people are paying attention to the same object' (Mastrangelo 2009: 36). Difficulties with joint attention can limit opportunities to learn about object properties and functions. Engaging in joint-attention during exploratory play supports children acquiring the foundational knowledge needed to engage in more advanced forms of play. Play with objects, particularly more malleable or sensory materials, can provide a soothing and relaxing experience for the child with ASD (Josefi and Ryan 2004). Such experiences support emotional regulation and it may be counterproductive to redirect the child to more exploratory play. Careful observation will ensure that adult responses are attuned to children's immediate play needs.

When constructing and making, children demonstrate self-regulation as they plan what to make; creativity as they solve problems and mathematical understanding when counting, measuring and exploring spatial concepts (Sarama and Clements 2009). Many children with ASD do not demonstrate typical patterns in constructing and making (Granpeesheh, Tarbox, Najdowski and Korneck 2014). Issues with inhibitory control can make it difficult to engage with the salient features of objects, which then impacts on children's ability to use them creatively (Jarrold and Conn 2011). A child who experiences a strong response to the colour of blocks might be compelled to sort the blocks by colour, which inhibits the facility to use them to construct something. Furthermore, if children have not had adequate opportunities to explore, they may not have the necessary understanding of object properties to build or make something (Wolfberg 2003). With support, children with ASD can broaden their repertoire of strategies and designs when constructing and making (Napolitano, Smith, Zarcone, Goodkin, and McAdam 2010). When children with ASD are ready to construct and make, modelling and describing how to build simple stacks and rows can encourage functional use of construction materials. Difficulties with executive function and self-regulation mean that children with ASD may need help generating ideas, planning and translating ideas into form (Granpeesheh et al. 2014). When adults have knowledge of children's interests, they can suggest meaningful and interesting things to make. Replicas or photographs of objects that the child wants to reconstruct can assist planning and translation of ideas into form. Providing materials that appeal to children's interests also encourages motivation to construct and make, which can be particularly powerful when children demonstrate a preference for open-ended or structured objects. Many children with ASD find constructing and making more rewarding and appealing than other types of play, which therefore provides a readily available playful context through which important social, cognitive and academic learning goals can be worked towards (Dewey, Lord and Magill 1998; Owens et al.).

Key Signposts: Object Play

- Children with ASD can be more object than people orientated in their play.
- Engaging in joint-attention during exploratory play supports children acquiring knowledge of object properties and functions.
- Modelling and describing can encourage functional use of construction materials.
- During constructing and making, children with ASD may need help generating ideas, planning and translating ideas into form.

Pretend Play

In pretend play, children transform objects, people and contexts with pretending being closely related to emotional wellbeing, language, creativity, self-regulation and social competence (O'Sullivan 2016; O'Sullivan and Ring 2016). The research suggests that while children with ASD both understand and produce pretend play in more structured conditions, they are less likely to spontaneously generate pretend play (Kasari et al. 2013). When children with ASD generate pretence, it tends to involve imitation of modelled behaviours or representing something exactly as it is in reality, rather than the generation of impossible or novel ideas (Scott 2013). It is then questionable whether the pretence many children with ASD engage in can be truly labelled pretence if it lacks the spontaneity and novelty typically associated with pretend play Kasari et al. 2013. Another issue relates to how motivating pretend play is for children with ASD. Given that they experience challenges when participating in their social world, they may not have the requisite social understanding to generate pretend play. Alternatively, such cultural reproduction might simply not be rewarding for them (Jarrold, Boucher and Smith 1993).

From an educational perspective, teaching children with ASD pretend play skills is considered to be an important aspect of the curriculum given its potential to foster knowledge and understanding, emotional expression and understanding, self-regulation, language, communication and friendship (Wolfberg 2003). Even if pretence is not children's preferred play activity, it still offers a more child-centred collaborative context within which to support these important aspects of learning. Careful assessment is needed to determine if children need to develop foundational skills before embarking on pretend play. If children spend much of their time engaged in repetitive and stereotypical manipulations of objects, then object exploration and joint attention might be a necessary first step. When children have accrued experience of exploratory play and joint attention, functional play where objects are used for their intended purposes can be encouraged (Mastrangelo 2009). Functional pretence can be supported through modelling object attributions, such as pretending to drink from an empty cup, and enacting simple scripts such as pretending to pour tea and milk into a cup and stirring it before pretending to drink it.

When children are ready for more advanced pretence involving roles and elaborate scripts, everyday themes which are meaningful and in which the child demonstrates an interest should be selected. To take the theme of 'shopping' as an example, adults could facilitate visits to the supermarket and engage in dialogue about what happens there. This ensures children have adequate knowledge of the roles and scripts associated with the theme. A pretend 'supermarket' which includes props such as a cash register, money and grocery items could be set up. Visual prompts of items, people and events characteristic of the supermarket could be provided to support children deciding what to play and to communicate their intentions to others. During play, adults can model specific roles, such as how the shop assistant scans the grocery items in addition to the relationships between different roles, for example, how the shop assistant might ask the customer if they need help packing their bags. It is also important to make suggestions for the child as to how the play could progress. The adult might suggest that after filling the basket with items, the child takes them to the check-out to pay. As children with ASD can find it difficult to imagine non-literal or impossible worlds, targeting metacommunication during pretence can help children understand reality/pretence boundaries (Josefi and Ryan 2004). Metacommuncation allows children to create a play-frame within which it is accepted that behaviour, while acted as if it were real, is not real (Whitebread and O'Sullivan 2012). The use of the word 'pretend', for example, can help children to understand this boundary between fantasy and reality. In this context, the adult can explicitly ask the child if he/she wants to pretend to be the shopkeeper. Using visual cues to signal the beginning and end of the pretend activity can also support children's understanding of pretend play contexts. Supporting children with ASD in developing metacommunication can also equip them with the tools needed to engage in social pretend play with peers (Douglas and Stirling 2012).

> ### *Key Signposts: Pretend Play*
>
> - Children with ASD are less likely to spontaneously generate pretend play. They seem to find pretence less motivating than other types of play.
> - Teaching children with ASD pretend play skills is important, given its potential to foster knowledge and understanding, emotional expression and understanding, self-regulation, language, communication and friendship.
> - Careful assessment is needed to determine if children need to develop foundational skills before embarking on pretend play.

Symbolic Play

While the term symbolic play is often used interchangeably with pretend play, here it is used to denote play with various symbolic systems such as language, music, visual media, writing, reading and mathematical graphics (Whitebread et al. 2012). Play with language involves having fun with language through playing around with sounds, words, rhymes and jokes, rather than using it to communicate meaning (Freeman Davidson 2006). As practice is so important for language learning, adult-directed activities should be balanced with opportunities for children to play around with language in their own unique ways. If echolalia is a feature of the language repertoire of the child with ASD, then they should have some opportunity to freely engage in this. While music may be overwhelming for children who are highly sensitive to auditory input, it can be highly appealing for children who seek out auditory stimulation. As play with music employs verbal and non-verbal modes of communication it can provide a context through which non-verbal children can easily communicate (Boucher 1999). Play with music can support joint attention when music is made collaboratively; self-regulation through the playing of soothing music to regulate anxiety; using songs to signal transitions during the school day or to remember the sequence of daily routines, such as tidy up time (Wimpory and Nash 1999; Pound 2015).

Children are also eager to use a range of media including drawing, painting and collage, in addition to writing, reading and mathematical graphics, for the purpose of representing their ideas (Whitebread et al. 2012). During early drawing, children learn that their marks and symbols can convey meaning. They also learn that letters and words convey meaning and enjoy playing around with scribbles, letter shapes and letters (Mayer 2007; Coates and Coates 2015). Children develop strong preferences for certain storybooks and enjoy opportunities to return to these books during play where they learn skills, such as how to hold a book and turn pages and how to use graphics to decipher the meaning of text (Bissex 1980).

While the exceptional drawing abilities of some children with ASD are well documented, all children with ASD have the capacity to use visual media to represent ideas (Jolly 2010). Similar to pretend play, children with ASD can generate realistic representations but typically have difficulty generating more novel images when drawing (Scott 2013; Allen and Craig 2015). As illustrated through tasks such as the 'draw a man task' and 'draw an impossible man task', children with ASD can produce 'a man' but it is the 'impossible man' which proves problematic (Scott 2013). It seems that children with ASD can think imaginatively as they demonstrate the capacity to represent, through visual media, mental images of previously experienced objects, events and people. Creativity, or using mental images to create new and novel representations, seems to present more of a challenge (Scott 2013).

Play with visual media provides multipe possibilities for children to communicate their ideas. Adults can support play with visual media through providing materials that appeal to individual interests and through modelling the possibilities of such materials to represent ideas. It is also important to consider the conditions that best suit children, such as a preference for working at an easel or a table. Children with ASD might need more support with planning and deciding how they will use visual media to represent ideas (Allen and Craig 2015). It is important that children with ASD have opportunities to engage playfully with visual media on account of the fact that when opportunities are confined to adult prescribed tasks, children experience difficulty using visual media to communicate their own personal meanings.

The main benefit of play with reading and writing is its capacity to foster children's motivation to become readers and writers (Bissex 1984). Through tapping into children's interests, story-books and concept books related to children's individual interests can be sourced and non-book materials can be provided, such as train tickets and timetables if the child is interested is trains. To foster emergent writing it is important to consider children's prefered writing tools and writing materials. Providing a wide selection of writing tools and materials for children with ASD was observed to increase children's engagement and absorption in drawing during the evaluation conducted by Daly and colleagues (2016). It is also helpful when adults model literacy behaviours during play, such as writing down an order in the restaurant in pretend play, given that skill generalization is an important goal in the education of children with ASD.

Play with mathematical graphics involves exploring and communicating mathematical thinking through graphical representation (Carruthers and Worthington 2011) Children attach mathematical meanings to their drawings and writing when they represent quantities that are counted, refer to their marks as numbers and use numbers as labels (Carruthers and Worthington, 2011). This type of play supports children developing the foundational knowledge needed to engage with more standardized mathematics (Davenall 2015). While some children with ASD demonstrate particular islets of ability in terms of mathematical skills, many will be attracted to numbers, quantities and calculations that are often included in their drawings (Lewis and Boucher 1991). When adults tune into the potential of drawings and paintings to represent mathematical thinking they create a meaningful context in which to work towards mathematics learning goals.

Key Signposts: Symbolic Play

- Symbolic play involves play with various symbolic systems, such as language, music, visual media, writing, reading and mathematical graphics.
- As practice is important for language learning, children with ASD should have opportunities to play around with language in their own unique ways.
- Play with music can appeal to children who seek out auditory stimulation.

- Play with visual media, such as drawing and painting, provides multiple possibilities for children with ASD to represent and communicate their ideas.
- Opportunities to play around with reading and writing can foster children's motivation to become readers and writers.
- Children with ASD can be attracted to numbers, quantities and calculations which are often included in their drawings in the form of mathematical graphics.

Games with Rules

Games with rules include simple turn-taking games, chase games, music games, physical games, fantasy games, board games, electronic games and organized sports. Physical games and sports contribute to physical wellbeing while social games contribute to language, communication and social competence (Pellegrini 2009). Games also contribute to self-regulation as children employ executive function skills, such as working memory, when they are required to keep the rules of the game in mind while playing. They also promote inhibitory control when waiting in turn and attentional flexibility through paying attention to other players' actions (McClelland and Tominey 2015).

Simple games, such as finding hidden objects or ball games, can be particularly useful when supporting children with ASD developing joint attention (Josefi and Ryan 2004). Children with ASD can find games with rules particularly appealing, given that they offer more structure than improvisational forms of play, such as pretence (Dewey et al. 1988). Adults can support children with ASD engaging in games through selecting games which are interesting, and which offer an appropriate level of challenge. The provision of activity schedules which provide visual step by step cues can further support children with ASD participating in social games (Betz, Higbee and Reagon 2008). Moreover, an interest in games can easily be promoted across the curriculum to support learning in areas such as self-regulation through playing Simon Says and through sorting and matching games in mathematics, for example.

Key Signposts: Games with Rules

- Children with ASD can find games with rules particularly appealing, given that they offer more structure than improvisational forms of play, such as pretence.
- Simple games, such as ball games, can be useful when supporting children with ASD developing joint attention
- Adults can support children with ASD engaging in games through selecting games which are interesting to them and which offer an appropriate level of challenge.

Social Play

Children with ASD engage more in solitary play and are less likely to spontaneously initiate social interactions with peers (Wolfberg 2003; Owens et al.). Most likely, many factors contribute to the challenges associated with social play. Differences with language and communication clearly make social play much more demanding for children with ASD. Differences with theory of mind development can make understanding the perspectives of others difficult (Jarrold and Conn 2011). Moreover, the play preferences of children with ASD may be less interesting to their peers, which can further diminish opportunities for social interaction (Jarrold, Boucher and Smith 1993). From a motivational perspective, social play might simply not be as rewarding for some children with ASD, or repeated failures to establish social play relationships might also decrease motivation to engage in social play (Jarold et al. 1993).

Given the socially mediated nature of learning, targeting social skills in addition to play skills, is an important part of the curriculum for children with ASD. While one-to-one work makes a powerful contribution to certain social skills, such as developing joint attention, peer interaction can contribute in ways which complement learning mediated by adults. El-Ghoroury and Romanczyk (1999), for example, found that while parents tended to overcompensate for the child with ASD through assuming the responsibility for initiating social interaction. On the other hand, siblings were less likely to do this, giving the child with ASD more responsibility for initiating interactions. Careful assessment of children's play preferences can inform planning as they will be more motivated to initiate social interaction when activities are interesting to them (Owens et al. 2008). Children in the peer group can also be supported to develop strategies that allow them to collaboratively organize and maintain social play with their peers with ASD (El-Ghoroury and Romanczyk, 1999). When adults mediate social play with peers, they are simultaneously promoting social skills, and play skills with a net effect being gains in language, problem-solving and creativity (Kasari et al. 2012).

Key Signposts: Social Play

- Children with ASD engage more in solitary play and are less likely to spontaneously initiate social interactions with peers.
- Targeting social skills in addition to play skills is an important part of the curriculum for children with ASD.
- Children in the peer group can be supported to develop strategies that allow them to collaboratively organize and maintain social play with their peers with ASD.
- When adults mediate social play with peers, they are simultaneously promoting social skills, and play skills with a net effect being gains in language, problem-solving and creativity.

Conclusion

Clearly there is a myriad of possibilities for adopting a playful pedagogy for children with ASD from early years to post-primary level. Through participating in the five types of play, children with ASD can develop play skills and social skills in addition to working towards a broad range of important curriculum learning goals. However, it is clear that children with ASD require additional support to receive the maximum learning benefits from play. Crucially, a balance needs to be maintained between freely chosen play and play where adults become involved so as to subtly guide learning (O' Sullivan and Ring 2016). Such a balance recognizes that opportunities for children to direct their own activity are necessary for overall wellbeing, while adult guidance can extend learning across curricular areas. Supporting children with ASD engaging in social play with peers creates an inclusive culture where all children have opportunities to play and learn together. All children have a right to play and a capacity to do so spontaneously. While all children remain reliant on us to facilitate this right, children with ASD require us to be tireless advocates and ensure their right to play becomes a reality. This chapter is the beginning of that journey.

Bibliography

Allen, M. L., and Craig, E. (2015). 'Brief Report: Imaginative Drawing in Children with Autism Spectrum Disorder and Learning Disabilities', *Journal of Autism and Developmental Disorders*, 46(2), 704–712.

Barnett, L. A., and Owens, M. H. (2015). 'Does play have to be playful?' In J. E. Johnson, S. G. Eberle, T. S. Henricks and D. Kuschner (eds), *The Handbook of the Study of Play*, pp. 453–460. Lanham, MD: Rowan and Littlefield.

Betz, A., Higbee, T. S., and Reagon, K. A. (2008). 'Using Joint Activity Schedules to Promote Peer Engagement in Preschoolers with Autism', *Journal of Applied Behavior Analysis*, 41(2), 237–241.

Bieberich A. A., and Morgan, S. B. (2004). 'Self-regulation and Affective Expression during Play in Children with Autism or Down Syndrome: A Short-Term Longitudinal Study', *Journal of Autism and Developmental Disorders*, 34(4), 439–448.

Bissex, G. L. (1980). *GNYS AT WRK: A Child Learns to Read and Write*. Cambridge, MA: Harvard University Press.

Boucher, J. (1999). 'Editorial: Interventions with Children with Autism – Methods based on Play', *Child Language Teaching and Therapy*, 15(1) 1–5.

Carruthers, E., and Worthington, M. (2011). *Understanding Children's Mathematical Graphics: Beginnings in Play*. Berkshire: McGraw Hill Open University Press.

Coates, E., and Coates, A. (2015). 'Recognising the sacred spark of wonder: Scribbling and related talk as evidence of how young children's thinking may be identified'.

In S. Robson and S. Flannery Quinn (eds), *The Routledge International Handbook of Children's Thinking and Understanding*, pp. 306–317. Abingdon: Routledge.

Daly, P., Ring, E., Egan, M., Fitzgerald, J., Griffin, C., Long, S., McCarthy, E., Moloney, M., O'Brien, T., O'Byrne, A., O'Sullivan, S., Ryan, M., Wall, E., Madden, R., and Gibbons, S. (2015). *An Evaluation of Education Provision for Students with Autism Spectrum Disorder in Ireland*. Trim: National Council for Special Education.

Davenall, J. (2015). 'Young Children's Mathematical Recording', *Mathematics Teaching*, November, 46–50.

Dewey, S., Lord, C., and Magill, J. (1988). 'Qualitative Assessment of the effect of Play Materials in Dyadic Peer Interactions of Children with Autism', *Canadian Journal of Psychology*, 42(2), 242–260.

Douglas, S., and Stirling, L. (2012). 'Metacommunication, Social Pretend Play and Children with Autism', *Australasian Journal of Early Childhood*, 37(4), 34–43.

El-Ghoroury, N. H., and Romanczyk, R. (1999). 'Play Interactions of Family Members towards Children with Autism', *Journal of Autism and Developmental Disorders*, 29(3), 249–258.

Freeman Davidson, J. I. (2006). 'Language and Play: Natural Partners'. In D. Fromberg and D. Bergen, (eds), *Play from Birth to Twelve – Contexts, Perspectives and Meaning* (2nd edn), pp. 31–40. New York: Routledge.

Goldschmeid, E., and Jackson, S. (1994). *People under Three: Young Children in Day-Care*. Abingdon: Routledge.

Granpeesheh, D. Tarbox, J., Najdowski, A. C., and Korneck, J. (2014). *Evidence-based Treatment for Children with Autism: The CARD Model*. Oxford: Academic Press.

Gray, P. (2013). *Free to Learn: Why Unleashing the Instinct to Play will make our Children Happier, more Self-reliant and better Students for Life*. New York: Basic Books.

Holmes, E., and Willoughby, T. (2005). 'Play Behaviour of Children with Autism Spectrum Disorders', *Journal of Intellectual and Developmental Disability*, 30(3), 156–164.

Howard, J., and McInnes, K. (2013). *The Essence of Play: A Practice Companion for Professionals working with Children and Young People*. London: Routledge.

Jarrold, C., and Conn, C. (2011). 'The Development of Play in Children with Autism'. In A. Pellegrini (ed.), *The Oxford Handbook of the Development of Play*, pp. 308–321. Oxford: Oxford University Press.

Jarrold, C., Boucher, J., and Smith, P. (1993). 'Symbolic Play in Autism: A Review', *Journal of Autism and Developmental Disorders*, 23(2), 281–307.

Jolly, R. P. (2010). *Children and Pictures: Drawing and Understanding*. Sussex: Wiley Blackwell.

Jordan, R. (2003). 'Social Play and Autistic Spectrum Disorders: A Perspective on Theory Implications and Educational Approaches', *Autism*, 7(4), 347–360.

Josefi, O., and Ryan, V. (2004). 'Non-Directive Play Therapy for Young Children with Autism: A Case Study', *Clinical Child Psychology and Psychiatry*, 9(4), 533–551.

Kasari, C., Chang, Y., and Patterson, S. (2013). 'Pretending to Play or Playing to Pretend: The Case of Autism', *American Journal of Play*, 2(4), 124–135.

Lewis, V., and Boucher, J. (1991). 'Skill, Content and Generative Strategies in Autistic Children's Drawings', *British Journal of Developmental Psychology*, 9, 393–416.

Mayer, K. (2007). 'Emerging Knowledge about Emergent Writing', *Young Children*, 62 (1) 34–40.

McClelland, M. M., and Tominey, S. L. (2015). *Stop, Think, Act: Integrating Self-Regulation in the Early Childhood Classroom*. New York: Routledge.

Mastrangelo, S. (2009). 'Harnessing the Power of Play: Opportunities for Children with Autistic Spectrum Disorders', *Teaching Exceptional Children*, 42(1), 34–44.

Memari, A. H., Panahi, N., Ranjbar, E., Moshayedi, P., Shafiei, M., Kordi, R., and Ziaee, V. (2015). 'Children with Autism Spectrum Disorder and Patterns of Participation in Daily Physical and Play Activities', *Neurology Research International*, 2015, 1–7.

Moylett, H. (2013). *Active learning*. London: Practical Preschool.

Napolitano, D. A., Smith, T., Zarcone, J. R., Goodkin, K., and McAdam, D. B. (2010). 'Increasing Response Diversity in Children with Autism', *Journal of Applied Behavior Analysis*, 43(2), 265–271.

National Council for Curriculum and Assessment (2009). *Aistear: The Early Childhood Curriculum Framework*. Dublin: National Council for Curriculum and Assessment.

O'Sullivan, L. (2016). 'Social Pretend Play and Self-regulation', *Early Education Journal*, 80, 12–15.

O'Sullivan, L., and Ring, E. (2016) 'Supporting a Playful Approach to Learning in the Early Years: Early Years Education-Focused Inspections: A Licence to Play', *Childlinks*, 1, 2–6.

Owens, G., Granader, Y., Humphry, A., and Baron-Cohen, S. (2008). 'LEGO Therapy and the Social Use of Language Programme: An Evaluation of Two Social Skills Interventions for Children with High Functioning Autism and Asperger Syndrome', Journal *of Autism and Developmental Disorders*, 38, 944–1957.

Paul, R. (2008). 'Interventions to Improve Communication in Autism', *Child and Adolescent Psychiatric Clinics of North America*, 17(4) 835–856. DOI: 10.1016/j.chc.2008.06.011.

Pellegrini, A. D. (2009). *The Role of Play in Human Development*. New York: Oxford University Press.

Pellegrini A. (2011). 'The Development and Function of Locomotor Play'. In A. Pellegrini (ed.), *The Oxford Handbook of the Development of Play*, pp. 172–183. Oxford: Oxford University Press.

Pound, L. (2015). 'In Tune with Play'. In J. Moyles (ed.), *The Excellence of Play* (3rd edn), pp. 201–212. Buckinghamshire: Open University Press.

Ring, E., McKenna, M., and Wall, E. (2014). 'Quality educational experiences for children with autistic spectrum differences. Perspectives for the classroom in the 21st century – an Irish perspective'. In P. M. Rabensteiner and G. Rabensteiner (eds), *Internationalisation in Teacher Education*, pp. 207–229. Batlmannsweiler: Schneider Verlag Hohengehren GmbH.

Ring, E., Mhic Mhathúna, M., Moloney, M., Hayes, N., Breathnach, D., Stafford, P., Carswell, D., Keegan, S., Kelleher, C., McCafferty, D., O'Keeffe, A., Leavy, A., Madden, R., and Ozonyia, M. (2016). *An Examination of Concepts of School Readiness among Parents and Educators in Ireland*. Dublin: Department of Children and Youth Affairs.

Sarama, J., and Clemments, D. H. (2009). 'Building Blocks and Cognitive Building Blocks: Playing to Know the World Mathematically', *American Journal of Play*, 1, 313–337.

Scott, F. J. (2013). 'The Development of Imagination in Children with Autism'. In M. Taylor (ed.), *The Oxford Handbook of the Development of Imagination*, pp. 499–515. Oxford: Oxford University Press.

Tomchek, S. D., and Dunn, W. (2007). 'Sensory Processing in Children with and without Autism: A Comparative Study using the Short Sensory Profile', *The American Journal of Occupational Therapy* 61(2) 190–200.

Whitebread, D., Basilio, M., Kuvalja, M., and Verma, M. (2012). *The Importance of Play: A Report on the Value of Children's Play with a Series of Policy Recommendations* (Toy Industries of Europe). Accessed online on 25 January 2018 at <http://www.importanceofplay.eu/IMG/pdf/dr_david_whitebread_-_the_importance_of_play.pdf>.

Whitebread, D., and O'Sullivan, L. (2012). 'Preschool Children's Social Pretend Play: Supporting the Development of Metacommunication, Metacognition and Self-Regulation', *International Journal of Play*, 1, 197–213.

Wimpory, D. C., and Nash, S. (1999). 'Musical Interaction Therapy – Therapeutic Play for Children with Autism', *Child Language Teaching and Therapy*, 15(1), 17–28.

Wolfberg, P. J. (2003). *Peer Play and the Autism Spectrum: The Art of Guiding Children's Socialization and Imagination*. Kansas: Autism Asperger Publishing Co.

SARAH FEENEY

3   Addressing Children's Sensory Differences: Strategies for Practice

ABSTRACT

All of us have sensory preferences, varying tolerances, likes and dislikes. For children with autism spectrum difference (ASD), these sensory differences can have a pervasive impact on both the child's wellbeing and ability to engage with the environment and learning (Ayres 2005; Stock Kranowitz 2005; Murray-Slutsky and Paris 2014; Grandin 2015). By observing and acknowledging these differences, adaptations can be made that can help the child's sensory system, thus helping the child reach the ultimate goal of a calm alert state (Ayres 2005; Kuypers 2011).

This chapter aims to explain sensory integration processes in the body by outlining each sensory system and addressing both normative and atypical development. Examples of sensory differences are offered and strategies are suggested for parents, teachers and anyone working with, and supporting, children with ASD. A list of suggested resources is also provided that the author has found to be particularly useful in her work with children with sensory differences. As the language used in this field can be both perplexing and ambiguous, a glossary of terms is available at Appendix A of this chapter, which can be consulted as you read the chapter.

Introduction

Many children can have a sensory processing difference (SPD) without having ASD. However, it is widely accepted that all children with ASD experience some degree of SPD (Stocl Kranowitz 2005; Horwood 2009; Koomar 2014; Miller 2014). The 'hallmark feature' of SPD in children is that their sensory differences are 'chronic' and disrupt their everyday life. (Miller 2014). 'Hypo- or hyper-reactivity to sensory input/ unusual interests in sensory aspects of the environment' is now a diagnostic feature in the criteria for ASD in the fifth edition of the Diagnostic and Statistical Manual of Mental Disorders (DSM V) (American Psychological Association (APA) 2013: 50).

It is important to acknowledge the central role of the occupational therapist (OT) or sensory integration (SI) therapist in assessing and addressing sensory differences. Sensory processing is a biological neuroscience, and challenges with sensory integration can present in a number of ways, thus the need for careful professional evaluation (Ayres 2005; Stock Kranwowitz 2005; Dunn 2008; Murray-Slutsky and Paris 2014). A multi-disciplinary team (MDT) approach is preferable, with input from OT, psychologist, physiotherapist and speech and language therapist in evaluating and planning intervention for a child with ASD and sensory needs.

In the recently published evaluation of education provision for children with ASD in Ireland, reference was repeatedly made to the limited availability of MDTs to support both parents and schools (Daly et al. 2016: 197). This is also an issue internationally and is recognized as a barrier for ASD diagnosis, alongside access to interventions and services, which negatively impacts a child's development (Wallace et al. 2012; Wan et al. 2013; Cummings, Case, Ji, and Marcus 2015; Elder, Brasher and Alexander 2016; Antezana, Scarpa, Valdespino, Albright and Richey 2017).

Therefore, while affirming the need for MDT approaches, we must also concede that there are long waiting lists for both initial diagnosis, and further sensory assessments. However, in the interim parents, teachers and other professionals can gain a basic understanding of sensory differences and be confident of offering some sensory input, which is safe and helpful.

According to Aspy and Grossman (2011) the sensory differences a person with ASD might encounter include, but are not limited to, responding unusually to sound, smell, taste, light, colour and temperature. Individuals may seek or avoid activities that provide touch, pressure or movement. Studies on the prevalence of sensory differences suggest an incidence of 69–95 per cent for individuals with ASD (Leekam, Libby, Wing, Gould, and Taylor 2002; Baranek, David, Poe, Stone, and Watson 2006; Tomcheck and Dunn 2007). These figures include those who are either over-responsive or under-responsive to a range of sensory stimuli, as well as those who are sensory seeking. Often, the experience is a mix of these, with individuals found to be both under- and over-responsive simultaneously (Baranek 2002; Baranek et al. 2006, Lane and Reynolds cited in Murray-Slutsky and Paris 2014).

The Ziggurat Model, developed by Aspy and Grossman (2011), depicted in Figure 3.1, presents a useful framework to support us in designing interventions for children with ASD. The model focuses on children's sensory and biological needs through placing them at the heart of intervention, while prioritizing the need for a sensory diet and the monitoring of environmental stressors and movement needs in conjunction with appetite, fatigue and medical needs. If children's sensory needs are a basic biological prerequisite, then we must address sensory difference through this lens. The Evaluation Framework developed by Middletown Centre for ASD (MCA) and the National Council for Special Education (NCSE) (MCA and NCSE 2013) specified 'access to sensory resources' as a stress-reducing initiative to enhance children's wellbeing.

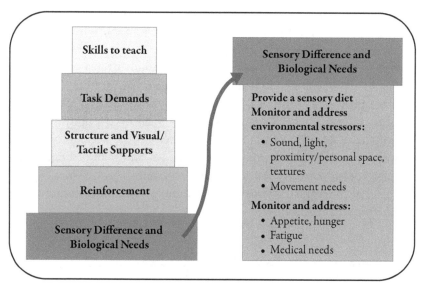

Figure 3.1: Ziggurat Model (adapted from Aspy and Grossman 2011)

Key Signposts: Introduction

- It is widely accepted that all children with ASD experience some degree of sensory processing difference, being over- and/or under-responsive to a range of sensory stimuli.
- Parents, teachers and other professionals can gain a basic understanding of sensory differences and be confident of offering some sensory input which is safe and helpful.
- Viewing children's sensory needs as a basic biological prerequisite is the first step on the path to intervening effectively.

What is Sensory Integration?

Sensory integration (SI) is a neurological process that takes place automatically in the typically developing child (Ayres 2005). Sensory integration theory was developed in the 1970s by Dr Jean Ayres, whose ideas and theories were rooted in occupational therapy and her research studies in educational psychology and neuroscience. Sensory integration theory and research provide a theoretical framework, a lens through which we can examine and explain behaviour. As a process, SI allows the body to receive and organize sensations from the environment, process the information and make an effective adaptive response (Case-Smith and Bryan 1999). For SI to occur correctly, Anzalone and Williamson (2000) identify five interrelated components, namely: registration; orientation; interpretation; organizing and executing a response.

Registration

Sensory registration is the '*when and how*' of becoming aware of input. For us to become aware of sensations they must firstly reach our own individual threshold. However, this threshold is affected by stress, expectations and environmental conditions. For example, if a noise awakens you from sleep you are on '*high alert*' and may hear or register sounds around you that ordinarily you would not. For children with ASD, their threshold may be out of synchronization with what's expected, they may be over- or under-responsive to sensory input because their level of registration is higher or lower than the circumstance would normally warrant. It is very common for children, and adults, with ASD to be over-responsive to touch and sound (Williamson and Anzalone 2001; Dunn 2008; Grandin 2015; MCA 2017).

It is very important to note that responses to sensory input can fluctuate greatly, even within a day, and that some children who appear unresponsive can actually be highly sensitive, leading them to 'shut down' as a form of self-protection (Yack, Aquilla and Sutton 2015).

Orientation

Sensory orientation, also called sensory modulation, is the '*paying of attention*' to the required sensory input. Typically developing children are able to regulate what information they need to tune into and what information can be ignored. For example, they can focus on the voice of the teacher rather than sounds outside the classroom. Many children with ASD tend to focus on insignificant sensory inputs and thus miss out on the important messages being communicated. Ayres (2005) likens this sensory orientation/modulation to volume control. Ayres also observes that children with ASD can have difficulty adjusting their 'volume control' and become overwhelmed.

Interpretation

Interpretation is crucial in order for the body to form the appropriate response. Interpretation of sensory information in the brain is linked with the synapses between the parts of the brain responsible for, memory, where for example a taste may remind us of a time we had similar food and got sick, resulting in us developing a dislike for this taste. Here there are some readily identifiable issues for children with ASD. If the child has previously made negative associations with events, it can affect the child's reaction to sensory input, which can sometimes be difficult to observe and interpret out of context. For example, the child might associate a taste with the last time the taste was experienced – and being in the park where it was very noisy and too bright. The child's immediate reaction might be to spit out the food to avoid the environment again becoming noisy and bright.

Interpretation of sensory input is the point of the response where the body can execute 'fright, fight or flight' reaction. One reason those with ASD strive for routine is because the world is so unpredictable for them, and bombards them with sensory input on a daily basis (Stock Kranowitz 2005; Miller 2014; Grandin 2015). This 'sensory bombardment' can be very difficult to process and sensations may be interpreted consistently as new and unfamiliar, thus engaging the child's fight or flight reaction all the time, thereby leading to the child being described as sensory defensive.

Organize a Response

After sensory input has been interpreted, the next step for the brain is to organize a response. Responses can be physical, emotional, cognitive, or a combination of all. For example, 'I hear a sound, I recognize it is coming from the telephone, I know this means the phone is ringing. Now I can decide to pick up the phone and answer it, or not'.

If someone has difficulty with registration, orientation and interpretation, it is at this point where others can begin to identify it, through observing an inappropriate reaction or difficulty at the stage of forming a reaction or response.

Execute a Response

Finally, we react, the last stage of the process of SI. Those who experience problems with motor planning can also have inappropriate physical responses to sensory input. Conversely, this is a two-way street as issues with sensory integration have also been linked to poor motor planning (Ornitz 1974; Donnellen, Hill and Leary 2013).

Sensory processing can be interrupted at any, and many, points along the way, resulting in many difficulties for the child and ranging in severity. Sensory integration dysfunction is the term used by Ayres to describe atypical responses that some have to sensory stimuli due to the nervous system's inability to receive and integrate sensory input from the environment (Ayres 2005). Sensory dysfunction points to difficulty with either the sensory message being received or else the message not making the correct connection in the brain. Sensory processing issues in ASD can be categorized as sensory modulation differences, sensory discrimination differences and sensory-based motor differences (Stock Kranowitz, 2005; Murray-Slutsky and Paris 2014). Poor motor ability in those with ASD can be related to sensory issues, such as sensory discrimination/sensory modulation, as well as neurodevelopmental differences related to core stability and motor organization. Children who experience sensory dysfunction can have problems across multiple areas, they may appear disorganized and offer inconsistent performance. The implications for children with ASD have been described as:

> Atypical language, memory and emotional development in individuals with ASD may interfere with the ability to interpret sensory information. Sensory experiences may not be adequately labelled or remembered. Familiar, pleasurable sensory experiences may not be connected with positive emotions. Individuals with ASD may also have problems with the stages of sensory registration and orientation subsequently hampering the interpretation process. (Yack et al. 2015: 20)

When senses develop in the neuro-typical child, development is automatic and takes unconscious effort. Children without sensory issues do not have to learn the steps and processes associated with SI. It is somewhat difficult then to consider how sensory input, for example, jumping on a trampoline, could potentially help a child to listen more carefully in the time period following the exercise. It can be even more confusing to consider that jumping for five minutes may not be alerting enough and jumping for ten minutes might be too much and overstimulate the child.

Because we are all on a sensory-processing continuum, we all at some time experience sensory processing problems where we become deregulated

(Stock Kranowitz 2005). An important caveat to note is that a child might be over- *and* under-responsive in one sensory system and across all sensory systems. For example, a child may be oversensitive to an alarm clock but tolerate a fire alarm. Sometimes practitioners can disregard a sensory problem if we don't see it in every context, but context is of very considerable importance (Miller 2014; Yack et al. 2015: 20; Grandin 2017). The child who usually finds assembly totally overwhelming may be able to cope when assembly is directly after time in the sensory room. If a child is in a state of high alert, new sensations may trigger reactions and, similarly, if a child is calm and alert, usual triggers that upset may be tolerated.

Key Signposts: What is Sensory Integration?

- Sensory integration (SI) theory is a theoretical framework developed by Jean Ayres.
- As a process, SI allows the body to receive and organize sensations from the environment, process the information and respond.
- For correct SI to occur, there are five interrelated steps: registration, orientation, interpretation, organizing and executing a response
- Children with sensory differences can have problems at any or many stages of SI.
- When observing sensory responses in children, context is of huge importance and a major consideration when deciding if a response is sensory or behavioural.

What Can We Do?

When any child presents with a behaviour, it is fundamental to check for underlying medical issues (Grandin 2017). Sometimes, we can wrongly associate behaviours with a diagnosis of ASD and a related sensory-processing issue, but this is not always the case and assessment by a qualified professional should always be the first step. For example, the child who covers his ears, bangs his head or doesn't respond to calling may be suffering from persistent ear infections and require treatment. The child who drools and chews may indeed have some oral motor issues but may also have a tooth infection. It is always important to rule these possibilities out first before embarking on sensory-based therapies.

Best practice in education now advocates a universal design for learning for all (Burgstahler 2009; Katz 2013; Johnson-Harris and Mundschenk 2014). We all have sensory preferences, regardless of the presence or absence of any other diagnosis, and creating a learning environment to suit and benefit all sensory preferences reflects the principles of Universal Design. Having various seating options available, various writing utensils and supports, being able to control light, temperature, background noise to a certain extent will both reduce stigma attached to those with sensory differences and promote access to learning for everyone. It is well documented that all types of learners benefit from movement breaks (Kwak, Kremers, Bergman, Ruiz, Rizzo and Sjostrom 2009; Donnelly and Lanbourne 2011; Webster, Russ, Vasou, Goh, and Erwin 2015). The National Behaviour Support Service (NBSS) states that 'incorporating planned movement breaks within lesson plans is an effective way of 'feeding' the children's sensory systems and maintaining their levels of alertness' (NBSS, 2017:1).

'Ayres Sensory Integration' (ASI®) is a trademarked therapy based on fidelity to certain circumstances and can be carried out only by a certified SI therapist (Fisher, Murray and Bundy 1991; Kimball 1993; Ayres 2005; Miller 2014). However, in the absence of a certified therapist, ASI® provides a useful frame of reference to begin to understand how behaviours may be linked to sensory processing and help us identify meaningful interventions (Case-Smith and Bryan 1999). If interventions are not ASI®, then they are termed 'sensory-based interventions' (Murray-Slutsky and Paris 2014; Watling and Hauer 2015). Sensory-based interventions can be very effective in helping the functioning of a child with ASD and include sensory diets, sensory stories, access to multi-sensory rooms, specific equipment and any sensory stimulation or enhancement offered to a child or made to their environment (Miller 2014).

The exact neuroscience of SI is based in occupational therapy and physical therapy. So for teachers, parents and those working with children with ASD, sensory diets and sensory-based interventions can be intimidating and seem outside our remit. What we can do, however, is closely observe and monitor. Observing and monitoring behaviour, attempting to identify possible causes and effects in the child's environment can lead to better understanding and, therefore, lead to better provision. Both Yack, Acquilla and Sutton (2015) and Stock Kranowitz (2005) offer teacher and parent assessment checklists to guide observation of sensory differences. Daly and colleagues reported that 'excellent practice was often evident in supporting children to self-regulate' (Daly et al., 2016: 199). Once we follow the child's lead and watch their responses there are many things we can try. Children won't readily engage in and/or positively respond to a sensory activity which displeases them. If the aim of a sensory input is to relax and calm, then simply following the child's lead is often a safe strategy to use. However, caution must be used as the 'sensory seeker' may happily over-stimulate himself/herself; therefore, careful monitoring of reactions and outcomes is critical (Horwood 2009; Yack et al. 2015).

A 'sensory diet' is a carefully designed activity plan that provides the desired amount of sensory input a child needs to stay focused and organized during the day (Wilbarger and Wilbarger 2002). Sensory diets, while executed by parents and/or supporting practitioners, should be designed and reviewed by OTs, SI therapists or physiotherapists.

Sensory stories are a useful tool in assisting a child with ASD to cope with undesirable but unavoidable sensory input (Marr and Nacklev 2006). Similar in approach to Carol Gray's Social Story approaches (Gray 2000), sensory stories detail the steps involved in a sensory activity, for example getting a haircut, in a meaningful way related to the child's level of understanding. The story is read by or to the child frequently in a bid to teach the child the skills needed to successfully engage in the targeted activity.

Multi-sensory rooms are designated spaces where light and sound can be controlled and sensory stimulating equipment is used to create a relaxing space to calm and gently stimulate the sensory systems in the body. They are often used by children with ASD as a calming, relaxing time-out from classroom situations. With sensory-based interventions, we are fundamentally seeking to take away or change the stressor for the child; to give the child structure and routine, visuals and sensory activities and to teach the child self-regulatory coping strategies and replacement behaviours (Murray-Slutsky and Paris 2014). An understanding of the sensory systems is an important pre-requisite for devising sensory-based interventions.

Key Signposts: What Can We Do?

- Firstly, rule out any underlying medical issues.
- Monitor, observe, assess and get to know the child.
- When considering behaviour, always ask yourself 'what *else* could it be?'.
- Seek support from an Occupational Therapist or Sensory Therapist.
- Apply the principles of Universal Design and offer sensory supports and movement breaks to all children.
- Sensory diets, sensory stories, multi-sensory rooms and equipment are useful tools to help.

Understanding the Sensory Systems

A child with ASD may have sensory differences in each or a number of the body's sensory systems. As stated previously, it is always worthwhile to start with an assessment by an OT, or SI therapist with input from a physiotherapist also, if available. In the absence of this, or while awaiting it, practitioners and parents can refer to books and sensory programmes commercially available as a starting point (see section on suggested resources at the end of the chapter). It is always beneficial to start with a parent/teacher-based questionnaire or checklist to gain an overview of a child's sensory differences and begin to understand possible triggers.

The sensory systems of the body are

- Visual (Sense of sight)
- Auditory (Sense of hearing)
- Olfactory (Sense of Smell)
- Gustatory (Sense of taste)
- Tactile (Sense of Touch)
- Vestibular (Sense of balance and movement)
- Proprioception (sense of body in space)

Sometimes interoception is included in this list also. This sense provides information from our internal organs, for example, sensations of hunger, thirst, temperature and the urge to urinate. According to Stock Kranowitz (2005), many children can have inefficient interoception, and Ayres (2005) claims poor interoception has an impact on the development of the vestibular, proprioceptive, tactile, auditory and visual senses. The cumulative effect of this is difficulty in using our body, in developing concentration and academic skills, confidence and self-esteem (Fisher et al. 1991; Ayres, 2005).

Signposts are provided in Tables 3.1 to 3.7 in relation to accommodating each of these sensory systems for children with ASD in early years, primary, post-primary and special school settings. These tables have been collated and adapted from Stock Kranowitz (2005); Marr and Nacklev (2006); Horwood (2009); Kuypers (2011); Murray-Slutsky and Paris (2014); (Yack et al. 2015); Grandin (2017) and MCA (2017).

Table 3.1: Signposts for Accommodating Visual Differences in Early Years, Primary, Post-Primary and Special School Settings

- Keeping environments free of visual clutter is important and helps the child focus on the relevant information.
- Using symbolic visual representation that are meaningful to the individual child – e.g. objects of reference, photographs, symbols, words in visual timetables and communication systems.
- Reduce visual distractions in classroom – turning off computers/whiteboards when not in use.
- Remove florescent lighting and consider using dimmer switches.
- Reduce and limit the amount of visual information, data on a page etc. that is presented to the child.
- Consider where child is placed in room, use physical structure to limit visual overloading, as is used in the TEACCH approach.
- If children seem overly interested in some particular visual stimuli, firstly consider how this can be used as a teaching and learning tool: Can it be incorporated to initiate /maintain interest and if not can its use be limited/honed? Can it be used before a lesson to help child reach calm alert state, or can it be used as a motivator? Can you observe and isolate what it is that is of particular interest for the child and can you build upon this?

Table 3.2: Signposts for Accommodating Auditory Differences in Early Years, Primary, Post-Primary and Special School Settings

Auditory Sense	Common Responses	Sensory-Based Interventions
Over-Sensitive	• Avoids noisy situations. • Makes noise to block out other sounds. • Distracted by background sounds, distressed by sounds that do not bother others, such as the hum of the fridge. • Difficulties in giving and maintaining attention.	• Overall goal is to decrease sound sensitivity so that the child can cope with sounds around them – a delicate balance that can take time. • Provide ear defenders – it is very important to ensure that these are not used all the time but as a tool on the road to desensitization. For example, allow the child to wear them in the supermarket but not in the classroom, and in the kitchen but not in the living room. • Allow the child to control the sound that bothers them through allowing them to turn off the source of the sound. • Provide enjoyable activities as a distraction in noisy situations – or for use on desensitization programmes. For example, provide child with favourite toy/comforter/book when at a whole-school event. • Use first/then schedules and/or timers so that the child knows how long they are expected to tolerate noise. • Deep pressure input often helps children in these situations. • Insofar as possible, monitor and control the sound levels in the child's home and school environment. • Teach child strategies for 'time out' breaks or for requesting ear defenders for when they are getting overwhelmed. Try to help the child to develop this awareness in themselves. • Provide quiet working areas in the classroom.

(Continued)

Table 3.2: (Continued)

Auditory Sense	Common Responses	Sensory-Based Interventions
Under-Sensitive	• Slow to respond, lethargic, passive, 'daydreamer'. • Can go 'under the radar', as is usually quiet and well behaved. • Does not interact well with others. • Displays a general lack of awareness. • Doesn't react to the environment and/or • Heavily reliant on visual cues. • Speaks in a soft tone of voice.	• Increase sensory input to gain the child's attention and allow for the input to register on the child's higher threshold. • Offer physical activity before a lesson – e.g. trampolining, running, jumping jacks, and provide frequent movement breaks. • For the under-responsive child with ASD an activity might need to be scaffolded – i.e. rather that expecting this child to do five jumping jacks, they may need to co-ordinate this with another activity – complete a five-piece jigsaw but do one jumping jack between each piece placement. Maybe time the activity and try to increase times each go. • Use visual supports. • Allow this child to hum, sing and chat to themselves as this may be keeping them alert.

Table 3.3: Signposts for Accommodating Olfactory Differences in Early Years, Primary, Post-Primary and Special School Settings

- This is often an area that only needs addressing when it's a pervasive issue.
- When children don't like sitting near others at mealtimes, it can be related to the particular smells of other plates/lunch boxes. Following observation, the complexities of the issue need to be acknowledged and a pragmatic approach adopted:
  - In some cases, global accommodations may be required. For example, if a particular brand of food is observed to be generating the response, asking all children not to bring this brand may be the solution or asking children to eat this at a different time.
  - If a more pervasive issue is emerging, a targeted programme aimed at desensitizing the child, similar to sound desensitization may be required. Using First/ Then and timers to allow the child to understand for how long he/she will be near the source of smell, or adjusting the intensity of the smell can be explored. Incorporating smell into sensory place and using liked scents to promote positive outcomes may all help.
- For the smell seeker, and to desensitize others, smelling jars can be used as a sensory activity and also providing the child with cloths with varying strong scents can help.
- Sensory stories can be used to explain to children who seek sensory stimulation through inappropriately smelling people and objects in their environment.

Table 3.4: Signposts for Accommodating Gustatory Differences in Early Years, Primary, Post-Primary and Special School Settings

- Allow favoured foods at mealtime.
- Any desensitization efforts regarding food should not be associated with meal times at first.
- Introduce new foods in sensory play first, and follow immediately with an object/ activity of high interest in order to create positive associations and reward the child for interacting with new food.
- When introducing new food, maintain the child's preferred texture, and when introducing a new texture, use a favoured food. Do not introduce new food *and* new texture together.
- For some children, strong flavours (sour sweets, strong mints etc.) may contribute to improving children's alertness and can be used effectively for this purpose.

Table 3.5: Signposts for Accommodating Tactile Differences in Early Years, Primary, Post-Primary and Special School Settings

Responses to Touch	Common Responses	Sensory-Based Interventions
Over-Sensitive	• Avoids touches – both initiating and receiving. • Dislikes getting dirty. • Dislikes certain textures and labels on clothes. • May insist on long sleeves/trousers regardless of season.	• Implement desensitization strategies. • Ensure a gradual exposure to messy play. For example, use dry ingredients first; allow the child to wear gloves at first.
Under-Sensitive	• Seems unaware of touch. • Unaware of tactile experiences, such as food on face or having clothes in disarray. • Under-responsive to pain and temperature. • Lack of motivation to touch anything.	• Massage (either use of massagers or having person massage child, can be helpful to make child aware of body part/limb). • Use of vibrating toys (to 'wake up' body part, electric toothbrushes are often used on mouth area before speech and language work). • Textured mediums (having varying materials for child to touch – on a wall or in a book).
Sensory-Seeking	• May seek tickles/massage/deep pressure. • Enjoys vibration or major movement activities, such as on the trampoline. • Seems to be driven to touch and feel everything in environment. • Likes to be barefoot.	• Physical activities. • Use of theraputty (similar to 'play dough' but comes in different resistances making it harder or easier to manipulate). • Add resistance to fine motor activities – pencil weights, etc. • Messy play.
Issues with Tactile Discrimination	• Displays poor body awareness. • Displays trouble orientating body during dressing and self-care routines. • Can potentially limit the child's vocabulary and impact negatively on imaginative capacity due to lack of tactile experiences. • Needs to use vision in conjunction with touch. The child displays difficulty in recognizing items without looking at them also.	• Deep pressure (can be applied to child by another person or through use of weighted garments, lap weights, weighted toys under guidance of OT).

| Issues with Praxis/ Motor Planning | • Exhibits poor gross motor skills.
• Has poor hand-eye co-ordination.
• Limited fine motor skills in precise use of fingers/toes/mouth.
• Experiences challenges in following sequences in both physical and cognitive tasks, for example, dressing and/or following a recipe. | • Use of therabands (stretchy bands used to create muscular resistance – can be used as fidgets when tied to chair legs).
• Trampolining.
• Lots of high activity dispersed throughout child's day.
• Proprioception activities
• Tactile treasure hunts.
• Use of 'feelie bags'/sensory bins (a selection of different materials and textures for child to engage with).
• Cookery activities – stirring, mixing, washing up.
• Exposure and exploration of different types of textures.
• Multi-sensory approaches to learning.
• Blindfold games – pin the tail etc. (if child is comfortable with it, it allows them to focus on tactile sense rather than vision).
• Tactile stepping stones – tactile obstacle course. |

Table 3.6: Signposts for Accommodating Vestibular Differences in Early Years, Primary, Post-Primary and Special School Settings

Responses on Vestibular Input	Common Responses	Sensory-Based Interventions
Over-Sensitive	• Presents as 'intolerant' to movement. • Dislikes and/or avoids swings, slides, roundabouts, lifts and escalators. • A child may have 'gravitational insecurity', resulting in an abnormal fear of falling. • Displays anxiety when the feet are not touching the ground. • Dislikes head being inverted or tilted – for example during hair washing. • Is fearful of climbing.	Vestibular input should be planned and supervised by experienced OTs/ SI therapists. Overload is easily achieved with vestibular activities and can have negative effects on the body for up to twenty-four hours after input. Signs of overload include: excessive yawning, change in pallor, increased anxiety levels, pupil dilation and significant changes in overall demeanour and arousal levels (Yack et al., 2015). The following activities may mitigate vestibular issues: • Gymnastics. • Skipping (with/without rope). • Trampoline. • Dancing. • Rotary Swinging (swings that can spin around, use only under OT supervision) • Different seating aids e.g. Move and Sit cushions (inflatable cushion with textured top), ball chairs (yoga ball stabilized to sit on). • Prone extension (lying on belly with arms and legs off the ground. Sometimes can be done with child inverted but only under OT supervision). • Climbing activities.
Under-Sensitive	• Doesn't notice or react to movement/being moved. • Doesn't notice when falling and shows no signs of self-correction or attempts to protect him/herself.	
Sensory-Seeking	• Has trouble sitting still. • Repeatedly rocks, or jumps, shakes/bangs head (often without signs of distress). • Craves intense movement – 'thrill-seeker'. • Doesn't seem to get dizzy after spinning/ swinging.	

- Allowing the child to rock.
- Providing opportunities for the child to spin.
- Having a selection of trikes, bikes and/or scooters available for the child to freely choose.
- Swimming.
- Outdoor play.
- Upside down play.

Calming Vestibular Activities:

- Linear Swinging (swing that only goes forwards and backwards).
- Gentle rocking using a rocking chair.
- Gentle bouncing (perhaps on mini trampoline, space hopper or yoga ball).

Table 3.7: Signposts for Accommodating Proprioceptive Differences in Early Years, Primary, Post-Primary and Special School Settings

Responses to Proprioception	Common Responses	Sensory-Based Interventions
Over-Sensitive	• Avoids activities that stretch and contract the muscles. • Resists high input activities, such as, jumping, hopping and spinning due to experiencing high intensity feedback. • Dislikes passive input, such as being hugged and touched or being lifted and moved. • Resists foods that need to be chewed.	• Proprioceptive activities can be passive (deep pressure) or active (heavy work). • Both types can be calming and alerting. • Use of weighted products (vests, lap mats, backpacks, blankets – OT advice needed). • Massage (either use of massagers or having person massage the child, can be helpful to make child aware of body part/limb).
Under-Sensitive	• Displays a low muscle tone. • Holds limbs tight to compensate (elbow held into ribs, knees held together when standing). • Difficulty with somatosensory discrimination – how much strength to apply, child can overshoot with muscle force and break things easily. • May sit in uncomfortable position and not notice. • Experiences difficulty dressing and requires assistance for many ADLS.	• Deep pressure (can be applied to child by pressing or gently squeezing on their shoulders/limbs – if warranted and enjoyed by the child). • Providing oral motor strategies, such as blowing bubbles/harmonicas/balloons. • Including elements of heavy work in the child's curriculum, such pushing, lifting and/or carrying. • Climbing stairs. • Crawling through tunnels. • Crashing (running into crash mats, jumping into ball pit, onto couch/bed – essentially being able to throw body onto something safe).

Sensory-Seeking	<ul><li>May be described as a 'crasher' as the child seems to deliberately bump into items (and people) in the environment seeking sensory feedback.</li><li>Craves active movement and is observed pushing, pulling and throwing him/herself around.</li><li>Craves passive pressure/deep pressure and enjoys being pressed and squeezed.</li><li>Seeking sensory experiences – may present as aggressive behaviours to others through biting and hitting or to own self through self-injurious behaviours, such as banging head and/orbiting skin.</li></ul>	<ul><li>Rough-housing (rough and tumble play with parent).</li><li>Catching, throwing kicking balls.</li><li>Big ball activities.</li><li>Scooter board activities.</li><li>Cookery activities.</li><li>Biting and chewing tubing or resistive foods (there are commercially available safe chew toys, but also chewy sweets/foods can be used.</li><li>Deep breathing exercises.</li><li>Wheelbarrow walking.</li><li>Reading/doing a puzzle with feet positioned higher than head in prone position, e.g. over a therapy ball</li><li>Hanging from monkey bars.</li><li>Body stretches.</li><li>Joint compressions.</li></ul>

Key Signposts: Understanding the Sensory Systems

- The sensory systems of the body are:
— Visual (Sense of sight)
— Auditory (Sense of hearing)
— Olfactory (Sense of smell)
— Gustatory (Sense of taste)
— Tactile (Sense of touch)
— Vestibular (Sense of balance and movement)
— Proprioceptive (Sense of body in space)
- Sensory-Based Interventions are listed in Tables 3.1–3.7 above. Remember, where possible, always seek guidance from an OT.
- Parents, teachers and child must work together to see what interventions are *safe and appropriate* to be used in each setting.

Conclusion

We need to watch, learn and get to know each child, to see where they are in relation to sensory differences and to provide appropriate and effective support. Sensory integration as a process leads to self-regulation, leaving the child calm, comfortable and ready to learn. The ultimate goal of sensory-based therapy is that the child will recognize his/her sensory issue, and possibly what is causing it, in order to ensure access to input that addresses this need and succeed in calming the child's sensory system (Kuypers 2011).

Best practice suggests that children with ASD should be educated in an appropriate, visually structured, sensory-friendly environment (NSCE 2016). Sensory input should be offered to children before, during and after learning opportunities (Ayres 2005, Dunn 2008; Murray-Slutsky and Paris, 2014; Grandin 2017). Sensory regulation leads the child to their 'calm alert state', which allows for 'optimal learning' opportunities and 'participation in everyday activities and routines' (Yack et al. 2015: 28). We must be flexible enough to respond to children's sensory differences and remember the importance of the Ziggurat model in Figure 3.1. It is imperative to understand that sensory input is non-negotiable, it is not a reward, not something to be earned or lost on any behavioural management programme (Horwood 2009). Improving SI for children, and providing them with opportunities for achieving a balancing of their senses, may at the very least improve daily functioning and most certainly will contribute to their comfort, confidence and wellbeing across all education settings.

Bibliography

Antezana, L., Scarpa, A., Valdespino, A., Albright, J., and Richey, J. A. (2017). 'Rural Trends in Diagnosis and Services for Autism Spectrum Disorder', *Frontiers in Psychology*, 8, 590.

American Psychiatric Association (2013). *Diagnostic and Statistical Manual of Mental Disorders* (5th edn) (DSM-V). Washington: American Psychiatric Association.

Anzalone, M. E., and Williamson, G. G. (2000). 'Sensory processing and motor performance in autistic spectrum disorders'. In A. Wetherby and B. Prizant (eds), *Communication and language issues in autism and pervasive developmental disabilities: A transactional developmental perspective*, pp. 143–166. Baltimore, MD: Paul H. Brookes.

Aspy, R., and Grossman, B. G. (2011). *The Ziggurat Model: Release 2.0 A Framework for Designing Comprehensive Interventions for High-Functioning Individuals with Autism Spectrum Disorders*. Kansas: AAPC Pub.

Ayres, A. J. (2005). *Sensory Integration and the Child: 25th Anniversary Edition*. Los Angeles, CA: WPS.

Baranek, G. T. (2002). 'Efficacy of Sensory and Motor Interventions for Children with Autism', *The Journal of Autism and Developmental Disorders*, 32(5), 397–422.

Baranek, G. T., David, F. J., Poe, M. D, Stone, W. L., and Watson, L. R. (2006). 'Sensory Experiences Questionnaire: Discriminating Sensory Features in Young Children with Autism, Developmental Delays, and Typical Development', *The Journal of Child Psychology and Psychiatry*, 47(6), 591–601.

Burgstahler, S. (2009). *Universal Design of Instruction (UDI): Definition, Principles, Guidelines (Report)*. Washington, DC: Do It.

Case-Smith, J., and Bryan, T. (1999). 'The Effects of Occupational Therapy with Sensory Integration Emphasis on Preschool-age Children with Autism', *American Journal of Occupational Therapy*, 53, 489–497.

Cummings J. R., Case B. G., Ji, X., Marcus S. C. (2016). 'Availability of Youth Services in U.S. Mental Health Treatment Facilities', *Administration and Policy in Mental health*, 43(5), 717–727.

Daly, P., Ring, E., Egan, M., Fitzgerald, J., Griffin, C., Long, S., McCarthy, E., Moloney, M., O'Brien, T., O'Byrne, A., O'Sullivan, S., Ryan, M., Wall, E., Madden, R., and Gibbons, S. (2016). *An Evaluation of Education Provision for Students with Autism Spectrum Disorder in Ireland*. Trim: National Council for Special Education.

Donnellen, A. M, Hill, D. A., and Leary, M. R. (2013). 'Rethinking Autism: Implications of Sensory and Movement Differences for Understanding and Support', *Frontiers in Integrative Neuroscience*, 6(124), 1–11.

Donnelly, J. E., and Lanbourne K. (2011). 'Classroom-Based Physical Activity, Cognition, and Academic Achievement', *Preventive Medicine*, 52 (supplement), S36—S42.

Dunn, W. (2008). *Living Sensationally: Understanding your Senses*. London: Jessica Kingsley Publishers.

Elder, J. H., Brasher, S., and Alexander, B. (2016). 'Identifying the Barriers to Early Diagnosis and Treatment in Undeserved Individuals with Autism Spectrum Disorders (ASD) and their Families: A Qualitative Study', *Issues in Mental Health Nursing*, 37(6), 412–420.

Fisher, A. G., Murray, E. A., and Bundy, A. C. (1991). *Sensory Integration Theory and Practice*. Philadelphia, PA: F.A Davis Company.

Grandin, T. (2015). *Temple Talks: About Autism and Sensory Issues*. Arlington, TX: Sensory World.

Grandin, T. (2017). 'Autism: Different Kinds of Minds', *Building Capacity Conference, Middletown Centre for Autism*, 12 May 2017, Belfast: Titanic.

Gray, C. (2000). *The New Social Story Book*. Arlington, TX: Future Horizons.

Horwood, J. (2009). *Sensory Circuits: A Sensory Motor Skills Programme for Children*. Cambridge: LDA.

Johnson-Harris, K. M., and Mundschenk, N. A. (2014). 'Working Effectively with Students with BD in a General Education Classroom: The Case for Universal Design for Learning', *Clearing House*, 87(4), 168–174.

Katz, J. (2013). 'The Three Block Model of Universal Design for Learning (UDL): Engaging Students in Inclusive Education', *Canadian Journal of Education*, 36(1), 153–194.

Kimball, J. (1993). 'Sensory Integration Frame of Reference'. In P. Kramer and J. Hinojosa (eds), *Frames of Reference in Paediatric Occupational Therapy*, pp. 87–167. Philadelphia: Williams and Wilkins.

Koomar, J. (2007). *Answers to Questions Teachers ask About Sensory Integration (Including Sensory Processing Disorder)*. Arlington, TX: Future Horizons.

Kuypers, L. M. (2011). *The Zones of Regulation: A Curriculum Designed to Foster Self-regulation and Emotional Control*. Santa Clara, CA: Think Social Publishing, Inc.

Kwak, L., Kremers, S. P. J., Bergman, P., Ruiz, J. R., Rizzo, N. S., and Sjostrom, M. (2009). 'Associations between Physical Activity, Fitness and Academic Achievement', *The Journal of Paediatrics*, 155(6), 914–918.

Leekam, R. S., Libby, S. J., Wing, L., Gould, J., and Taylor, C. (2002). 'The Diagnostic Interview for Social and Communication Disorders: Algorithms for ICD-10 Childhood Autism and Wing and Gould Autistic Spectrum Disorder', *The Journal of Child Psychology and Psychiatry*, 43(3), 327–342.

Marr, D., and Nacklev, V. (2006). *Sensory Stories*. Framingham, MA: Theraproducts.

Middletown Centre for Autism (2017). *Sensory Processing Resource*. Accessed online on 30 January 2018 at <http://sensory-processing.middletownautism.com/>.

Middletown Centre for Autism and National Council for Special Education (2013). *Evaluation Framework to Underpin the Evaluation of Educational Provision for Students with ASD*. Trim: National Council for Special Education.

Miller, L. J. (2014). *Sensational Kids*. New York: Penguin.

Murray-Slutsky, C., and Paris, B. A. (2014). *Autism Interventions: Exploring the Spectrum of Autism*. Texas, TX: Hammill Institute on Disabilities.

National Behaviour Support Service (NBSS) (2017). *Movement Breaks: Occupational Therapy Tips*. Accessed online on 30 January 2018 at <https://www.nbss.ie/sites/default/files/publications/movement_breaks_tip_sheet_o.pdf>.

National Council for Special Education (2014). *Information for Parents/Guardians of Children and Young People with Autism Spectrum Disorder*. Trim: National Council for Special Education.

Ornitz, E. M. (1974). 'The Modulation of Sensory Input and Motor Output in Autistic Children', *Journal of Autism and Childhood Schizophrenia* (4), 197–215.

Stock Kranowitz, C. (2005). *The Out-of-Sync Child*. New York: Penguin.

Tomcheck, S. D., and Dunn, W. (2007). 'Sensory Processing in Children with and without Autism: A Comparative Study using the Short Sensory Profile', *The American Journal of Occupational Therapy*, 61(2), 190–200.

Wallace, S., Fein, D., Rosanoff, M., Dawson, G., Hossain, S., Brennan, L., Como, A., and Shih, A. (2012). 'A Global Public Health Strategy for Autism Spectrum Disorders', *Autism Research* (5), 211–217.

Wan Y, Hu Q, Li T, Jiang, L., Du, Y., Feng, L., Wong, J. C. M., Li, C. (2013). 'Prevalence of Autism Spectrum Disorders among Children in China: A Systematic Review', *Shanghai Archives of Psychiatry*, 25(2), 70–80.

Watling, R., and Hauer, S. (2015). 'Effectiveness of Ayres Sensory Integration® and Sensory Based Interventions for People with Autism Spectrum

Disorder: A Systematic Review', *American Journal of Occupational Therapy*, 69(5), 1–12.

Webster, C. A., Russ, L., Vasou, S., Goh, T. L., and Erwin, H. (2015). 'Integrating Movement in Academic Classrooms: Understanding, Applying and Advancing the Knowledge Base', *Obesity Reviews*, 16(8), 691–701.

Wilbarger, J., and Wilbarger, P. (2002). 'Clinical Application of the Sensory Diet'. In A. Bundy, S. J. Lane and E. A. Murray (eds), *Sensory Integration: Theory and Practice* (2nd edn), pp. 339–341. Philadelphia PA: Davis.

Williamson, G. G., and Anzalone, M. E. (2001). *Sensory Integration and Self-Regulation in Infants and Toddlers: Helping Very Young Children Interact with Their Environment*. Washington, DC: Zero to Three.

Yack, E., Aquilla, P., and Sutton, S. (2015). *Building Bridges through Sensory Integration* (3rd edn), Arlington, TX: Sensory World.

Appendix A: Glossary

(Adapted from <http://www.therakids.org/> and <http://www.inha.ie/sensory-processing-disorder/>.)

Auditory defensiveness: an oversensitivity to sounds in the environment.

Auditory discrimination: the ability to receive, identify, differentiate, understand and respond to sounds.

Gustatory: sense of taste.

Hypersensitivity/over-sensitive/over-responsive: terms used to describe observable over-reactive behaviour produced in reaction to sensory stimuli.

Hyposensitive/under-sensitive/under-responsive: terms used to describe an under-reaction to sensory stimuli that is observed as either being passive and lethargic or by a child craving and seeking out more sensory input.

Interoception: the body-centred sense involving both the conscious awareness and the unconscious regulation of bodily processes.

Modulation: the brain's regulation of its own activity.

Motor planning/praxis: the ability to organize and sequence steps in body movement in a co-ordinated manner.

Olfactory: sense of smell.

Over-reactivity and under-reactivity: exaggerated neurological and physiological processes that we cannot observe, which may cause over- and under-responsive behaviour.

Proprioception: the unconscious awareness of sensations coming from muscles and joints, telling the brain how much they are moving and stretching, where the body and its parts are in space, and how the body is moving.

Self-regulation: the ability to control one's activity level and state of alertness, emotional wellbeing and one's responses to sensations.

Sensory diet: a planned activity programme that an occupational therapist develops to aid a person with self-regulation.

Sensory discrimination disorder: problems in discerning the characteristics of sensory stimuli and problems with telling the differences between stimuli.

Sensory integration: the organization of sensory input in human bodies.

Sensory integration difference/sensory processing difference: an irregularity in brain function which makes it difficult to integrate sensory information effectively.

Sensory Modulation: The brain's regulation of its own activity. Modulation involves
    facilitating some neural messages to maximize a response, and inhibiting other
    messages to reduce irrelevant activity processing.
Tactile: sense of touch.
Tactile defensiveness: when sensations of touch create negative emotional reactions.
Vestibular system: the sensory system that provides the individual in relation to bal-
    ance, spatial orientation and motion.

Appendix B: Resources

Ayres, A. J. (2005). *Sensory Integration and the Child: 25th Anniversary Edition.* Los Angeles, CA: WPS.

———*This book provides the overview and theory from the seminal author in the field.*

Dunn, W. (2008). *Living Sensationally: Understanding your Senses.* London: Jessica Kingsley Publishers.

Fisher, A. G., Murray, E. A., and Bundy, A. C. (1991). *Sensory Integration Theory and Practice.* Philadelphia, PA: F.A Davis Company.

Grandin, T. (2015). *Temple Talks: About Autism and Sensory Issues.* Arlington, TX: Sensory World.

———*First-hand insight into autism and sensory issues.*

Horwood, J. (2009). *Sensory Circuits: A Sensory Motor Skills Programme for Children.* Cambridge: LDA.

———*An excellent resource for schools to set up sensory obstacle courses for all that will hugely benefit those with sensory issues. Activities are listed in terms of what are alerting, calming, organizing, etc., for the senses.*

Koomar, J. (2007). *Answers to Questions Teachers ask About Sensory Integration (Including Sensory Processing Disorder).* Arlington, TX: Future Horizons.

———*Good selection of teacher- and parent-based checklists, brief and easy to follow.*

Kuypers, L. M. (2011). *The Zones of Regulation: A Curriculum Designed to Foster Self-regulation and Emotional Control.* Santa Clara, CA: Think Social Publishing, Inc.

———*A complete programme to develop self-regulation – all materials provided.*

Middletown Centre for Autism (2017). *Sensory Processing Resource.* Accessed online on 30 January 2018 at <http://sensory-processing.middletownautism.com/>.

Miller, L. J. (2014). *Sensational Kids.* New York: Penguin.

Murray-Slutsky, C., and Paris, B. A. (2014). *Autism Interventions: Exploring the Spectrum of Autism.* Texas, TX: Hammill Institute on Disabilities.

Stock Kranowitz, C. (2005). *The Out-of-Sync Child.* New York: Penguin.

———*An excellent overview of all sensory issues, a good starting point and reference tool.*

Yack, E., Aquilla, P., and Sutton, S. (2015). *Building Bridges through Sensory Integration* (3rd edn), Arlington, TX: Sensory World.

———*This book suggests numerous activities to provided sensory input at home and in school.*

CLAIRE GRIFFIN

4   Supporting Children with Autism Spectrum
    Difference: The Role of the Special Needs
    Assistant/Inclusion Support Assistant[1]

ABSTRACT

This chapter seeks to critically explore the role of the Special Needs Assistant (SNA)/
Inclusion Support Assistant (ISA) in supporting children with autism spectrum difference (ASD) in Ireland's educational system. The author will firstly present an overview of
the SNA scheme, emphasizing the exponential growth of the scheme in recent years. The
unique care role of the Irish SNA will be outlined and compared with paraprofessional roles
in other international countries. Following this, key findings from the National Council
for Special Education (NCSE) evaluation of education provision for students with ASD
will be presented and critically reviewed (Daly et al. 2016), with particular reference to
the role of the SNA in supporting children with ASD. Similarities and differences will be
discussed across three main educational settings comprising early intervention, mainstream
and special schools. Based on such findings, future suggestions for the evolving role of
the SNA/ISA will be presented, with reference to the comprehensive review of the SNA
scheme conducted by the NCSE over 2016/2017 (NCSE 2018). Such suggestions will aim
to inform both policy and best practice within the field.

Introduction

Ireland's educational landscape has undergone significant changes
over recent years. Fuelled by national and international policy changes
(Government of Ireland (GOI) 1998; 2004; 2005), the drive towards

---

[1]   In March 2018, the National Council for Special Education (NCSE) recommended
      that 'Special Needs Assistants' (SNAs) be referred to as 'Inclusion Support Assistants'
      (ISAs) (NCSE 2018). In this chapter, the term SNA encompasses the role of the SNA
      and the ISA and both terms are used interchangeably throughout the chapter.

inclusive education has resulted in a myriad of developments within Irish schools. Of particular note is the special needs assistant (SNA) scheme, which presents as one of the largest support systems implemented within Irish education across recent years. Originating from the Child-Care Assistant Scheme in the 1980s, the SNA scheme was firmly established in 1998 to support children who present with significant care needs arising from a disability (Department of Education and Science (DES) 2002). This scheme aimed at allowing such children 'to participate fully in the education system ... [and] to enable them to reach their potential' (GOI 1998, as cited in Department of Education and Skills (DES) 2011a: 127–128). Notably, in March 2018, the National Council for Special Education (NCSE) recommended that SNAs should be renamed 'Inclusion Support Assistants' (ISAs), a title that was deemed to better reflect the increased focus on the development of student independence inherent in the role. In addition, it was thought that the ISA title moves away from special needs terminology which is often disliked by students and parents (NCSE 2018). Accordingly, throughout this chapter, the terms SNA and ISA will be used interchangeably, with reference to the non-teaching care-support role within Irish schools. Focusing specifically on children with autism spectrum difference (ASD), SNA allocation is assigned at a minimum of two SNAs for every six children with ASD within early intervention and special classes. In contrast, the sole diagnosis of ASD does not automatically equate to SNA access within mainstream class settings. Rather, SNAs are sanctioned on the basis of one of three criteria. These include when a child has significant care needs arising from:

i.   A significant medical need;
ii. A significant impairment of physical or sensory function;
iii. For the care needs of pupils whose disability categorisation is that of Emotional Behaviour Disorder (EBD) or Severe Emotional Behavioural Disorder (SEBD), or where the care needs specified relate to behavioural disturbance or behavioural related care needs. (DES 2014: 4–5)

Notably, the 'non-teaching' focus of the SNA role stands in stark contrast to numerous international models of paraprofessional support, whereby a teaching assistant or auxiliary educational role is emphasized. In the Irish context, however, this educational focus is substituted by a care role, with the additional aim of 'developing [the child's] independent living skills' (DES 2014: 3).

Considering children with ASD, recent data from the National Council for Special Education (NCSE) illustrates that 69 per cent of all children with ASD have access to SNA support, accruing to an annual governmental spend of €152 million (NCSE 2015). Table 4.1 provides a snapshot of this provision, spanning mainstream classes, special classes and special schools. In addition, cutting-edge data from the Irish Government Economic and Evaluation Service (IGEES) (2016) reveals that ASD now presents as the most common diagnosis for children obtaining SNA access in mainstream schools. In fact, this population has witnessed a 17 per cent average annual growth in SNA access since 2011/2012. Undoubtedly, the significance of the SNA scheme in seeking to support children with ASD stands clear.

Table 4.1: Snapshot of SNA Support in Schools for Children with ASD
(NCSE 2015: 39)

Classes	Number of Students with SNA Access
Mainstream classes	4,489
Special classes in mainstream schools (including early intervention classes)	3,229
Special schools (including early intervention classes)	1,919
Total number of students	9,637

In spite of this exponential growth in the SNA scheme over recent years, a review of the literature illustrates how a dearth of related national research prevails. Nonetheless, the recent work of Daly et al. (2016) has served to address this significant research gap, focusing specifically on children with ASD in an Irish context. This chapter seeks to critically review a subset of the research findings, concentrating solely on the role of the SNA in supporting children with ASD. Reflecting on statements and criteria from work of Middletown Centre for Autism (MCA) and the NCSE (2013), a selection of key research findings will be presented and critiqued under three themes comprising (i) *The role of the SNA*, (ii) *The child's independence* and (iii) *Knowledge, qualifications and continuing professional development* (CPD). Reference will also be made to child-centred, collaborative planning and review, which is further explored in Chapter 5 of this publication. In light of these themes, examples of positive practices will be contrasted with discrete areas for development, with comparisons drawn across educational settings. Finally, future suggestions for the evolving role of the ISA will be presented, with reference to the comprehensive review of the SNA scheme conducted by the NCSE over 2016/2017 (NCSE, 2018). Such suggestions will aim to inform both policy and best practice within the field.

Key Signposts: Introduction

- The move towards a more inclusive education system in Ireland over recent decades has been paralleled by an exponential growth in the national Special Needs Assistant (SNA) scheme.
- The SNA scheme originated from the Child-Care Assistant Scheme of the 1980s.
- The SNA scheme was established in Ireland in 1998 to support children who present with significant care needs arising from a disability. This support was aimed at allowing such children to participate fully in the education system and to enable them to reach their potential.
- The care role of the SNA contrasts significantly with many international models of paraprofessional support which comprise an educational remit.
- In March 2018, the NCSE recommended that SNAs should be renamed Inclusion Support Assistants (ISAs) to better reflect the increased focus on the development of student independence inherent in the role and to move away from special needs terminology.
- A minimum of two SNAs are assigned for every six children with ASD in early intervention and special classes.
- Access to SNA support for a child with ASD in mainstream education is associated with the child having a specified significant care need.
- In addition to care support, SNAs are also required to support the development of children's independent living skills.
- ASD now presents as the most common diagnosis for children obtaining SNA access in mainstream schools.
- 69 per cent of all children with ASD have access to SNA support, accruing to an annual governmental spend of €152 million (NCSE 2015).

The Varied and Stretched Role of the SNA/ISA

Considering the role of the SNA, primary findings verify that SNAs are serving to support a culture of inclusion within schools, including for children with ASD (Daly et al. 2016). This finding echoes that of previous research in the field (Logan 2006; DES 2011a). In contrast, the NCSE notes that confusion still prevails regarding SNA duties, with variances in practices evident across classrooms and settings (NCSE 2015). In particular, the diverse role of the SNA was documented, such that SNA duties both aligned with, and stretched beyond, their prescribed care role (DES 2002; DES 2014).

At an early intervention level, data illustrated how SNAs were particularly involved in supporting children's self-care needs, including toileting and behaviour support. Special needs assistant practices were rated as 'excellent' in terms of supporting a sensitive and differentiated approach to children's involvement in activities (Daly et al. 2016: 59). At a primary school level, the role of the SNA in supporting movement breaks and gross-motor activities was outlined. Of note was the 'excellent' focus within primary settings on promoting positive mental health and relationships (Daly et al. 2016: 88). This is a positive finding, whereby the caring, relational role of the SNA resonates with international data in the field (Broer, Doyle and Giangreco 2005). Moving to post-primary settings, SNA duties were observed to shift more towards supporting curriculum access and support of learning. Examples included note-taking, providing opportunities for rehearsal of answers and using verbal and visual prompts. Conversely in one site, SNAs were observed to engage in teaching activities and instructional roles, assuming high levels of SNA responsibility for children's learning. This 'unacceptable' finding (Daly et al. 2016: 105) resonates with a plethora of previous research in the field which points to the stretched role of the SNA (Carrig 2004; Elliott 2004; DES 2011a; Spens 2013).

Focusing on special schools, SNAs were observed to work at a more one-to-one level, reflecting children's individual needs, particularly for those with severe or profound general learning disabilities. Teachers were observed to create lists of activities to guide SNAs' work with children at personal workstations. Such practices are in line with policy documents which emphasize the need for SNAs to assist in enabling curriculum access for children 'under the direction of the teacher' (DES 2014: 6).

Across all settings, the role of the SNA in positively supporting children's behaviour was recognized. Examples included SNA awareness of potential triggers for behavioural outbursts and SNAs' use of prompts and token-economies to scaffold positive behaviour. In contrast, data revealed the necessity for staff development when working with children with SEBD, particularly during episodes of violent behaviour. The NCSE (2015: 14) acknowledges the need for specific DES guidance on 'realistic and appropriate emergency procedures to be used in crisis situations, involving episodes of extremely challenging or violent behaviour'. Schools need to ensure that evidence-based approaches to behavioural support are adopted and employed consistently by all school personnel, including SNAs. Previous research has illustrated the considerable involvement of SNAs in behaviour management such that in some instances, SNAs were more involved in the 'containment' of problematic behaviours rather than in their prevention (DES 2011a: 73). The complexity of challenging behaviour cannot be underestimated, whereby the need for a 'focused and consistent approach, which is embedded in a whole-school policy' must be prioritized within schools (DES 2011a: 68). Reference to recent publications by the NCSE (Cooper and Jacobs 2011), the National Educational Psychological Service (NEPS) (DES 2010) and the National Behaviour Support Service (NBSS) (NBSS 2008) may help to provide settings with additional support in this regard.

The role of SNAs in supporting children's sensory needs was also acknowledged across all settings, but particularly, within special schools. One principal outlined the significant impact of sensory issues on children's learning and behaviour, referring to it as 'a big interfering factor in their education' (Daly et al. 2016: 136). Although some SNAs outlined their prior engagement in sensory-based courses, the level of SNA knowledge and skills in this domain remains questionable. Notably, national policy supports SNA involvement in assisting children with access to therapy, but highlights how it must occur under the direction of 'qualified personnel' (DES 2014: 7). This sentiment is echoed in the most recent NSCE policy advice paper no. 6, as based on the comprehensive review of the SNA scheme (NCSE 2018). Specifically, the NCSE recommended that moving forward, ISAs may be deployed to mediate therapy programmes, but only when the programme is carried out under the direction of qualified personnel and where the ISA has the appropriate training and skills.

Beyond sensory-based issues, data highlighted the role of the SNA in supporting children's anxiety and stress. This issue comes as no surprise as data reveals how approximately 40 per cent of individuals with ASD present with symptoms of at least one anxiety disorder, compared with up to 15 per cent in the general population (Galanopoulos, Robertson, Spain and Murphy 2014, as cited in The National Autistic Society 2017: n.p.). Changes to routines and transitions, both on a daily basis and between settings, were highlighted as particularly challenging for children. SNAs were observed to employ a range of supportive strategies including movement breaks and time-out from the classroom. Other strategies included written schedules, oral and pictorial cues, site visits, short school placements and meetings between school personnel (Daly et al. 2016). At the post-primary level, anxiety issues appeared even more significant, with SNAs used to facilitate children's breaks from classrooms and the supervision of children in designated social areas. Considering the recent focus on child wellbeing and mental health (DES 2013: 2015), it is clear that issues related to anxiety and stress are gaining prominence in a national sphere, with 'wellbeing' specifically identified as one of the key themes of *Aistear: The Early Childhood Curriculum Framework* (National Council for Curriculum and Assessment (NCCA) 2009). The need for further guidance and CPD for all staff must be considered by the DES and school management to ensure appropriate support for all children. With regard to wellbeing and transitions, the NCSE (2015; 2016) has recently recognized the potential role of the SNA in supporting children's transitions across educational settings. Nonetheless, it remains paramount that SNA sanctioning occurs within time-bound parameters, with the overall aim of promoting the child's independent functioning (DES 2014).

Ultimately, a review of the research illustrates the significant role of the SNA in supporting children with ASD in educational settings. In particular, the varied but stretched role of the SNA stands clear, whereby data revealed a host of positive and negative practices across classrooms and settings. In light of the long-standing issues inherent in the SNA scheme, it is envisaged that the *New School Inclusion Model*, as proposed by the NCSE (2018), will serve to provide an improved support model to children with additional care needs, with the aim of providing the right supports to children at the right time, as delivered by appropriately qualified and trained personnel. In the interim, however, school management must seek to ensure that SNAs are assigned duties appropriate to their current job description and tailored to children's needs. By employing a clear school policy on the management and deployment of SNAs, in addition to a personalized care plan for each child accessing SNA support, the drive towards effective care support of all children with additional needs can be realized.

Key Signposts: The Varied and Stretched Role of the Special Needs Assistant

- Primary findings from Daly et al. (2016) verify that SNAs are serving to support a culture of inclusion within schools.
- Confusion still prevails regarding SNA duties, with variances in practices evident across classrooms and settings.
- Findings illustrated that SNA duties continue to align with, and stretch beyond, their prescribed care role. There was some evidence of SNAs' engagement in pedagogical and instructional activities which extend beyond their care remit.
- SNA support in early settings predominantly related to children's self-care needs. In contrast, primary and post-primary SNA support shifted more towards curriculum access and support of learning.
- SNA support in special schools was more at an individualized, one-to-one level, particularly during children's work at personal workstations.
- Although SNAs were recognized to provide positive support to children's behaviour, higher levels of CPD and whole-school approaches to behavioural support were deemed necessary, given the complexity of challenging behaviour.
- The role of SNAs in supporting children's sensory needs was acknowledged across all settings, but particularly, in special schools.
- SNAs were recognized to support children's wellbeing, particularly during times of anxiety, stress and transitions. Movement breaks were particularly used during the school day.
- The need for further national clarity on the SNA role, in addition to clear school policies in relation to SNA deployment, is essential in addressing longstanding issues with the SNA scheme.
- It is envisaged that the *New School Inclusion Model*, as proposed by the NCSE (2018), will serve to provide an improved support model to children with additional care needs, with the aim of providing the right supports to children at the right time, as delivered by appropriately qualified and trained personnel.

Special Needs Assistant Support Versus the Child's Independence

When considering the prescribed care role of the SNA, it is also paramount that the development of children's independent living skills is given precedence. In fact, this issue has been at the heart of the SNA scheme since the outset, such that original documentation stressed that 'a balance must be struck between allocating necessary care support and the right of the child to acquire personal independence skills' (DES 2002: 2). This focus also dominates most recent SNA policy, as outlined in Circular 30/14 (DES 2014), and is emphasized throughout the NCSE policy advice paper no. 6 (NCSE, 2018). Conversely, previous national and international research has pointed to potential drawbacks of the paraprofessional role, whereby it can serve to foster dependency in children. Examples include the paraprofessional maintaining physical contact with the student; sitting in a chair immediately next to the child and/or accompanying the student to virtually every place within the school (Giangreco, Edelman, Luiselli and MacFarland 1997; Giangreco 2010a; 2010b). Such practices have been shown to result in a host of negative implications for children, including adult dependency, reduced peer interactions and loss of personal control (Giangreco et al. 1997; Malmgren and Causton-Theoharis 2006; Giangreco 2010a; Blatchford, Webster and Russell 2012).

Findings from the national ASD evaluation (Daly et al. 2016) revealed varied practices in this regard. Across early intervention and primary school settings, teachers showed awareness of the SNAs' role in supporting or inhibiting independence. This awareness was echoed by school leaders, whereby the rotation of SNA support at a whole-school level was deemed an effective mitigating strategy. The developmental nature of care needs was also acknowledged within primary school settings, with one mainstream class teacher observing that as children get older, they often prefer to work independently. In this setting, the principal outlined how he had deliberately reduced SNA support for children, acknowledging how some SNAs 'don't always have the ability to pull back' (Daly et al. 2016: 85). This finding resonates with previous Irish research in the field which highlighted issues relating to children's overreliance on SNA support, learned helplessness and evidence of a 'velcro' model between the SNA and child (Elliott 2004; Logan 2006; Shevlin, Kenny and Loxley 2008; Keating and O'Connor 2012).

Focusing on special schools, strategies observed to support children's independent functioning included the use of individual workstations, assistive technology, visuals and differentiated SNA support. Special needs assistants in special schools expressed strong awareness of children's growing independent needs. This was reflected in SNA comments including, 'In the senior section of the school I shadow and prompt and step back and promote independence' (Daly et al. 2016: 146). Such findings are particularly positive, illustrating awareness among some SNAs of the impact of their physical proximity on children's functioning.

At post-primary level, data revealed that across many settings, SNAs were being effectively used to increase children's independence and participation in school activities. School staff showed awareness of children's changing needs over time. Within some post-primary settings, higher levels of support were deployed in initial years to support children's social skills and their transition from primary school. As children continued through the Junior Cycle, SNA support was reduced and then re-focused towards the Senior Cycle to support children's self-management strategies. As stated by one principal, 'we might enable dependency by allocating support evenly across the years of the post-primary school – earlier interventions in first year matter' (Daly et al. 2016: 118). Despite the strength of these practices, shortfalls were also evident at post-primary level. Examples included a lack of navigational strategies in large school buildings to promote children's independent mobility, coupled with disproportionate levels of SNA support. As stated by one SNA, 'Wherever the boys go, we go' (Daly et al. 2016: 112). Akin to previous international research in the field (Harris 2011; Blatchford et al. 2012), this 'unacceptable' level of support for children was observed to have negative implications for their engagement and participation in learning activities (Daly et al. 2016: 10).

Reflecting on cumulative findings, it is clear that examples of both positive and negative practices were evident across settings. On one hand, some SNAs showed strong awareness of their potential role in impacting on children's independence through supportive strategies and appropriate levels of proximity. Moreover, principals and teaching staff reported strong awareness of the need to promote children's independent functioning. This is in accordance with DES (2014) guidelines, whereby schools now have autonomy and flexibility in the deployment of SNA resources.

On the other hand, it is questionable the degree to which all SNAs are aware of specific strategies to support children's independence growth. Undoubtedly, the complexities inherent in moving a child from significant levels of support to independent functioning must be acknowledged. Challenging this issue, Giangreco (2010b: 341) queries how 'teacher assistant utilisation has advanced steadily and their roles have expanded instructionally despite lacking both a theoretically defensible foundation and a substantive evidence base'. On reflection, it appears essential that SNAs are encouraged to adopt theoretically grounded, evidence-based approaches to supporting children's needs (Griffin, 2015). This may require high levels of teacher-led skill-based instruction for the child, which is then paralleled by calibrated SNA support. Examples include sequential learning through backward and forward chaining, the support of children's communication strategies, such as through Lámh (Lámh 2009) or Picture Exchange Communication System (PECS) (Bondy and Frost 2002), or the promoting of children's self-management and self-regulatory strategies. In all cases, clear delineation of the SNA care role should be outlined and documented in the child's personalized plan.

At a broader level, the use of scaffolding theory, as originally proposed by Vygotsky (1978), offers a sociocultural framework for promoting a child's independence. Through this theoretical viewpoint, the role of the 'more able other' is deemed central in the promotion of learning and independence skills. In a recent systematic review of research in this domain, Van de Pol, Volman and Buishuizen (2010) highlighted three key characteristics of scaffolding which serve to foster independence in children. These comprise *contingency, fading* and *transfer of responsibility*. It is notable that in recent years, scaffolding theory has been applied to the work of teaching assistants in the United Kingdom in an effort to promote children's higher-order learning and independent functioning, with a strong focus placed on the teaching assistant's use of language (Radford, Bosanquet, Webster, Blatchford, and Rubie-Davies, 2014); Radford, Bosanquet, Webster, and Blatchford, 2015).

Moving forward, it is evident that SNAs' support of children must stem from theoretically grounded models of practice to ensure that a systematic and calibrated approach to child support is executed. Such strategies must be central to the collaborative planning process and clearly documented in children's individualized education plans, with reference to domains of target-setting, planning, monitoring and review. Such matters are further explored in Chapter 5, including the need for the SNA to contribute to the planning process and support the child to voice his/her views.

Key Signposts: Special Needs Assistant Support Versus the Child's Independence

- The development of children's independent living skills constitutes a key role of the SNA.
- Data revealed both positive and negative practices across educational settings in terms of SNAs fostering children's independence.
- Some teachers and school leaders showed awareness of SNAs' role in supporting or inhibiting independence, with some effective whole-school strategies evident to reduce pupils' dependence on the SNA.
- Some SNAs showed strong awareness of their potential role in impacting on children's independence through supportive strategies and appropriate levels of child proximity.
- Use of individualized approaches to support children's independent functioning was particularly evident in special schools.
- Across post-primary settings, varied practices were evident, with some schools showing a lack of environmental supports to support children's independence.
- Many SNAs across settings appeared unclear of specific strategies to support children's independence growth.
- Moving forward, it is recommended that SNA practices are underpinned by theoretically grounded, evidence-based approaches to supporting children's development.
- The developmental nature of children's growth in independence must be acknowledged, with due regard for each child's individual strengths and needs.
- School principals must seek to continuously review SNA deployment across school systems to promote children's independent functioning.
- Theoretical models, including behaviourist and sociocultural approaches offer potential frameworks for supporting more effective SNA practices.
- Plans for supporting children's care needs and independence development must be evidence-based and central to the child's individualized planning process.

Special Needs Assistants: Knowledge, Qualifications and Continuing Professional Development

Having considered the role of the SNA, both in terms of care and independence, the complexities inherent in the role stand clear. Stemming from this factor, cumulative findings from the ASD research (Daly et al. 2016) revealed strong dissatisfaction across data sources in terms of the level of required qualifications and CPD for SNAs. This issue is particularly relevant when one considers the current minimum required educational standard for SNA appointment in Ireland. This comprises (i) a Further Education and Training Award Council (FETAC) Level 3 major qualification on the National Framework of Qualifications *or* (ii) a minimum of three grade Ds in the Junior Certificate *or* (iii) equivalent (DES 2011b). Considering this low educational baseline, findings from the NCSE research illustrated variances in SNA knowledge across settings. This ranged from an 'acceptable' understanding of ASD to 'excellent' knowledge (Daly et al. 2016: 15); the latter particularly evident in special school settings. In such settings, SNAs were strongly aware of children's sensory and care needs, with the 'practical' knowledge and skills of SNAs of particular note (Daly et al. 2016: 138). In contrast, many SNAs across educational settings appeared to rely heavily on experiential learning for knowledge acquisition, with one SNA stating how they have 'learned by their mistakes over the years' (Daly et al. 2016: 149). In general, SNAs outlined how their knowledge had developed through working with specialist teachers and with teachers who had acted as mentors, sharing information from their own CPD experiences.

Considering professional development, a unified response to the 'unacceptable' level of initial qualifications and CPD for SNAs was highlighted across all settings (Daly et al. 2016: 98). Significant frustrations were expressed across almost all stakeholders, particularly in terms of the lack of systematic national opportunities for SNAs to develop knowledge and skills. This was contrasted with the availability of CPD for teachers. Interestingly, some SNAs perceived the lack of CPD to be associated with the lower status of the SNA job. This was deemed to impact negatively on SNAs' sense of morale and job satisfaction, whereby some SNAs felt that their contributions were not valued within their school. The desire for increased levels of CPD was noted by almost all SNAs, with one SNA stating, 'there is no development for SNAs. Zero. There is no career progression, there is no career ladder, there is nothing' (Daly et al. 2016: 150). For those SNAs that did avail of CPD, however, this generally occurred at a personal cost (both time and financial), with limited spaces on CPD courses highlighted as a further inhibitory factor. Special needs assistant feedback related to CPD was at times negative, with some courses reported as being too 'basic' and others pertaining only to the primary school setting (Daly et al., 2016: 50). The need for both generic and ASD-specific CPD was acknowledged across settings, with suggested areas including PECS (Bondy and Frost 2002), Lámh (Lámh 2009), Applied Behaviour Analysis, Treatment and Education of Autistic and related Communication-handicapped CHildren (TEACCH) (Schopler, Mesibov and Hearsey 1995), manual handling, sensory issues, socialization, challenging behaviour, Crisis Prevention Intervention and courses related to medical needs, such as epilepsy. Schools also highlighted the need for SNA CPD in terms of supporting children with mental health and anxiety issues. At post-primary level, the need for whole-school professional development in the Relationships and Sexuality Education strand of the curriculum was emphasized, Interestingly, data revealed that SNAs in special schools received significantly more in-house CPD than that of SNAs in other settings, organized and paid for by the schools in many sites. Such courses often took place during Croke Park[2] hours or in late August and particularly related to care needs, ASD-specific methodologies and communication programmes. Principals in such schools noted difficulty in providing after-school CPD for SNAs, as several SNAs worked also as bus escorts.

Looking forward, the need for a national, formalized and structured approach to initial and ongoing professional development for SNAs stands clear. In fact, the Organisation for Economic Co-operation and Development (OECD) (2012) has emphasized the central role of staff knowledge, qualifications and professional development in supporting high quality educational provision and positive outcomes for children's development. Notably, the

---

2   Croke Park hours constitute an additional seventy-two hours, or twelve school days, that SNAs are required to work outside of normal school opening hours and/or the normal school year, as mandated in the *Public Service (Croke Park)* Agreement (DES, 2011c).

NCSE policy advice paper no. 6 (NCSE, 2018) recommended that a national training programme be introduced at level 5 on the National Framework of Qualifications for existing SNAs who do not have the requisite level of relevant training and for new ISAs on appointment. In addition, they recommended that further focused training be made available, as tailored to the needs of specific children being supported, with additional training also provided for the entire school community on supporting children with additional care needs. Based on the findings from Daly et al. (2016), coupled with that from the comprehensive review of the SNA scheme (NCSE, 2018), it is questionable whether a Level 5 qualification will be sufficient in addressing the knowledge and skills required of ISAs to effectively support the range of care needs with which children with special educational needs can present, coupled with the evidenced-based strategies that ISAs require to develop children's independent living skills. It is suggested that a generic structured educational programme for all SNAs should firstly be devised to address the core skills required to successfully engage in the role. Thereafter, more specialized qualifications could be considered to increase domain-specific expertise across the work-force. High quality CPD must be prioritized to ensure consistency of approach for all children with additional needs and/ or ASD, particularly in complex areas such as behaviour management.

The examination of international models of professional development may offer avenues for renewed thinking in the field. Examples include the Finnish model of initial qualifications and CPD for SNAs, whereby professional competencies are developed through a vocational and apprenticeship model with a focus both on skills testing and proficiency requirements (Takala 2007; Mäensivu, Uusiautti and Määttä 2012). Similarly, the UK's work in the 'Maximising the Impact of Teaching Assistants' project (Webster, Russell and Blatchford 2012; 2016) and the 'Effective Deployment of Teaching Assistants Project' (Webster, Blatchford and Russell 2013) could aid to inform aspects of our national qualifications and CPD programmes, particularly in the areas of *preparedness, deployment and practice* of SNAs. Giangreco and Suter (2015: 115) emphasize how such international approaches should be used as 'an exemplar meant to ... spur discussion, creative problem solving, and action planning to explore model development suited to local contexts'. Ultimately, the Irish education system must seek to adopt a distinct model of professional development that aligns with our national context. In this way, practitioners can be facilitated to acquire 'the knowledge, skills and ongoing supports needed to implement inclusion effectively' (NCSE 2015: 29). At a school level, principals must also seek to

Key Signposts: Special Needs Assistants: Knowledge, Qualifications and Continuing Professional Development

- Minimum required educational standards for SNA appointment in Ireland (up to 2018) appear at odds with the varied role of the SNA and the knowledge and skills required to effectively support children with significant care needs.
- Research findings illustrated variances in SNA knowledge across settings, ranging from an 'acceptable' understanding of ASD to 'excellent' knowledge; the latter particularly evident in special school settings.
- SNAs in special schools received significantly more in-house CPD than that of SNAs in other settings.
- Many SNAs outlined an over-reliance on experiential learning for knowledge acquisition.
- A unified response to the 'unacceptable' level of initial qualifications and CPD for SNAs was highlighted across all settings.
- Significant frustrations were expressed across almost all stakeholders, particularly in terms of the lack of systematic national opportunities for SNAs to develop knowledge and skills.
- Current inhibitory factors to CPD for SNAs include lack of time, personal costs and a lack of availability of high quality SNA training.
- The need for both generic and ASD-specific CPD was acknowledged across settings, including areas such as mental health, anxiety and relationships and sexuality education at post-primary level.
- There is significant need for a national, formalized and structured approach to initial and ongoing professional development for SNAs.
- The NCSE policy advice paper no. 6 (NCSE, 2018) recommended that a national training programme be introduced at Level 5 on the National Framework of Qualifications for existing SNAs who do not have the requisite level of relevant training and for new ISAs on appointment, coupled with further focused training for ISAs and training at a whole-school level. It is questionable whether a Level 5 qualification will be sufficient in addressing the knowledge and skills required of ISAs to effectively support the range of care needs with which children with special educational needs can present, coupled with the evidenced-based strategies that ISAs require to develop children's independent living skills.
- The examination of international models of professional development may offer avenues for renewed thinking in the field.
- Principals have a central role in supporting the professional development of SNAs and all staff through whole-school CPD.

recruit staff with high levels of qualifications, knowledge, experience and expertise. The principal's role in supporting the professional development of all staff must also be emphasized, whereby CPD planning at a systemic level may serve to formalize processes across the whole school.

Conclusion

Reflecting on the data set from the national evaluation of education provision for students with ASD in Ireland (Daly et al. 2016), it is clear that SNAs hold a central role within our schools in supporting children with ASD. Based on these findings, this chapter sought to critically review the role of the SNA, with reference to three discrete themes. Firstly, the widespread role of the SNA was explored, spanning areas of children's self-care needs, motor activities, mental health, curriculum access, positive behaviour support and sensory needs. Examples of positive SNA practices were juxtaposed with a number of 'unacceptable' findings, particularly in relation to SNAs engagement in pedagogical activities and instructional roles. Such findings echo previous research in the field, which point to the stretched role of the SNA beyond its prescribed 'care role' (Carrig 2004; Elliott 2004; Lawlor and Cregan 2003; Logan 2006; O'Neill and Rose 2008; Shevlin et al. 2008; Spens 2013). The need for further national clarity on the SNA role, in addition to clear school policies in relation to SNA deployment, is deemed essential in addressing these longstanding issues in the field. Moreover, schools must ensure that child-centred, collaborative planning, target-setting, monitoring and review are central to the support process, including the voice of the SNA and child (DES 2014).

Secondly, the role of the SNA was explored in terms of supporting the development of children's personal independence skills. Across school settings, data revealed evidence of both positive and negative practices. At a whole-school level, the role of leadership in effectively deploying and reviewing SNA support was highlighted as a positive means of reducing SNA dependency. At a classroom level, some awareness was evident among SNAs of how to support children's independent functioning, with due respect given to the developmental nature of this learning. Nonetheless, the lack of theoretically grounded frameworks to guide SNAs' work was noted as a distinct issue in the field. Theoretical models, including behaviourist and sociocultural approaches, were forwarded, offering potential frameworks for supporting more effective SNA practices. Moving forward, schools need to adopt more collaborative, evidence-based approaches to building children's independent functioning, combining both skill-based instruction, as led by the teacher, with evidence-based calibrated SNA support (Griffin 2015).

Finally, this chapter reflected on SNA knowledge, qualifications and CPD, which together, were expressed as significant issues of frustration across staff in all school settings. The complexities inherent in the SNA role were contrasted strongly with factors including the current minimum required educational standards for SNA appointment in Ireland, the limited CPD opportunities for SNAs and the ad-hoc approaches that guide SNA learning and development. The need for a formalized and structured approach to the continuum of professional learning for SNAs was highlighted as a national priority to support high quality educational provision and positive outcomes for children (NCSE 2015; 2016). Although this has been recommended by the NCSE (2018) as part of their policy advice paper no. 6, it is questionable whether Level 5 qualifications on the National Framework of Qualifications will be sufficient in addressing the knowledge and skills required of ISAs to effectively support the range of care needs with which children with special educational needs can present, coupled with the evidenced-based strategies that ISAs require to develop children's independent living skills. An array of international models of professional development programmes was forwarded as potential exemplars to facilitate national reflection and progression in this field.

Overall, it is clear that a range of positive and negative practices are evident across all settings in terms of SNA support for children with ASD. On one hand, SNAs are clearly facilitating inclusive practices within our schools and supporting the significant care needs of children with ASD. In contrast, the stretched role of the SNA and the variety of ineffective SNA practices highlights the substantial issues that remain central to this national scheme. Considering the volume of SNAs within our education system, coupled with the significant annual expenditure on the scheme, the need to increase the effective utilization of this resource is deemed paramount. Not alone is this required to facilitate greater value for money, but rather, to maximize the potential of the SNA role and ensure effective support of all children with significant care needs. While the SNA scheme does not apply to early childhood care and education settings, an application can be made under the access and inclusion model for additional assistance in the preschool room (Inter-Departmental Group (IDG), 2015). Clearly the findings in relation to the effective utilization of SNA support are eminently applicable in early years contexts. Stemming from the comprehensive review of the SNA scheme and the proposed new school inclusion model aimed at delivering the right support at the right time to students with additional needs (NCSE, 2018), it is clear that changes are imminent, both in terms of policy and practice. It is only through renewed thinking and the integration of the best available research with clinical expertise that the original tenets of the SNA scheme can be realized. In this way, we can aim to 'allow such children to participate fully in the education system ... and enable them to reach their potential' (GOI 1998, as cited in DES 2011a: 127–128).

Bibliography

Blatchford, P., Webster, R., and Russell, A. (2012). *Challenging the Role and Deployment of Teaching Assistants in Mainstream Schools: The Impact on Schools. Final Report on Findings from the Effective Deployment of Teaching Assistants (EDTA) project*. Accessed online on 1 February 2018 at <http://maximisingtas.co.uk/assets/content/edtareport-2.pdf>.

Bondy, A., and Frost, L. (2002). *A Picture's Worth. PECS and Other Visual Communication Strategies in Autism*. Bethesda: Woodbine House.

Broer, S. M., Doyle, M. B., and Giangreco, M. F. (2005). 'Perspectives of Students with Intellectual Disabilities about their Experiences with Paraprofessional Support', *Exceptional Children*, 71, 415–430.

Carrig, M. (2004). 'Changing Role of the Special Needs Assistant: Perspectives of a Special School Staff', *Reach*, 17(2), 119–126.

Cooper, P., and Jacobs, B. (2011). *Evidence of Best Practice Models and Outcomes in the Education of Children with Emotional Disturbance/Behavioural Difficulties. An International Review.* Accessed online on 1 February 2018 at <http://aboutones. com/wordpress/wp-content/uploads/2014/10/7_NCSE_EBD.pdf>.

Daly, P., Ring, E., Egan, M., Fitzgerald, J., Griffin, C., Long, S., McCarthy, E., Moloney, M., O'Brien, T., O'Byrne, A., O'Sullivan, S., Ryan, M., Wall, E., Madden, R., and Gibbons, S. (2016). *An Evaluation of Education Provision for Students with Autism Spectrum Disorder in Ireland.* Trim: National Council for Special Education.

Department of Education and Science (2002). *Circular Special Education 07/02: Applications for Full-time or Part-time Special Needs Assistant Support to Address the Special Care Needs of Children with Disabilities.* Dublin: Department of Education and Science.

Department of Education and Skills (2010). *Behavioural, Emotional and Social Difficulties: A Continuum of Support.* Dublin: Department of Education and Skills.

Department of Education and Skills (2011a). *The Special Needs Assistant Scheme: A Value for Money Review of Expenditure on the Special Needs Assistant Scheme.* Dublin: Department of Education and Skills.

Department of Education and Skills (2011b). *Circular 0021/2011: Educational Qualifications for Appointment as Special Needs Assistant in recognized Primary and Post Primary Schools.* Dublin: Department of Education and Skills.

Department of Education and Skills (2011c). *Public Service (Croke Park) Agreement – Special Needs Assistants: Circular Number 0071/2011.* Accessed online on 1 February 2018 at <https://www.education.ie/en/Circulars-and-Forms/Active-Circulars/cl0071_2011.pdf>.

Department of Education and Skills (2013). *Well-being in Post-Primary Schools: Guidelines for Mental Health Promotion and Suicide Prevention.* Accessed online on 1 February 2018 at <https://www.education.ie/en/Publications/Education-Reports/Well_Being_PP_Schools_Guidelines_Summary.pdf>.

Department of Education and Skills (2014). *Circular 0030/2014: The Special Needs Assistant (SNA) Scheme to Support Teachers in Meeting the Care Needs of Some Children with Special Educational Needs, Arising from a Disability.* Dublin: The Stationery Office.

Department of Education and Skills (2015). *Well-being in Primary Schools: Guidelines for Mental Health Promotion.* Accessed online on 1 February 2018 at <https:// www.education.ie/en/Publications/Education-Reports/Well-Being-in-Primary-Schools-Guidelines-for-Mental-Health-Promotion.pdf>.

Elliott, S. (2004). 'The Role and Training of Special Needs Assistants for Students with Autistic Spectrum Disorders in Ireland', *Good Autism Practice*, 5(2), 22–34.

Giangreco, M. F. (2010a). 'One-to-one Paraprofessionals for Students with Disabilities in Inclusive Classrooms: Is Conventional Wisdom Wrong?' *Intellectual and Developmental Disabilities*, 48(1), 1–13.

Giangreco, M. F. (2010b). 'Utilization of Teacher Assistants in Inclusive Schools: Is it the Kind of Help that Helping is all About?' *European Journal of Special Needs Education*, 25(4), 341–345.

Giangreco, M. F., and Suter, J. C. (2015). 'Precarious or Purposeful? Proactively Building Inclusive Special Education Service Delivery on Solid Ground', *Inclusion*, 3(3), 112–131.

Giangreco, M. F., Edelman, S. W., Luiselli, T. E., and MacFarland, S. Z. (1997). 'Helping or Hovering? Effects of Instructional Assistant Proximity on Students with Disabilities', *Exceptional Children*, 64(1), 7–18.

Government of Ireland (1998). *Education Act 1998*. Dublin: The Stationery Office.

Government of Ireland (2004). *Education for Persons with Special Educational Needs Act 2004*. Dublin: The Stationery Office.

Government of Ireland (2005). *Disability Act*. Dublin: The Stationery Office.

Griffin, C. P. (2015). 'The Pursuit of Independence? Reconsidering the Role of the Special Needs Assistant in Inclusive Education'. In A. O'Donnell (ed.), *The Inclusion Delusion? Reflections on Democracy, Ethos and Education*, pp. 61–76. Oxford: Peter Lang.

Harris, B. A. (2011). 'Effects of the Proximity of Paraeducators on the Interactions of Braille Readers in Inclusive Settings', *Journal of Visual Impairment and Blindness*, 105(8), 467.

Inter-Departmental Group (2015). *Supporting Access to the Early Childhood Care and Education Programme for Children with a Disability*. Accessed online on 1 February 2018 at <http://nda.ie/nda-files/Supporting-Access-to-the-Early-Childhood-Care-and-Education-for-Children-with-a-Disability.pdf>.

Irish Government Economic and Evaluation Service (2016). *Focused Policy Assessment of Data on Special Needs Assistants*. Accessed online on 1 February 2018 at <http://igees.gov.ie/wp-content/uploads/2015/02/Focused-Policy-Assessment-of-Data-on-SNAs_Final.pdf>.

Keating, S., and O'Connor, U. (2012). 'The Shifting Role of the Special Needs Assistant in Irish Classrooms: A Time for Change?' *European Journal of Special Needs Education*, 27(4), 533–544.

Lámh (2009). *About Lámh*. Accessed online on 1 February 2018 at <http://www.lamh.org/About-Lamh.aspx>.

Lawlor, L., and Cregan, A. (2003). 'The Evolving Role of the Special Needs Assistant: Towards a New Synergy', *REACH Journal of Special Needs Education in Ireland*, 16(2), 82–93.

Logan, A. (2006). 'The Role of the Special Needs Assistant Supporting Pupils with Special Educational Needs in Irish Mainstream Primary Schools', *Support for Learning*, 21(2), 92–99.

Mäensivu, K., Uusiautti, S., and Määttä, K. (2012). 'Special Needs Assistants – the Special Characteristic and Strength of the School System of Finland', *European Journal of Educational Research*, 1(1), 23–36.

Malmgren, K. W., and Causton-Theoharis, J. N. (2006). 'Boy in the Bubble: Effects of Paraprofessional Proximity and ther Pedagogical Decisions on the Interactions of a Student with Behavioral Disorders', *Journal of Research in Childhood Education*, 20(4), 301–312.

Middletown Centre for Autism and National Council for Special Education (2013). *Evaluation Framework to Underpin the Evaluation of Educational Provision for Students with ASD*. Trim: National Council for Special Education.

National Behaviour Support Service (2008). *Behaviour Support Classroom Best Practice Guidelines*. Accessed online on 1 February 2018 at <https://www.nbss.ie/sites/default/files/publications/NBSS_TG_Col.pdf>.

National Council for Curriculum and Assessment (2009). *Aistear: The Early Childhood Curriculum Framework*. Accessed online on 1 February 2018 at <https://www.ncca.ie/en/early-childhood/aistear>.

National Council for Special Education (2015). *Supporting Students with Autism Spectrum Disorder in Schools: NCSE Policy Advice Paper No. 5*. Trim: National Council for Special Education.

National Council for Special Education (2016). *NCSE Policy Advice: Supporting Students with Autism Spectrum Disorder in Schools: A Guide for Parents/Guardians and Students*. Trim: National Council for Special Education.

National Council for Special Education (2018). *Comprehensive Review of the Special Needs Assistant Scheme. A New School Inclusion Model to Deliver the Right Supports at the Right Time to Students with Additional Care Needs. NCSE Policy Advice Paper No. 6*. Accessed online 7 June 2018 at <http://ncse.ie/wp-content/uploads/2018/05/NCSE-PAP6-Comprehensive-Review-SNA-Scheme.pdf>.

O'Neill, A., and Rose, R. (2008). 'The Changing Roles of Teaching Assistants in England and Special Needs Assistants in Ireland: A Comparison', *REACH Journal of Special Needs Education in Ireland*, 22(1), 48–58.

Organisation for Economic Co-operation and Development (2012). *Encouraging Quality in Early Childhood Education and Care*. Accessed online on 1 February 2018 at <http://www.oecd.org/education/school/49322232.pdf>.

Radford, J., Bosanquet, P., Webster, R., and Blatchford, P. (2015). 'Scaffolding Learning for Independence: Clarifying Teacher and Teaching Assistant Roles for Children with Special Educational Needs', *Learning and Instruction*, 36, 1–10.

Radford, J., Bosanquet, P., Webster, R., Blatchford, P., and Rubie-Davies, C. (2014). 'Fostering Learner Independence through Heuristic Scaffolding: A Valuable Role for Teaching Assistants', *International Journal of Educational Research*, 63, 116–126.

Schopler, E., Mesibov, G. B., and Hearsey, K. (1995). 'Structured Teaching in the TEACCH System', In E. Schopler, and G. B. Mesibov (eds), *Learning and Cognition in Autism*, pp. 243–292. New York: Plenum Press.

Shevlin, M., Kenny, M., and Loxley, A. (2008). 'A Time of Transition: Exploring Special Educational Provision in the Republic of Ireland', *Journal of Research in Special Educational Needs*, 8(3), 141–152.

Spens, E. (2013). 'Examining the Role of Special Needs Assistants in Mainstream Post-Primary Schools', *REACH Journal of Special Needs Education in Ireland*, 26(2), 104–117.

Takala, M. (2007). 'The Work of Classroom Assistants in Special and Mainstream Education in Finland', *British Journal of Special Education*, 34(1), 50–57.

The National Autistic Society (2017). *Mental Health and Autism*. Accessed online on 1 February 2018 at <http://www.autism.org.uk/about/health/mental-health.aspx>.

Van de Pol, J., Volman, M., and Beishuizen, J. (2010). 'Scaffolding in Teacher–Student Interaction: A Decade of Research', *Educational Psychology Review*, 22(3), 271–296.

Vygotsky, L. S. (1978). *Mind in Society: The Development of Higher Psychological Processes*. London: Harvard University Press.

Webster, R., Blatchford, P., and Russell, A. (2013). 'Challenging and Changing how Schools use Teaching Assistants: Findings from the Effective Deployment of Teaching Assistants Project', *School Leadership and Management*, 33(1), 78–96.

Webster, R., Russell, A., and Blatchford, P. (2012). *Maximising the Impact of Teaching Assistants: Guidance for School Leaders and Teachers*. Oxon: Routledge.

Webster, R., Russell, A., and Blatchford, P. (2016). *Maximising the Impact of Teaching Assistants: Guidance for School Leaders and Teachers* (2nd edn). Oxon: Routledge.

MICHELE DUNLEAVY-LAVIN, SHIRLEY HEANEY
AND SHARON SKEHILL

5   Individualized Planning: Bureaucratic Requirement or Critical for Effective Practice?

ABSTRACT

In this chapter the central role of the individual education plan (IEP) or individualized planning[1] will be examined in relation to educational provision within inclusive early childhood, primary, post-primary and special school environments for children with autism spectrum difference (ASD). The contribution of the IEP process to providing a structure for the systematic planning and evaluation of learning programmes for children with ASD will be considered (Mittler 1996). Additionally, concerns in relation to IEPs being viewed as a bureaucratic demand rather than as effective tools to support the inclusion of children with additional needs in educational settings will be explored.

Introduction

The concept of Individualized Education Plans (IEPs) for children with additional needs can be traced to Public Law 94–142 (1975) in the United States, which was subsequently re-authorized as the Individuals with Disabilities Education Act (IDEA) of 1990 (Meyen and Skrtic 1998). This coincided with the emergence of a rights-based approach to education, which had originated in the Universal Declaration of Human Rights (United Nations (UN) 1948), with Article 26 stating clearly that 'everyone has a right to an education'. As a result we have moved from a culture of

---

1   The terms Individual Education Plan and Individualized Planning Process are used
     interchangeably throughout this chapter.

institutionalization, where children with additional needs were perceived not to be in need of education, to one of inclusion of all children in the education system from early years to post-primary level and beyond. The IEP has become a central document in this inclusive process and while the organization of the IEP varies from country to country and between educational establishments, the process follows a similar pattern as encapsulated in Figure 5.1, with the child firmly located at the centre of the process.

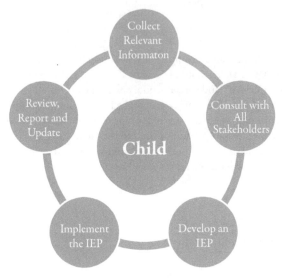

Figure 5.1: The Individual Education Plan Process

Collaborative practice between all stakeholders is critical to ensuring an effect IEP process. In this context, the guidelines compiled by the National Council for Special Education (NCSE) (NCSE 2006), which reflect international practice, suggest the following should participate in an IEP meeting:

- the child;
- the person co-ordinating the information being collected;
- the person, other than the child's teacher, who has responsibility for co-ordinating provision for children with additional needs in the setting;

- the child's early years/class or subject teacher(s) including, as appropriate, prospective setting personnel and any other key worker(s) involved with the child and
- any of a range of available and relevant professionals including psychologist, occupational therapist, speech and language therapist, physiotherapist, social worker, as appropriate.

Collaborative practice is an essential element of inclusive education (Interdepartmental Working Group (IDG) (2015), which is acknowledged within the philosophy of Ireland's early years curriculum framework, *Aistear* (National Council for Curriculum and Assessment (NCCA) 2009) and quality framework Síolta (Centre for Early Childhood Development and Education (CECDE) 2006). Moreover, the Diversity, Equality and Inclusion Charter (Department of Children and Young Affairs (DCYA) (2016) highlights that the best outcomes for children are achieved in inclusive settings that engage in 'meaningful collaboration with parents and other professionals to ensure access, equality and full participation for all children' (p. 4).

The NCSE (2006: 5) states 'that the IEP has an educational purpose'. This might suggest that IEPs, in Ireland, should have an exclusive academic focus. However, the NCSE also acknowledges that the Education for Persons with Special Educational Needs (EPSEN) Act (Government of Ireland (GOI) 2004) Section 8.5 states, that the IEP 'shall have regard to any needs, other than education needs of the child concerned which are specified in the assessments under Section 4, and shall ensure that the education plan is consistent with provision for needs'. This is also consistent with the foci of curricula in Ireland from early years to post-primary level, which are concerned with promoting the holistic development of the child (NCCA 1999; 2006; 2009; 2017). The NCSE (2006) further advises that IEPs should be individualized and child-centred; inclusive; collaborative and accessible. These characteristics clearly suggest that the foci of an IEP should extend beyond an academic focus. This has particular relevance for children with ASD, where differences in social and communication skills present most challenges and can impact negatively on the child's ability to integrate into the class and school community (Jordan and Jones 1999; Powell and Jordan 2002; Attwood 2007; Dunleavy-Lavin 2013). For this reason, one would expect that social and communication skills' development would be a key focus of the IEP for children with ASD.

In Ireland, unlike other countries such as the United Kingdom (UK), the United States of America (US), Australia and New Zealand, the IEP is not underpinned by legislation. Nevertheless, in 2006 the NCSE compiled comprehensive guidelines in relation to the IEP process. The aim being to provide national guidelines on IEPs 'which would underpin a uniform approach to work already in hand' (p. v) and begin preparations for the implementation of the EPSEN Act (GOI) 2004). Section 2 subsection 5 of the EPSEN Act states 'the principal shall ... within 1 month from the receipt by him or her of the assessment, cause a plan to be prepared for the appropriate education of the student'. However, this section of the Act has not been enacted and as a result IEPs do not have any legal status in Ireland. Although not underpinned by legislation the IEP process has been embraced by many teachers and education settings in Ireland concerned with promoting good practice for children with additional needs (McCarthy 2006).

The NSCE guidelines advocate for the 'effective' transition of children with additional needs from preschool to primary school education and strongly advise that transition is planned for, and included in the IEP process (NSCE 2006). Within the context of supporting children with additional needs in the early years setting the IDG (2015) developed a model of intervention to support the meaningful inclusion of children with additional needs accessing the Early Childhood Care and Education (ECCE) programme. Termed the Access and Inclusion Model (AIM), AIM provides a suite of supports ranging for universal to targeted under a seven step model of intervention. The supports provided under the model include, but are not limited to, 'expert' educational 'guidance and support' from early years specialists, a minor alterations capital grant for equipment and appliances and therapeutic intervention. An 'individual access and inclusion plan' and associated guidelines were developed to support the implementation of AIM (2017) and to promote the effective inclusion of children with additional needs in the early years setting. The individual access and inclusion plan is intended to support children's participation in the early setting through identifying 'access and participation goals' and providing the supports needed to achieve these goals. The plan is designed as a live document requiring collaboration and 'frequent reviews', it documents children's strengths and interests and identifies the child's needs through 'goal themes' which are located under access, participation and supports. These 'goal themes' can then be 'linked to the Pillars of Practice in the Aistear Síolta Practice Guide' (AIM 2017: 4).

In Ireland the IEP is the 'only document that is additional to or different from the differentiated curriculum plan that is already happening in the education setting. Individual education plans are not, therefore, a substitute for the curriculum' (NCSE 2006: VI). Additionally, the Special Education Support Service (SESS) provides guidelines that state 'the IEP is a written plan prepared for a named student, it is a record of what is agreed as "additional to" and "different from" the usually differentiated curriculum provision that is provided by very class/subject teacher' (SESS 2010: 1).

For the purposes of the study conducted by Daly and colleagues (2016), practice was evaluated with reference to the criteria set by the Evaluative Framework compiled by Middletown Centre for Autism (MCA) and the NCSE (MCA and NCSE 2013). In relation to the IEP process the main focus of this chapter will be the identification of children's strengths and needs, engaging in collaborative practice in order to compile a profile and set targets based on the assessed priority learning needs.

International and national guidelines on the IEP process suggest that the process is best supported by collaboration between parents, the child, teachers, and external professionals such as a psychologist, speech and language therapist, occupational therapist and others who are working with the child. A key challenge, which has been identified is providing for the inclusion of children in the IEP process and ensuring that their opinions are included in the final IEP (Bergin and Logan 2013). However, Bergin and Logan citing Mason et al. (2002) observe that when children have experience of being involved in their own IEP process, they have been observed to require less support from adult team-members and acquire greater self-confidence in relation to their own educational experience. The importance of listening to the child's voice in 'matters which affect them' is supported by national and international discourse, including the National Children's Strategy (Department of Health and Children (DoHC 2000: 11), and the United Nations Convention on the Rights of the Child (UNCRC) (UN 1989). While acknowledging that the 'age and maturity' of the child is an important consideration (DoHC 2000: 30) due attention must also be directed to the 'rich and vital information' that may remain uncovered if a child's ability to reflect on their experiences is underestimated (Zwiers and Morrissette 1999: 2).

It is critical therefore that children's contributions to the process are valued and their involvement clearly defined. In relation to target-setting, it has been suggested that targets should be specific; measureable; achievable; realistic and times (SMART) (Brown, Leonard and Arthur-Kelly 2016). McCarthy (2006) further highlights the importance of the IEP being understood in terms of a process rather than a product and notes that 'it is the quality of the process that dictates the quality of the efficacy of the IEP' (p. 112). Lordan (2002) highlights the importance of the generalization of skills being a target in the IEP process for children with ASD.

Key Signposts: Introduction

- The emergence of IEPS for children with additional needs coincided with the emergence of a rights-based approach to education, which had originated in the Universal Declaration of Human Rights (United Nations (UN) 1948).
- Individualized planning is central to effective inclusive practice for children with ASD.
- IEPS should be Individualized; child-centred; inclusive; collaborative; accessible and address the child's holistic development.
- The IEP process is best supported by collaboration between parents, the child, teachers, and external professionals.
- IEP targets should be specific, measurable, achievable, realistic and timed (SMART).

Individualized Planning

The research conducted by Daly and colleagues (2016) presents some valuable insights on the individualized planning process in early intervention classes, primary, post-primary and special school environments for children with ASD.

Early Intervention Classes

In the early intervention classes there was evidence of good written assessment policies. Policies provided evidence of assessment of, and for learning with a specific focus on children's functional language and communication, behaviour, social and emotional development, play, leisure skills and independence. However, there was no evidence of ASD specific assessments that could identify strengths and needs that are 'in addition to' and 'different from' the curriculum. Nevertheless, available assessments did inform the information gathering section of the IEP process. This in turn led to data indicating individualized planning as very good with explicit sectors detailing the child's strengths, needs and priority learning needs.

In the early years setting there was evidence of collaboration between parents, teachers and multidisciplinary team members as part of the IEP development process. However, while it would appear special needs assistants (SNAs) were involved in the implementation of the IEP, there was no evidence of their being part of the collaborative process mentioned above, as they did not attend IEP meetings. One SNA noted that 'we are not involved in IEP meetings but [are] given them [IEPs] and teachers [are] quite often open to get us to engage that might bring these elements out and with reward charts also' (Daly et al. 2016: 51). At this level the data suggested greater parental involvement in the IEP process with the opinions and contributions from parents being valued by school staff. Nevertheless, not all parents were satisfied with the process, with one parent expressing a wish for more than one meeting per year. The data indicates good informal involvement of children in the IEP process through discussion, interactions, teacher observations and planning based on the child's identified interests. Nevertheless, the formal involvement of children in their IEP compilation was unacceptable as this in turn leads to an undefined role for the child in the IEP process, which Bergin and Logan (2013) caution comprises the child's contribution to the process.

In terms of identifying targets, priority learning needs could be clearly linked to needs identified by assessments and SMART targets were compiled. It was evident that targets were informally reviewed on a regular basis and formal review dates were included in the IEP document. Although the use of ASD specific assessments was not evident, the need to include targets for social skills development, as highlighted by Baron-Cohen and Volkmar (1997) had been taken into account. Also, some parents reported that targets were not always reached. However, some parents were satisfied because the IEP not only focused on academic but also on skills that could transfer and make home life easier.

Within the mainstream early childhood settings, in addition to the incorporation of the Individual Access and Inclusion Plan previously referred to, there is an emphasis, through the implementation of the *Aistear* framework (NCCA 2009), of catering to the needs of every individual child in the preschool setting. Acknowledging that Ireland has only recently begun to focus on the importance of children's early years experiences (Ring 2015), there is now a shift towards the documentation and planning around the specific learning needs of every child. The *Aistear Síolta* Practice Guide (NCCA 2015) supports practitioners within the sector to devise individual learning journals for all children in the setting, using their strengths and their interests to devise learning goals to support their development. Children in ECCE settings are similarly encouraged to be active agents in their learning and development, through a playful and emergent curriculum.

In early childhood settings, there has been a shift away from this 'SNA' model under the AIM programme, with additional (Level 7) support in the classroom presenting as a Preschool Assistant employed by the service through government funding, to reduce the adult child ratio to 1:8. Indeed, a key principle of the Diversity, Equality and Inclusion Charter and Guidelines (DCYA 2016) notes the importance of utilizing the AIM programme effectively and recognizing that not all children with additional needs will require additional support. Síolta (CECDE 2006) advocates a Key Worker approach in the early years setting, which emphasizes the importance of the role of the adult working with the child in supporting their learning and development. The role of the Inclusion Co-ordinator, the graduate of the Leadership for INClusion (LINC) in the early-years programme under AIM, supports the key worker and the staff team in devising strategies and plans to ensure the participation and inclusion of all children in the preschool programme (Ring 2016). This new approach to preschool support for children with additional needs embraces the ideology of a more inclusive environment and culture for all children in the early years setting.

Key Signposts: Early Intervention Classes

- Assessment informed the information gathering section of the IEP process.
- Collaboration between parent, teachers and multidisciplinary team was part of the IEP development process.
- Priority learning needs were addressed in IEP targets.
- Targets were SMART and linked to needs identified by assessments.
- In early childhood settings, there has been a shift away from this 'SNA' model under the AIM programme, with additional (Level 7) support in the classroom presenting as a Preschool Assistant employed by the service through government funding, to reduce the adult child ratio to 1:8.
- The role of the Inclusion Co-ordinator, the graduate of the Leadership for INClusion in the Early Years (LINC) programme under AIM, supports the key worker and the staff team in devising strategies and plans to ensure the participation and inclusion of all children in the preschool programme.

Primary Schools

In the primary settings data indicate that there were variations in the planning process and that this ranged from very good, to unacceptable. In sites described as being good and very good the individualized planning process was structured and systematic and based on the children's assessed needs and strengths. The individualized plan included information on implementation and the children's learning and teaching.

In relation to targets identified, the data indicated that academic, social and communication, life skills and behaviour domains were included. Additionally, the data demonstrated a good level of understanding of the children's overall needs suggesting a holistic model of provision with the inclusion of social and communication skills' targets. A focus on SMART targets was evident and one principal added that 'the advice is to keep your targets nice and short and don't overcrowd the whole thing' (Daly 2016: 72). In the majority of schools, supplementary teaching was provided to address children's additional needs rather than to replace curriculum experiences. Copies of the IEP were held by the class teacher, special class teacher or resource teachers and parents. However, it was not clear if the SNA received a copy of the IEP although the data indicate that SNAs were involved in the IEP implementation where behaviour and care-related targets were set. Formal IEP meetings were scheduled on a bi-annual basis and attended by the class teacher, special class or resource teacher, parents and principal when possible. However, the data indicated that the SNA was not part of the collaborative process as they did not attend IEP meetings.

In this study the data suggest that parents of primary-aged children are involved in the IEP process and that the wishes/expectations of the parents were taken into account. In one school it was reported that a parent brought in video footage from a day at the leisure centre to help explain some of the difficulties experienced by the child. These were incorporated into target setting to assist both in school and at home. Whilst parents reported having a meaningful role within the IEP process, nevertheless some parents expressed confusion about the process.

In one school children's involvement was described as excellent. However, in the remaining schools it was deemed unacceptable as the role of the child was not clearly defined. However, it was something schools were willing to consider in the future, as one principal stated: 'it's not something we've done but it is something we might have a look at' (Daly et al. 2016: 73). It was clear that there was scope to consider providing teachers with continuing professional development (CPD) in relation to including children in the process (Bergin and Logan 2013). While schools expressed a willingness to engage with external professionals in the context of the IEP process, the limited availability of external professionals such as speech and language therapists, psychologists and occupational therapists was considered unacceptable.

Key Signposts: Primary Schools

- Targets included academic, social and communication life skills and behaviour domains.
- Supplementary teaching was provided to address additional needs rather than replacing curriculum experiences.
- In the majority of schools, IEPs were reviewed on a bi-annual basis.
- Teachers would benefit from additional CPD focused on including children in the IEP process.
- Schools were willing to engage with external professionals; however, their availability was limited.

Post-Primary Schools

Whilst there was documentary evidence of individualized planning in post-primary sites it was evident that the process was less developed at this level. This reflects similar findings by Tennant (2007) in relation to post-primary schools in the UK where he describes the perception of the IEP in terms of a 'bureaucratic encumbrance' (p. 204).

The data indicate that although mainstream teachers were given a copy of the IEP there was no evidence of collaboration with these teachers during the information gathering section of the process. The special educational needs co-ordinator in one school reported that 'it is really hard to collate multiple students and 11 subjects' (Daly et al. 2016: 101). There was no evidence of external professionals attending IEP meetings but there was some input on an informal basis. For example, one special educational needs co-ordinator stated that 'we indirectly get feedback from them [external services] should we need it to implement them into the IEP' (Daly et al. 2016: 101). It was explained that this input could be through reports or parental reporting. There was evidence of collaboration with parents with one parent stating that she was 'very involved and always have been. We would identify the targets with the unit teacher or with the classroom teacher and we would discuss them' (Daly et al. 2016: 101). Collaboration with children varied, however there was no evidence of children attending IEP meetings. Nevertheless, there was some evidence of informal input, for example, in one school the special class teacher stated that 'students would chat with myself or another staff member. There would be self-reflection about classes, what went well, what could be better what the challenges are' (Daly et al. 2016: 101). In other schools there was documentary evidence that children were involved in the IEP process although they did not attend the meetings. Here the children completed questionnaires and attended planning meetings. Bergin and Logan (2013) suggest that these aspects of involvement can be construed as the first stage in supporting involvement of children in the IEP process and developed further.

The report concluded that collaboration with parents and children was a strong feature of practice when compiling an IEP and acceptable in most sites. There was scope for development identified also in relation to target setting and the need for SMART targets in order to track progress.

The IEP was available to mainstream teachers with one class teacher observing that 'there is great benefit of being aware of their sensory needs' (Daly et al. 2016: 100). However, there was no evidence of a plan in place to observe and mitigate the impact of negative environmental sensory stimuli on children's engagement. Additionally, the implementation of the IEP was rarely in evidence outside of the special class. It would appear that class/

Key Signposts: Post-Primary Schools

- Although there was documentary evidence of IEPs, the process was less developed at this level.
- The level of collaboration with mainstream teachers at the information gathering stage of the IEP process required attention.
- The need for greater availability and involvement of external professionals in the IEP process was articulated.
- Parental collaboration and involvement in the IEP process was evident.
- Scope for development in relation to target setting and the need for SMART targets to track progress was identified.

subject teachers considered the implementation of the IEP to be the responsibility of the special education teachers as one teacher stated 'that's more special needs teachers' (Daly et al. 2016: 101). The data indicates an absence of methodical review and in some instances the absence of a formal review date in the IEP, thus potentially reducing the effectiveness of the process.

Special Schools

The practice of compiling individualized plans was evident in special schools, however there were differences in the structure and level of detail between schools. Therefore, the process ranged from fair to excellent and for this reason it can be argued that there was a lack of consistency in practice across schools. An example of this inconsistency can be seen when comparing practice. In one site in addition to individualized plans, the staff provided a record sheet for each child and these were used when compiling the individualized plan, while in another, individualized plans were incomplete and not time-bound. Nevertheless, the data suggest that special schools considered individualized plans as vital working documents that were used to inform teaching with one special class teacher noting that 'the IEPs are working documents. They get scribbled over and added to. Sometimes the targets are unachievable and I might have to go back to the parents' (Daly et al. 2016: 128). It was reported that all parents receive a copy of the IEP and while not all parents understood the term IEP they appeared satisfied with the progress being made by their children. As one parent observed 'I trust them really and as long as he is making headway I don't analyse or find out what they have done'. However, on the other hand one teacher described the IEP as 'a paper exercise' (Daly et al. 2016: 128). Whilst there were many variations in standards between sites, strategies, methodologies and resources for teaching the targets were clearly described in the IEP in five out of six special schools within the study.

Collaboration in relation to the IEP process was evident with a number of team-members attending the IEP meeting. These included the class teacher, the parent and when available, some members of the multidisciplinary team (MDT). When members of the MDT were not available information from their reports was used to inform the IEP. It would appear that special schools place a high value on parental input, with one teacher stating 'we would develop a plan with the parents. It is parent led really' (Daly et al. 2016: 129). One school had included a sheet from the parents entitled 'Hopes and Expectations' (Daly et al. 2016: 129) as they considered parental involvement to be central to the individualized planning process and their plans often contained direct quotes from parents.

In relation to children's participation in the IEP process, one special school reported involving children from the senior cycle through their own individual learning plan document. However, children rarely attended the individualized planning meetings. In other special schools, children were involved where appropriate but it was not stated what this meant or who decided if it was appropriate. However, one principal stated that 'none of the children would get involved in the process, none of them would be able to do that' (Daly et al. 2016: 130). Special needs assistants did not attend the IEP meetings but were often asked for input prior to the meeting. Following the compilation of the IEP the SNAs were made aware of targets either by the class teacher or at regular weekly or monthly meetings where the IEP was discussed. The SNA, in most cases, attended regular meetings either weekly or monthly to discuss the individual goals, progress and any issues that have arisen within the classroom.

In most schools the IEP included SMART targets, strengths and learning needs and targets were linked to the children's level of performance assessed using ASD specific assessment tools. This was demonstrated by the following example where the teacher reported that 'Tony finds it difficult to wait but is responding to the wait card' so his target is to learn to 'wait five seconds' (Daly et al. 2016: 128). In two schools IEPs were considered unacceptable as the targets were too general and not in accordance with SMART criteria.

As with other areas of the IEP process in special schools, the review dates varied with two out of the six schools not indicating a review date although in one school the IEP recorded the date the target was achieved. Three out of the six schools clearly stated bi-annual review dates with reviews usually occurring in September/October and January/February. One school indicated a monthly review date for each target with the special class teacher noting that 'we use the IEP as a working document. We do monthly targets and daily checklists and yearly reports' (Daly et al. 2016: 129).

Overall, there was some level of collaboration but this did not include parents and children in all schools and while members of the MDTs were invited to contribute to meetings, their attendance was not uniform. When parents were not directly involved in the IEP process they trusted the school to provide an appropriate plan for their child. Overall the structure of the IEP process ranged from very good to acceptable.

Key Signposts: Special Schools

- IEPs were a central feature of practice in special schools.
- Collaboration with class teacher, parents and when available multidisciplinary team was evident, this included children from the senior cycle in some sites.
- Targets were SMART and linked to the strengths and needs identified by ASD specific assessment.
- Review dates were not always indicated.

Conclusion

This chapter has examined the individual planning process in early intervention, primary, post primary and special schools for children with ASD in addition to reporting on recent developments to promote inclusion through the AIM in early childhood settings. The research findings by Daly and colleagues indicate that individualized planning is well developed and a feature of practice in early intervention classes, primary and special schools with greater scope for development at post-primary level (Daly et al. 2016). The introduction of an 'individual access and inclusion plan' and associated guidelines through the AIM present an opportunity to promote the effective inclusion of children with additional needs in the early years setting through individualized planning constructively linked to the early learning principles of *Aistear* (NCCA 2009).

Since the mid-twentieth century we have moved from a culture of segregation and institutionalization to one of inclusivity within the education system. This chapter suggests that rather than being a bureaucratic demand, individualized planning provides a mechanism for all children with ASD, regardless of ability, to gain meaningful access to the curriculum and achieve their full potential.

Bibliography

Access and Inclusion Model (2017). *Guidelines for Completing an Individual Access and Inclusion Plan.* Accessed online on 11 December 2017 at <http://aim.gov.ie/wp-content/uploads/2016/12/aim-level-4-individual-access-and-inclusion-plan.pdf>.

Attwood, T. (2007). *The Complete Guide to Asperger's Syndrome.* London: Jessica Kingsley Publishers.

Baron-Cohen, S., and Volkmar, F. (eds) (1997). *Handbook of Autism and Pervasive Developmental Disorders* (2nd edn). London: John Wiley and Sons.

Bergin, E., and Logan, A. (2013). 'An Individualized Education Plan for Pupils with Special Educational Needs: How Inclusive is the Process for the Pupil', *REACH Journal of Special Needs Education in Ireland*, 26(2), 79–91.

Brown, G., Leonard, C., Arthur-Kelly, M. (2016). 'Writing SMARTER Goals for Professional Learning and Improving Classroom Practices', *Journal of Reflective Practice*, 17(5), 621–635.

Center for Early Childhood Development and Education (2006). *Síolta: The National Quality Framework for Early Childhood Education.* Dublin: Center for Early Childhood Development and Education.

Department of Children and Youth Affairs (2016). *Diversity, Equality and Inclusion Charter and Guidelines for Early Childhood Care and Education.* Accessed online on 11 December 2017 at <http://aim.gov.ie/wp-content/uploads/2016/06/Diversity-Equality-and-Inclusion-Charter-and-Guidelines-for-Early-Childhood-Care-Education.pdf>.

Department of Health and Children (2000). *National Children's Strategy: Our Children-Their Lives.* Dublin: Department of Health and Children.

Dunleavy-Lavin, M. (2013). *The Inclusion of Pupils with Autistic Spectrum Disorder in Mainstream Primary Schools in Ireland.* Unpublished D.Ed. Thesis. Dublin: Trinity College Dublin.

Government of Ireland (2004). *The Education for Persons with Special Educational Needs Act.* Dublin: The Stationery Office.

Inter-Departmental Group (2015). *Supporting Access to the Early Childhood Care and Education (ECCE) Programme for Children with a Disability.* Accessed online on 11 December 2017 at <http://nda.ie/nda-files/Supporting-Access-to-the-Early-Childhood-Care-and-Education-for-Children-with-a-Disability.pdf>.

Jordan, R., and Jones, G. (1999). *Meeting the Needs of Children with Autistic Spectrum Disorder.* London: David Fulton Publishers.

Lordan, M. (2002). 'Assessment and IEP Development for Young Children with Autism', *REACH Journal of Special Needs Education in Ireland*, 15(2), 66–77.

McCarthy, J. (2006). 'The IEP Process: Current Practice and Perspectives', *REACH Journal of Special Needs Education in Ireland*, 19(2), 112–121.

Meyen, E. L., and Skrtic, T. M. (eds) (1994). *Special Education and Student Disability: Traditional, Emerging and Alternative Perspectives* (4th edn). Denver, CO: Love Pub Co.

Middletown Centre for Autism and National Council for Special Education (2013). *Evaluation Framework to Underpin the Evaluation of Educational Provision for Students with ASD.* Trim: National Council for Special Education.

Mittler, P. (1996). *Changing Policy and Practice for People with Learning Disabilities.* London: Cassell Education.

National Council for Curriculum and Assessment (1999). *The Primary School Curriculum.* Dublin: National Council for Curriculum and Assessment.

National Council for Curriculum and Assessment (2006). *Social, Personal and Health Education Curriculum Framework for Senior Cycle.* Dublin: National Council for Curriculum and Assessment.

National Council for Curriculum and Assessment (2009). *Aistear: The Early Childhood Curriculum Framework.* Dublin: National Council for Curriculum and Assessment.

National Council for Curriculum and Assessment (2015). The Aistear Síolta Practice Guide. Accessed online on 5 February 2018 at <http://www.aistearsiolta.ie/en/>.

National Council for Curriculum and Assessment (2017). *Junior Cycle Wellbeing Guidelines.* Dublin: National Council for Curriculum and Assessment.

National Council for Special Education (2006). *Guidelines on the Individual Education Plan Process.* Trim: National Council for Special Education.

Powell, S. and Jordan, R. (eds) (2002). *Autism and Learning: A Guide to Good Practice.* London: David Fulton Publishers.

Ring, E. (2015). 'Early Years Education-focused Inspections: A Reason to Celebrate', *Children's Research Digest*, 2(2), 42–46.

Ring, E. (2016). 'National Higher Education Programme for Inclusion Coordinators in Early Years' Settings', *Education Matters*, 131.

Special Education Support Service (2010). *Individual Education Planning.* Accessed online on 11 December 2017 at <http://www.sess.ie/sites/default/files/Resources/Classroom/SESS_IC_IEP.pdf>.

Tennant, G. (2007). 'IEPs in Mainstream Secondary Schools: An Agenda for Research', *Support for Learning*, 22(4), 204–208.

United Nations (1948) *Universal Declaration of Human Rights.* Accessed online on 5 February 2018 at <http://www.un.org/en/universal-declaration-human-rights/>.

United Nations (1989). *United Nations Convention on the Rights of the Child.* Accessed online on 5 February 2018 at <http://www.childrensrights.ie/sites/default/files/UNCRCEnglish.pdf>.

Zwiers, M. L., and Morrissette, P. J. (1999). *Effective Interviewing of Children.* United States: Taylor and Francis.

MARIE RYAN

6   Assessment and Children with Autism Spectrum Difference

ABSTRACT

This chapter explores how assessment can be used in inclusive education settings, with specific focus on the assessment of children with autism spectrum difference (ASD). Purposeful and appropriate assessment is essential for successful teaching and learning. The learning preferences of children with ASD must be considered if educators are to gather accurate evidence of learning for these children. Inclusive assessment approaches are based on having a deep appreciation of the distinct characteristics associated with ASD. This chapter will explore how learning evidence is gathered from children with ASD in Irish educational settings, drawing on data from the national evaluation of educational practices for children with ASD (Daly et al. 2016). In light of these findings and contemporary literature, suggestions will be offered for developing assessment approaches that are sensitive enough to capture valid evidence of learning amongst children with ASD in order to support teaching and learning across all education settings.

What Should We Assess?

Autism spectrum difference affects multiple domains of development and therefore requires a multi-layered assessment approach. In assessing the progress of children with ASD, it is important to consider behaviour, sensory and motor skills, life skills, communication skills, socialization skills, emotional skills, cognitive functioning and executive functioning. Assessment should also consider children's wellbeing and happiness (Vermeulen 2014). In the midst of all these complex domains of development which are important for assessment, we need to be careful however not to overlook the children's curricular goals. Dyson (2001: 101) suggests that once a child is 'labelled' educators tend to narrow their focus to an 'individual gaze' rather than a 'curriculum gaze' and that curricular assessment and subsequently curricular attainment are neglected for children with formal diagnoses. Ultimately, curricular attainment is a passport to employment and opportunity in today's society and we need to remain alert and not inadvertently jeopardize children's likelihood of successful inclusion in adult society by underestimating and underemphasizing the academic potential of these learners. Adults with ASD, when asked what assessment information was important for teachers to inform teaching and learning for children with ASD, advocated for assessment approaches, which identify students' strengths, special interests and motivators (Jones et al. 2014). Given the range and scope of assessment domains which are pertinent for children with ASD, an educator would be forgiven for feeling somewhat overwhelmed! It is unrealistic to expect any one educator to manage this depth of assessment on their own, which is why an assessment-team approach is recommended. By pooling the resources and expertise of mainstream educators, special needs assistants (SNAs), support teachers, parents and the children themselves, a comprehensive approach to assessment for children with ASD can be achieved.

Educators in Ireland are subject to significant national policy demands in terms of curriculum and assessment. For example, in early years settings, there is an expectation that all children's curricular experiences are underpinned by *Aistear: The Early Childhood Curriculum Framework* (National Council for Curriculum and Assessment (NCCA)) (NCCA 2009). Within the primary school context, the vast, diverse curriculum provides many opportunities for learners and teachers but can also pose barriers, as teachers can feel overwhelmed by pressure to cover the hundreds of curriculum objectives outlined for every year level. Assessing children's learning of all these objectives provides even further challenges. Mainstream class teachers are required to administer standardized assessments in literacy and numeracy from first class to sixth class and results from these assessments must be reported to parents on at least two occasions during the child's primary school experience (Department of Education and Skills (DES) 2011). Given the significant curriculum and assessment demands, it is unsurprising that the assessment practices observed in mainstream primary classrooms during the evaluation study predominantly focused on academic skills in literacy and numeracy. The most common assessment tools employed by mainstream teachers in the research sites were based on literacy and numeracy achievement; 'Friday tests' of spellings and tables; standardized tests; school/teacher devised assessments of sounds, sight words, maths skills and termly maths assessments associated with textbooks. Special needs assistants (SNAs) tended to be designated significant responsibility in terms of assessment of behaviour engaging in systematic frequency observations and antecedent-behaviour-consequence (ABC) observations. They were generally not involved in assessing children's academic progress. Support teachers were particularly focused on assessing children's social, emotional, functional, behavioural and communication skills. They assessed skills which were tied to the Individual Education Plan (IEP) process.

In this way, mainstream class teachers, SNAs and support teachers were essentially operating assessment partnerships such that children with ASD were experiencing a multi-domain, multi-assessment approach. Such assessment partnerships were also evident in early childhood and post-primary settings. In most cases these assessment partnerships worked co-operatively, with responsibility for various assessments being clearly designated according to separate roles, rather than collaboratively in terms of regularly sharing of assessment evidence and assessment roles. There is a danger that if each assessment team member is solely focused on one or a limited number of learning domains that the picture of the whole child may remain disjointed. Further underlining the importance of collaborative assessment, children with ASD can have difficulties with generalization which is linked to their differences in relation to information processing or flexibility of thought; therefore, it is important not to assume that a skill observed in one context will be able to be applied elsewhere (Farrell, Fidler, Christie and Lyn-Cook 2016). While planning time is a persistent barrier to collaboration across all education settings, the introduction of some team-teaching practices and secure file sharing technologies may help to foster a more collaborative assessment team. Findings indicated that educators had huge respect for parents' expertise and the intimate knowledge that they had of their children's strengths and needs (Daly et al. 2016). However, the potential to exploit this expertise and employ parents as co-assessors in a holistic assessment approach was not realized to the extent that it might have been. In many cases parents were kept well informed of their child's progress but rarely did they share responsibility in the assessment process with the teacher. For example, one parent responded that, while she didn't know what assessments her child completed, she had 'one hundred per cent confidence in the teacher' (Daly et al. 2016: 58). Parents can offer insights into both the generalization of learning and consolidation of learning, often identifying things that may not be as easily detected by someone who does not know the child as well. They can contribute hugely to the learning story (Bourke and Mentis 2014a) for their child.

Key Signposts: Reflecting on Assessment

When considering assessment reflect specifically on:

Domains of Learning: Gather assessment evidence relating to:

- all relevant domains of development for the child
- what motivates the child
- what makes the child happy
- the child's curricular performance

Assessment Team:

- Ensure a comprehensive assessment plan
- Involve parents, SNAs, support teachers any relevant multi-disciplinary personnel and the child in gathering assessment evidence
- Compile all assessment evidence and share evidence to build a complete picture of the child as a learner and to ensure generalization of learning *across contexts*

How Should We Assess: Considering Assessment for Learning for Children with ASD

The National Council for Curriculum and Assessment classroom assessment guidelines for primary teachers (NCCA 2007; 2009) suggest a spectrum of assessment approaches to be adopted by educators. The guidelines categorize assessment in terms of assessment of learning (AoL) and assessment for learning (AfL) and recommend a balanced approach to classroom assessment (NCCA 2007; 2009). Assessment of learning, as described in the guidelines reflects more formal, medium- to long-term (end-of-unit/ end-of-term) assessments such as checklists, weekly tests, termly tests, commercially available termly tests associated with relevant text-books and standardized assessments. Assessment for Learning describes more informal, frequent assessment practices, which inform daily teaching and planning and include observations of learning during individual or group tasks, questioning, conversations and self-assessment. Reflective of these recommendations, the findings of Daly et al. (2016) indicated that educators adopted approaches which spanned the assessment continuum; working with child-led assessment via self-assessment, portfolio approaches and teacher-led assessment through observation, weekly tests and standardized tests.

Assessment for Learning is often described as an inclusive assessment practice (Bourke and Mentis 2013; 2014a; 2014b; Hayward 2014). Wilkinson and Twist (2010) allude to the potential of AfL approaches for children with ASD while cautioning that there is a lack of empirical evidence on the challenges of using AfL approaches with children with ASD. The appropriateness of AfL for children with ASD was discussed by a team of European experts who concluded that AfL approaches were to be recommended with the exception of self-assessment which was deemed to be overly difficult and challenging for children with ASD (European Agency for Development in Special Needs Education (EADSNE) 2009). Jackie Ravet (2013) is much more dubious about the suitability of AfL for children with ASD, cautioning against blindly implementing these methods without sufficient consideration of the key characteristics of ASD. She argues that the characteristics associated with ASD are likely to impede many of the perceived benefits of AfL approaches and could potentially serve to exclude children from educational success if they are not adapted appropriately. However, if we look at the definition of AfL as provided by the Assessment Reform Group (2002), it is difficult to argue with those who consider AfL as an inclusive assessment approach: 'the process of seeking and interpreting evidence for use by learners and their teachers to decide where the learners are in their learning, where they need to go and how best to get there' (p. 2). The principles or process of

AfL as articulated here reflects the essence of inclusive practice. Concerns expressed are unlikely to reflect an issue with AfL as an assessment system, using assessment evidence to inform teaching and learning, but rather reflect concerns regarding the congruence between the assessment tools most commonly associated with AfL and the characteristics of ASD. As concluded by the EADNSE (2009) report 'students with profound difficulties do not need different assessment systems, but only different methods/ tools of assessment' (p. 4).

Harlen (2007) identifies the following tools for AfL; discussions; observations; self-assessment; peer-assessment; teacher debate; comment-only feedback; dialogue and questioning. Many of these tools could be considered constructivist and social constructivist teaching tools. The majority of AfL proponents couch their work within these theoretical perspectives with Hayward (2012) claiming that AfL is a practice situated most comfortably within socio-cultural learning theories. Some authors have questioned the suitability of constructivist modes of teaching for children with ASD, arguing that the available evidence supports more behaviourist approaches than constructivist approaches for children with ASD (McMahon and Cullinan 2016). Polarizing pedagogical debates pitting behaviourist and constructivist/social-constructivist philosophies against each other has yielded little practical advice for teachers. Both perspectives offer insights into learning. Applied behavioural approaches have been used successfully with children with ASD and a wealth of research evidence has demonstrated how task analysis, discrete skill training, reinforcement schedules and continuous assessment of skills to inform teaching, for example, precision teaching, can support the children's learning (Peters-Scheffer, Didden, Korzilius, and Sturmey 2011; Odom, Hume, Boyd, and Stabel 2012;). The findings from our national evaluation study indicated that these types of practices were used extensively, albeit not exclusively, amongst learning support and resource teachers who were providing additional support teaching to children with ASD. (Daly et al. 2016). Continuous progress monitoring, curriculum-based measurement (both commercial and teacher-designed), regular checklists, and precision teaching tracking were used to inform planning and teaching, particularly as part of the Individual Education Plan (IEP) process. Children's progression on skills were evaluated through a a range of performance scales, such as; 'presented-practised-perfected'; 'can complete with prompting – can complete without prompting'. These teachers used assessment in a skilful and targeted way to identify gaps in the children's learning and to address those gaps. While the tools used by these teachers are not generally associated with AfL, it is clear that the teachers were using the evidence derived from these tools to inform teaching and learning in a manner worked effectively for the children that they were working with.

Constructivist assessment tools are more concerned with what children are thinking and understanding than what they know and don't know. The aim of these tools is to provide a window into the child's mind, enlightening the educator with regard to what the children are interested in, what they understand or where confusions lie, in order to guide the knowledge building journey with the child. In general, the AfL tools used to make children's thinking visible involve oral questioning; group-work; whole-class dialogue; conversations and peer assessment. Given that children with ASD experience difficulties with social interaction and communication, it is reasonable to suggest that these methods may not give the most accurate representation of children's thinking and level of understanding. This does not mean that we should abandon constructivist principles; we still need to know what these children are thinking, what they understand, and what they want to know. Rather, we need to reflect on how we can modify these approaches to make them more effective and to think about alternative ways to make children's thinking visible. Concept mapping is one useful approach to make thinking visible which has been found to capitalize on the visual processing strengths of children with ASD and to facilitate them in overcoming the limitations of a cognitive style that encourages them to focus on detail rather than the overarching connections between concepts (Roberts and Joiner 2007). Many educators in the evaluation study spoke about the success that they had experienced when using approaches based on Information and Communication Technology (ICT) to capture children's thinking with one educator articulating the advantages of the approach for children with ASD as 'ICT assessment is fantastic ... it motivates pupil and at the end I have a record ... it is very visual and the visual works' (Daly et al. 2016: 71). Project work and asking the children to create illustrations to demonstrate understanding were also found to be successful methods of tapping into children's thinking. Analysis of children's drawings can offer important insights into their thinking and can serve as a scaffold for children with ASD when they are attempting to communicate their thoughts.

Observation emerged as the most relied upon tool for children with ASD amongst all educators; with teachers identifying it as 'the most important assessment of all' (Daly et al. 2016: 70). I would argue that observation in and of itself is not an assessment tool. Observation only becomes an assessment tool when the observer has attuned him/herself to the observable assessment criteria of the moment, and has a frame of reference for interpretation, knowing what he/she is looking for and what 'good' looks like. While it is difficult to record every observation of every child every day, documentation of our observations needs to be enhanced if we wish to fully exploit this most important evidence source. If we do not record our observations consistently and somewhat systematically we can find ourselves over-relying on more formal, narrow assessment information from tests when it comes to compiling IEPs and long-term educational planning as this is the only data that we have easy access to.

Assessment will only promote children's learning when learning intentions and success criteria are clearly outlined and when children receive feedback which guides the next steps in their learning (Black and Wiliam 2012). Educators in both mainstream and support roles, across a number of sites were found to share learning intentions and success criteria, for example, using statements such as: 'we are learning to ...' and 'what I am looking for ...', with the children and found this approach to be very effective in terms of keeping learners focused and on task with their learning. The more descriptive this information was the more helpful children with ASD found it. For example, when educators used exemplars to demonstrate success criteria the quality of work produced was likely to be better, as children had a better understanding of what 'good' work looked like. Feedback practices varied across sites. Some good examples of practice included the following; short, unambiguous, learning-focused comments;

feedback which pointed out examples of good performance; feedback given close to the learning event and feedback which explicitly outlined the next steps in learning.

The promotion of autonomous learning is a key principle underlying the AfL philosophy (Pedder and James 2012). Self-assessment, the primary means by which this aim is addressed, is the most contentious AfL approach when it comes to children with ASD. Researchers highlight the challenges that children with ASD experience in terms of metacognition and theory of mind (ToM) and argue that these barriers minimize the benefits of self-assessment (EADSNE 2009; Ravet 2013). In order for children with ASD to truly benefit from self-assessment and become self-regulated learners, additional support should be provided alongside basic strategies. Self-assessment strategies were employed in a number of the research sites (for example; Self-Assessment Learning Folders; '2 Stars and a Wish') but there was room for improvement in terms of how children with ASD were supported to use these approaches. For example, children were asked to include their 'best' work in their Self-Assessment Learning Folders but were not given any clear guidance or criteria, visual or otherwise, to help them to determine what their best work might look like.

Assessment for Learning is central to effective teaching and learning for all children. Different AfL tools assess different types of learning. Comprehensive assessment for children with ASD will require the use of many different types of AfL tools to complement each other. Some assessment tools commonly associated with AfL may pose particular difficulties for children with ASD. As these tools give important insights into children's thinking it is important to adjust these tools to make them more accessible and consider alternative ways of capturing children's thinking. Rather than designating some assessment tools as 'autism assessment tools', adopting a universal design for learning (UDL) approach, whereby children are given multiple options for expressing their learning, is a more suitable means of ensuring all children can demonstrate their learning without conveying low-level expectations or reducing opportunities for children with learning differences (Ryan 2015). Some suggestions to consider when using AfL approaches with children with autism are offered below.

Key Signposts: Reflections for Using Assessment for Learning Approaches with Children with ASD

Making Thinking Visible

- UDL – ensure choice and flexibility for children to demonstrate their learning.
- If asking oral questions, be aware that a child with ASD might not volunteer an answer even though they might know how to respond. Be aware that a child with ASD may actually know and understand more than they are willing/able to communicate orally in front of a large group.
- If questioning, you might need to call a child's name to get his or her attention. Try to keep questions short. Support questions visually if possible and appropriate (see Ravet, 2013 for further suggestions).
- Consider the child's visual strengths and encourage opportunities to present their thinking visually through illustrations, concept maps, ICT, projects, etc.
- If using group-work consider structure and length of time for tasks. Think about clearly defined roles and responsibilities.
- Peer-assessment is likely to require a lot of preparatory work. Assessment and particularly peer assessment can leave many children feeling quite vulnerable. Children with ASD may need specific guidance on delivering feedback to others, particularly negative feedback.
- Social stories could be used to demonstrate appropriate social conventions during group-work and peer assessment.

Sharing Success Criteria & Self-Assessment (see Ravet 2013 for further suggestions)

- Use clear, unambiguous language.
- Try to be as specific as possible.
- Use exemplars to demonstrate what 'good' looks like.
- Use rubrics with visuals where possible/appropriate.

Feedback (see Ravet 2013 for further suggestions)

- Use clear, unambiguous language.
- Short, explicit-learning focused feedback.
- Give reasonably close to time of assessment.
- Clearly outline next steps in learning.
- Check for understanding.

Progress Monitoring

- For skill development, consider precision teaching, CBM and checklists.
- Use assessment information to guide IEP process.
- Involve children in tracking and graphing progress.

Triangulation

- Ensure that all assessment information is considered when evaluating children's learning and making educational decisions.

How Should We Assess: Considering Assessment of Learning for Children with ASD

Researchers and educators alike have debated whether or not students with significant learning challenges should be included in the more formal classroom or standardized assessments associated with assessment of learning (AoL), with many arguing that it is not fair on the children to subject them to experiences in which they are not likely to succeed (Katsiyannis, Zhang, Ryan and Jones 2007; Thurlow and Kopriva 2015). Similarly, many educators in this study of educational provision for children with ASD in Ireland highlighted particular concerns with regard to the appropriateness of formal AoL assessment tools for children with ASD. In one primary school it was reported that children with ASD do not complete any of the weekly or termly tasks and tests. Teachers cited genuine concern for children's self-esteem as the primary justification for this decision. Evidence suggests however that such arguments could potentially have a negative impact on the learning and achievement of children with learning differences. If we consider assessment as integral to teaching and learning and if we use assessment information to guide our teaching and support children's learning, then without this information for children with ASD, we would have to question whether we can really teach them as effectively as every other child. Research suggests that including children with learning differences in formal assessments serves to raise expectations for these children and has a positive long-term influence on learning and achievement (Ysseldyke et. al. 2004). Following a large-scale analysis of assessment practice for children with special educational needs across a number of EU member states, the EADSNE was unequivocal in its conclusion that *all* children should be entitled to be part of *all* assessments and that appropriate accommodations must be made to make sure that this is possible (Watkins 2007). Murchan and Shiel (2017) suggest that assessment accommodations should be considered in the context of the UN Convention on the Rights of Persons with Disabilities (2006). They cite Section 24.2c in their argument that assessment accommodations are necessary and appropriate to enable students with learning differences the opportunity to demonstrate their learning and achievement on a level playing field with other students. The issue therefore, is not whether children with ASD should engage with formal classroom assessment, but rather how we can make these assessments more accessible for children with ASD.

While normative standardized assessments should be interpreted with caution for children with high level learning differences and while all evidence from these types of assessment should be triangulated with more meaningful evidence sources such as observations and criterion-referenced assessments (Bourke and Mentis 2014b), it is important that children with ASD have access to all assessment opportunities. As normative standardized tests are used to report to parents, designate learning resources and inform whole-school decision making in Irish primary schools in particular, it is important that data relating to the learning of children with ASD is available for these purposes.

Across all primary sites in our evaluation study, teachers reported that standardized tests posed particular problems for children with ASD (Daly et al. 2016). Teachers described many different ways in which they attempted to address the various challenges that children may experience when undertaking these assessments, as noted by one teacher's observation that 'we have to modify them because they are not able to sit for the length of time' (Daly et al. 2016: 69). Some teachers described reading the questions for the children and asking them to repeat the questions to check for understanding. Another teacher reported that she found that a child with ASD in her class performed better on these standardized assessments when she completed them in the less distracting support teaching room than when the assessment was conducted in the busy mainstream classroom. Teachers acknowledged the dilemma posed by these modifications in administration procedures, given that they deviate significantly from the recommended procedures, and would likely affect the reliability of the scores obtained. In some cases, teachers felt it unfair to put the children through the standardized assessment process. They expressed frustration at a lack of appropriate assessment tools and helplessness in terms of how these tools should be modified appropriately. They were concerned that there were gaps in terms of the assessment evidence available to reflect the academic learning of children with ASD.

The concerns expressed by these Irish primary teachers are echoed internationally and are relevant for all educators dealing with formal assessment systems. Wilkinson and Twist (2010), in their review of UK policy and practice with regard to ASD and educational assessment, concluded that formal accommodations for standardized assessments do not relate specifically to the needs of children with ASD. They note that it is not always clear where the line should be drawn between adapting assessments and providing alternative assessments for children with significant additional needs and cite evidence from the United States which reports that schools generally choose the most common or easy way to implement accommodations for all children with additional needs, regardless of the specific needs of the individual child. Educators are struggling to make appropriate assessment accommodations for children with ASD; it is apparent that there is a critical need for clearer, evidence-based guidance and increased professional development for educators to enable confident, appropriate and consistent assessment accommodations. Emphasizing the necessity for appropriate assessment accommodations for learners with ASD, adults with ASD have identified the assessment context as being of critical importance and suggested that teachers should consider the sensory sensitivities and learning differences of children with ASD when assessing their learning

(Jones et al. 2014). In an effort to support teachers in adjusting assessments for children with learning differences, Davies, Elliott and Cumming (2016) present a sixty-seven item checklist for educators in Australia to use when considering modifications to learning and assessment approaches in light of learning differences. The checklist reflects the following potential areas for consideration: motivational adjustments; scheduling adjustments; setting adjustments; assistance with directions; assistance during assessment; assistance prior to assessment administration; specialized equipment or assistive technology and learning and assessment formats. The checklist emphasizes the importance of ensuring alignment between instructional adaptations and assessment modifications, for example if a child receives a treat for completing tasks during instruction, the same approach should be considered during assessment and vice versa. While some educators found the checklist overly burdensome, the majority found it a useful method for recording adjustments and providing guidance for teachers on the various adjustments that might be applied (Davies, Elliott and Cumming 2016).

In the absence of a similar tool for the Irish context, I have compiled an *Autism Standardized Assessment Considerations Checklist* (ASACC) as a potential support for Irish educators in adjusting standardized assessments for children with ASD. This tool has been developed in light of findings from the national evaluation of educational provision for children with ASD in Ireland (Daly et al. 2016) and builds upon the work of Davies, Elliott and Cumming (Davies et al. 2016). A key consideration, when using this tool to determine appropriate assessment adaptations for children with ASD, is to consider alignment with instructional adaptations and to establish whether strategies that you use to support learning for children with ASD are also useful to support the assessment for children with ASD. This checklist is not exhaustive and it is likely that there are other accommodations that teachers may find appropriate to support the learners in their classrooms. As per standardized assessment guidelines, adherence to the standardized administration procedures is essential for the integrity of the assessment process, therefore any deviation from recommended procedures must be recorded and reflected in score interpretation. The purpose of the ASACC, presented in Table 6.1, is to provide a reflective framework for considering the specific needs of children with ASD in the context of standardized assessment and to provide a consistent method of recording assessment modifications.

Table 6.1: Autism Standardized Assessment Considerations Checklist (ASACC)

Assessment Preparation Considerations: *Children with ASD often experience significant anxiety, particularly in unfamiliar or unexpected situations. Standardized test procedures differ significantly from generally classroom practice – e.g. tables are separated, children are not permitted to seek help etc. This can be particularly unnerving for children with autism. Children with ASD often have a tendency towards literal interpretation of language – they may not understand to give more information than is directly requested by the question.*	
1. Does this child get anxious when there are changes to routines? Do I need to explain the change in routine in advance? Would a Social Story help? Would a 'mock' assessment in advance help?	
2. Does this child rely on visual schedules generally? Given that the assessment is likely to last much longer than regular lessons do I need a visual schedule to support this child in the assessment process,	
3. Does this child have a particular strategy to reduce anxiety e.g. sensory supports? Will this child have access to anxiety reducing supports if necessary?	
4. Does this child understand examiner expectations with regards to question stems such as; *discuss, give reasons for your answer, consider, evaluate* etc. Would preparatory work explaining marking expectations with regards to these types of phrases support this child?	
Motivational Considerations: *Children with ASD who are used to ABA type systems of instruction are likely to require motivational supports during formal assessments.*	
5. Does this child need reinforcers to engage purposefully in tasks (e.g. rewards, treats etc.)? Will a reinforcement schedule be required for this assessment? How often will reinforcers be used?	
6. Does this child need verbal encouragement for effort? Will he/she require verbal encouragement for the assessment?	

(Continued)

Table 6.1: (*Continued*)

7.	Does this child generally need encouragement to commence work? Will this be required for the assessment?	
8.	Does this child generally need encouragement to sustain effort? Will this be required for the assessment?	
9.	Does this child need encouragement so that he/she will not quit? How will I provide this encouragement if it is required?	
	Scheduling Considerations: *Due to hyperactivity and over-stimulation many people with autism find that concentrating on one thing for a long period of time can be very challenging.*	
10.	Does this child generally need extra-time to complete written, independent tasks? How much time? Would extra-time help him/her demonstrate their best work?	
11.	Does this child require frequent or extended rest-breaks during written, independent tasks? How do I know when a break is required – does the child given me signs? How can I address this need during the assessment? Would it make sense to complete the assessment over a few days?	
12.	Is there a time of day when this child works best? Is it possible to schedule the assessment during this time?	
	Environmental Considerations: *Many people with ASD feel the need to move around and find it difficult to sit still for lengthy periods of time. Sensory sensitivities can mean that things such as lighting, noise, smells, or the teacher walking up and down the room could all be distracting.*	
13.	Does this child work well on independent written tasks in the classroom environment in general? Would a change of seating help to remove distractions? Is the LS/RS room a more appropriate environment to complete this assessment?	
14.	Does adaptive furniture work for this child? Would it help during the assessment?	

15.		Does this child usually use headphones if noise becomes overwhelming? Will these be accessible to the child during the assessment if required?
16.		Does this child usually need movement breaks? Will he/she be allowed the freedom to move, stand or pace during the assessment?
		Considerations during assessment: Temporal and short-term serial order processing can be difficult for children with ASD. A detail-focused cognitive style could lead children to become overly focused on one particular question or one part of a question.
17.		Does this child generally need assistance with multi-step questions? Will assistance be required for this assessment? What generally works? Colour-coding to emphasize steps? Having the child re-read/re-state questions in his/her own words?
18.		Does this child need prompting to move onto the next question? What type of prompt would be appropriate? Does this child need regular reminders with regards to the amount of time remaining? Would a sand-timer or visual support assist in this regard?
19.		Are there significant auditory working memory demands placed on children in any of the assessments i.e. where the children have to remember sentences called out by the teacher in order to answer the question (e.g. Word Analysis in the Drumcondra Primary Reading Test or the NRIT assessments). Would a listening prompt before each sentence help e.g. *is everyone ready? Put your finger on the next one?*
20.		Does this child generally need a prompt to turn pages, move on to the next question? Does he/she get bogged down in minor details to the detriment of his/her performance? What sort of prompts generally help this behaviour? How can I use these types of prompts to help this child during the assessment?

(Countinued)

Table 6.1: (Continued)

21.	Does this child require support with written organization skills in class? Would lined/squared 'rough-work' paper help for math assessments? Some assessments provide very little space for children to work out their computations and to mistakes being made due to mess and lack of organization.
22.	Does this child generally track text effectively without skipping words or sections of text? Would cues such as stop signs/arrows on the test form help? Would a tick-off strategy for each question help? Would tracking the test items by pointing or by placing child's finger on the items help? Would separate copies of diagrams/tables needed be helpful that the child does not have to flip back and forth in materials?
23.	Does this child usually use assistive technology for independent written tasks? Laptop/iPad for presentation/recording of responses? Text-Speech Converter? Visual/Auditory magnification device? Audio-recorder? Manipulatives? Specialized pencils/grips, rulers? Etc.
24.	Is sign-language or oral interpretation likely to be required? Is a reader or scribe used for independent written tasks in class? Will one be required for the assessment?
25.	Are there irrelevant items on the text booklet likely to distract this child e.g. examiner scoring boxes? Can I cover these in some way?

Conclusion

This chapter focused in particular on the data from the national evaluation of education provision for children with ASD that emerged from mainstream primary schools. However, it is likely that the implications emerging from this data have applicability for early years, primary, post-primary and special school settings. Both the analysis of data and contemporary research on inclusive assessment practices revealed the barriers and challenges posed by traditional assessment approaches and offered insights for overcoming these issues. This chapter outlined the importance of a collaborative team approach to assessment to ensure that a wide range of assessment evidence, offering insights into all areas of development and competence can be compiled to present a comprehensive learning story. A broad definition of AfL was adopted to facilitate consideration of both wide-ranging and narrow-focused assessment tools and suggestions were offered for adapting and modifying AfL tools to enable children with ASD to give a genuine demonstration of what they know and what they can do. The case was made for ensuring that children with ASD have access to all assessments, including more formal assessments and standardized assessments. An autism specific considerations checklist was proposed as a reflective and recording tool for educators. It is hoped that this chapter will support educators across all education settings in using assessment to enhance learning opportunities for children with ASD and support them in realizing their full potential in a holistic manner.

Bibliography

Assessment Reform Group (2002). *Assessment for Learning: 10 Principles. Research-based Principles to Guide Classroom Practice.* Accessed online on the 18 December 2017 at <https://www.aaia.org.uk/content/uploads/2010/06/Assessment-for-Learning-10-principles.pdf>.

Black, P., and Wiliam, D. (2012). 'Assessment for Learning in the Classroom'. In J. Gardner (ed.), *Assessment and Learning*, pp. 11–32. London: SAGE.

Bourke, R., and Mentis, M. (2013). 'Self-Assessment as a Process for Inclusion', *International Journal of Inclusive Education*, 17(8), 854–867.

Bourke, R., and Mentis, M. (2014a). 'Self-assessment as an "Insider" Lens for Learning and Assessment'. In L. Florian (ed.), *The SAGE Handbook of Special Education Vol. 2*, pp. 537–552. London: SAGE.

Bourke, R., and Mentis, M. (2014b). 'An Assessment Framework for Inclusive Education: Integrating Assessment Approaches', *Assessment in Education: Principles, Policy and Practice*, 21(4), 384–397.

Daly, P., Ring, E., Egan, M., Fitzgerald, J., Griffin, C., Long, S., McCarthy, E., Moloney, M., O'Brien, T., O'Byrne, A., O'Sullivan, S., Ryan, M., Wall, E., Madden, R., and Gibbons, S. (2016). *An Evaluation of Education Provision for Students with Autism Spectrum Disorder in Ireland*. Trim: National Council for Special Education.

Davies, M., Elliott, S. N., and Cumming, J. (2016). 'Documenting Support Needs and Adjustment Gaps for Students with Disabilities: Teacher Practices in Australian Classrooms and on National Tests', *International journal of inclusive Education*, 20(12), 1252–1269.

Department of Education and Skills (2011). *Literacy and Numeracy for Learning and Life: The National Strategy to Improve Literacy and Numeracy Among Children and Young People, 2011–2020*. Dublin: Department of Education and Skills.

Dyson, A. (2001). 'Special Needs in the Twenty-first Century: Where We've Been and Where We're Going', *British Journal of Special Education*, 28(1): 24–29.

European Agency for Development in Special Needs Education (2009). *Assessment for Learning and Pupils with Special Educational Needs*. Accessed online on 18 December 2017 at <https://www.european-agency.org/sites/default/files/assessment-for-learning-and-pupils-with-special-educational-needs_assessment-for-learning-graphic-en.pdf>.

Farrell, S., Fidler, R., Christie, P., and Lyn-Cook, L. (2016). *The Development of a Progression Framework for Children and Young People with Autism*. Autism Education Trust. Accessed online on 11 December 2017 at <http://www.aettraininghubs.org.uk/wp-content/uploads/2016/02/PF-report.pdf>.

Harlen, W. (2007). *Assessment of Learning*. London: SAGE.

Hayward, L. (2012). 'Assessment and Learning: the Learner's Perspective'. In J. Gardner (ed.), *Assessment and Learning*, pp. 125–139. London: SAGE.

Hayward, L. (2014). 'Assessment for Learning and the Journey towards Inclusion'. In L. Florian (ed.), *The SAGE Handbook of Special Education Vol. 2*, pp. 523–535. London: SAGE.

Jones, G., Milton, D., Bradley, R., Guldberg, K., MacLeod, A., Thomas, G., Simpson, P., Stanyer, A., and Wiseman, A. (2014). AET Early Years Autism Competency Framework. London: AET. Accessed online on 15 December 2017 at <http://www.aettraininghubs.org.uk/wp-content/uploads/2014/09/AET-early-years-autism-competency-framework_final.pdf>.

Katsiyannis, A., Zhang, D., Ryan, J. B., and Jones, J. (2007). 'High-Stakes Testing and Students with Disabilities: Challenges and Promises', *Journal of Disability Policy Studies*, 18(3), 160–167.

McMahon, J., and Cullinan, V. (2016). 'Exploring Eclecticism: The Impact of Educational Theory on the Development and Implementation of Comprehensive Education Programmes (CEPs) for Young Children with Autism Spectrum Disorder (ASD)', *Research in Autism Spectrum Disorders*, 32, 1–12.

Murchan, D., and Shiel, G. (2017). *Understanding and Applying Assessment in Education*. London: SAGE.

National Council for Curriculum and Assessment (2007). *Assessment in the Primary School Curriculum: Guidelines for Schools*. Dublin: National Council for Curriculum and Assessment.

National Council for Curriculum and Assessment (2009). *Aistear: The Early Childhood Curriculum Framework*. Dublin: National Council for Curriculum and Assessment.

Odom, S., Hume, K., Boyd, B., and Stabel, A. (2012). 'Moving Beyond the Intensive Behavior Treatment Versus Eclectic Dichotomy: Evidence-Based and Individualized Programs for Learners with ASD', *Behavior Modification*, 36(3), 270–297.

Pedder, D., and James, M. (2012). 'Professional Learning as a Condition for Assessment for Learning. In J. Gardner (ed.), *Assessment and Learning*, pp. 33–48. London: SAGE.

Peters-Scheffer, N., Didden, R., Korzilius, H., and Sturmey, P. (2011). 'A Meta-Analytic Study on the Effectiveness of Comprehensive ABA-based Early Intervention Programs for Children with Autism Spectrum Disorders, *Research in Autism Spectrum Disorders*, 5(1), 60–69.

Ravet, J. (2013). 'Delving Deeper into the Black Box: Formative Assessment, Inclusion and Learners on the Autism Spectrum. *International Journal of Inclusive Education*, 17(9), 948–964.

Roberts, V., and Joiner, R. (2007). 'Investigating the Efficacy of Concept Mapping with Pupils with Autistic Spectrum Disorder'. *British Journal of Special Education*, 34(3), 127–135.

Ryan, M. C. (2015). Time for inclusion to detach from differentiation? In A. O' Donnell (ed.), *The Inclusion Delusion*, pp. 77–94. Bern: Peter Lang.

Thurlow, M. L., and Kopriva, R. J. (2015). 'Advancing Accessibility and Accommodations in Content Assessments for Students with Disabilities and English learners', *Review of Research in Education*, 39(1), 331–369.

United Nations (2006). United Nations Convention on the Rights of Persons with Disabilities. Accessed online on 18 December 2017 at <http://www.un.org/disabilities/documents/convention/convention_accessible_pdf.pdf>.

Vermeulen, P. (2014). 'The Practice of Promoting Happiness in Autism'. In Jones, G., and Hurley, E. (eds), *Good Autism Practice: Autism, Happiness and Wellbeing*, pp. 8–17. Birmingham: British Institute for Learning Disabilities.

Watkins, A. (2007). 'Assessment in Inclusive Settings: Key Issues for Policy and Practice'. Odense, Denmark: European Agency for Development in Special Needs Education. Accessed online on 18 December 2017 at <https://www.european-agency.org/sites/default/files/assessment-in-inclusive-settings-key-issues-for-policy-and-practice_Assessment-EN.pdf>.

Wilkinson, K., and Twist, L. (2010). *Autism and Educational Assessment: UK Policy and Practice*. Berkshire: National Foundation for Educational Research.

Ysseldyke, J., Nelson, J. R., Christenson, S., Johnson, D. R., Dennison, A., Triezenberg, H., and Hawes, M. (2004). 'What We Know and Need to Know about the Consequences of High-Stakes Testing for Students with Disabilities', *Exceptional Children*, 71(1), 75–95.

PART II

Creating an Inclusive Culture

ANNE O'BYRNE

7 Including Parents Right From the Start

ABSTRACT

Using data from the research conducted by Daly and colleagues (2016) as a foundation, this chapter invites early years, primary, post-primary and special school settings to reflect on how positive communication with parents can support the development of inclusive cultures. Research evidence is presented to support the practice of working together to support the best possible outcomes for children with autism spectrum difference (ASD). In particular, communication, decision-making, and the role of fathers is examined, as is an invitation to educators to create their own personal philosophy of parental involvement in order to support the development of inclusive cultures across all education settings. Throughout the chapter are various children's drawings from the research to remind us that the children are at the centre of our work and that developing inclusive school cultures supports the provision of high-quality education for children and young people with ASD.

Introduction

The effects of having a child with autism spectrum difference (ASD) can have a profound impact on the life of a family (DePape and Lindsay 2015). This impact is often both life-affirming and existentially challenging. In a review of research on parenting a child with ASD, Lashewicz, Shipton and Lien report on how raising a child with ASD made parents 'better people, increased their awareness and empathy for other people's experiences, and strengthened their family bonds' (2017: 2). Alongside this were reports of profound challenges which parents encountered at various stages of their child's development, including the struggle to obtain a diagnosis, coping with feelings of guilt, experiencing judgement from others and a lack of public understanding of ASD. From the beginning, teachers and personnel in education settings play a central role in the identification of

children with ASD and the provision of targeted support for children and
their families. However, many teachers remain unaware of the distinct and
unique experiences of parents of children with ASD. This chapter sets out
to highlight the importance of communication between education settings
and parents, with a particular focus on fathers, and identifies how effective
communication, including decision-making, can contribute to the creation of environments characterized by inclusive cultures. The chapter also
issues an invitation to educators to create their own personal philosophy
of parental involvement to support the development of inclusive cultures
across all education settings in order to provide high-quality education for
children and young people with ASD.

Inclusive Cultures

Developing inclusive cultures for children both with and without additional
needs requires education settings and parents to work together (Ferguson
2008; Walton and Moonsamy 2015). An abundance of research demonstrates that children have better outcomes when schools and parents work
in partnership with each other (Marjoribanks 1979; Epstein 1984; 1986;
Henderson and Berla 1994; Broussard 2000; Jeynes 2005; Green, Walker,
Hoover-Dempsey and Sandler 2011; Zablotsky, Boswell, and Smith 2012;
Wilder 2014; Sheridan, Holmes, Smith and Moen 2016). Sheridan et al.
'the benefits of engaging families in children's education are among the
most convincing and consistent findings in the educational literature'
(2016: 1). In particular, the research tells us that children benefit not only
in their academic outcomes but also in their behavioural outcomes when
parents and education settings work together to support their learning and
wellbeing (Hornby 2011). Moreover, when parents and teachers experience positive relationships and work together children succeed not just in
school, but more importantly throughout their adult life (Henderson and
Berla 1994).
    One way all education settings can engage with parents and families is
by taking a family-centred approach. A family-centred approach is based on

establishing mutually trusting relationships between teachers and families, based on a set of principles and practices that respect families and build on their strengths and competencies (Moore 2010). According to King, Law, Kertoy, Rosenbaum, and Hurley (2002), this approach recognizes that parents have a unique insight into their child. In particular, parents of children with ASD 'have expert knowledge that can inform our understanding of ASD' and how it impacts on family life (DePape and Lindsay 2015: 570). The family-centred approach begins in early childhood intervention where there is an effort to move away from professionally based models of service to family-centred models where the child's main environment, which is the family, is acknowledged as being the main learning environment (Moore 2010). Ultimately, this approach to working with parents and families is based on a respectful relationship that recognizes the importance of the family in the child's life and the belief that when families and organizations, like education settings, work together in this way, the child benefits. In fact, the evidence suggests that when parents and education settings partner together to meet the needs of children with ASD, there are often dramatic positive results in terms of the child's cognitive, social, and emotional development (Murray, Ackerman-Spain, Williams and Ryley 2011).

Adopting a family-centred approach challenges those of us who work across and with early years, primary, post-primary and special school settings to put the child within the family at the center of what we do. This requires education settings to commit to meeting with, and listening to families and to be sensitive to what parents may be experiencing (Schultz, Able, Sreckovic and White 2016; Griffin and Shevlin 2007). It can be challenging for education settings and families to make the time to do this. However, the evidence suggests that when we do, the child benefits. The Education Act (Government of Ireland 1998), the Education for Persons with Special Educational Needs Act (Government of Ireland 2004), *Aistear* (National Council for Curriculum and Assessment (NCCA) 2009) and the Irish Primary School Curriculum (NCCA 1999) all stress the importance of having regular consultations with parents, not only to inform parents about their child's progress, but also to hear what parents have to say about their child and to benefit from this expert knowledge. The findings from our ASD research study suggest that education settings have a very deep awareness of the impact on families of having a child with ASD with personnel demonstrating empathy for parents regarding the challenges experienced by them as a result of their child having ASD. Throughout the study, there was a clear belief held by many staff that the parents have expert knowledge of their own children as articulated in the following quote from a research participant: 'they [parents] know the child more than we do' (Daly et al. 2016: 86).

Key Signposts: Inclusive Cultures

- All children, including children with ASD, have better outcomes, not just in education settings, but more importantly throughout their adult life, when educators and parents work together to create inclusive cultures.
- Adopting a family-centred approach means putting the child within the family at the centre of creating our inclusive cultures.
- Acknowledging parents as the experts on their own children is central to creating inclusive cultures in our education settings.

Figure 7.1: Drawing by a Child in a Mainstream Primary School

Communication

Cultivating and nurturing positive relationships between home and education settings is dependent upon effective communication with parents
of children with ASD (Gazi and Mandell 2016). Furthermore, a study by
Syriopoulou-Delli, Cassimos, and Polychronopoulous (2016) found that
both teachers and parents identified communication between home and
school as being critical for positive educational outcomes for children with
ASD. Schultz et al. (2016) propose communication between parents and
teachers as the foundation of support for children with ASD. Similarly,
Stoner, Bock, Thompson, Angell, Heyl, and Crowley (2005) call for open
and regular communication between teachers and parents of children with
ASD. The importance of communication between schools and parents is
clearly evident in the ASD research study. All twenty-four sites explored
in the study displayed an understanding and appreciation of the importance of developing effective and positive communication with parents
and an extensive range of formal and informal communication was evident in all of the primary school sites (Daly et al. 2016). It is important,
however, that communication between education settings and parents is
two-way.

Two-way communication enables parents to hear from education settings and enables education settings to listen and respond to parents and
value their perspectives and insights into their child. The National Parents
Council (NPC) in Ireland, advocating for parents to be actively engaged
in their children's education, recommend that 'all communication and
dialogue with parents must be regular, open, two-way and meaningful'
(NPC 2013: 4). According to O'Connor (2008), when dialogue is not two-
sided, an incomplete perspective is only available on the child. However,
when parents and education settings are in dialogue and the conversation
is two-way, a fuller picture of the child is presented and home and setting
have a better chance of working together in the best interests of the child
with ASD. Research also tells us that 'one of the most powerful incentives

for parents to attend school is for their child to send a personal invitation' (Morgan 2017: 91). In our ASD research study, a parent reported experiencing one-sided communication and highlighted for us the importance of two-way dialogue so that the child with ASD can achieve the best possible outcomes (Daly et al. 2016). This two-way communication is of particular importance when parents and teachers come together for parent-teacher meetings.

The manner in which meetings with parents are conducted can support or inhibit communication. In a 2006 Report by the Department of Education and Skills (DES), it was found that parent-teacher meetings, in the main, involved one-sided communication (DES 2016). Even though evidence in the report suggested that, in theory, education settings were aware of the need to consult with and listen to parents, the evidence found that practice primarily involved teachers talking to parents with very little responsive listening evident. Moreover, in 2008, a report commissioned by the NCCA to report on practices in primary schools had similar findings (NCCA 2008). In this report, while parents were recognized as partners in education and teachers were sensitive to the need to engage with parents and hear what they had to say, the evidence suggested that due to the short time frame associated with parent-teacher meetings, progress was given from the teacher's perspective only and, consequently, communication tended to be one-sided.

Key Signposts: Communication

- Cultivating and nurturing positive relationships between home and education settings is dependent upon effective communication.
- Effective communication involves two-way communication.
- Two-way communication is particularly important when educators and parents come together for meetings.

Figure 7.2:   Drawing by a Child in a Special School

Decision-making

Involving parents in key educational decisions about their child is something that is really important to parents of children with additional needs (Lamb 2009). According to King et al. (2002), recognizing parents as the experts on their child promotes partnership, and allows parents a voice when key decisions have to be made about their child with ASD. As far back as 1937, the Irish Constitution in Article 42 (Government of Ireland 1937) recognized parents as the primary educators of their children and subsequent legislation and policy supports parents in decision-making about the education of their children. This legislation includes the Education Act (Government of Ireland 1998) and The Education Welfare Act (Government of Ireland 2000). It is also a requirement under the Education of Persons with Special Educational Needs Act (EPSEN) (Government of Ireland 2004), which is yet to be fully enacted. The involvement of parents in decision-making is also promoted in *Aistear* (NCCA 2009) and the Primary School Curriculum (NCCA 1999). However, in reality there are few opportunities for parents to get involved in decision-making in our schools (Bleach 2010). In 2006, the DES indicated that decision-making was conducted by schools with very little involvement from parents (DES 2006). In fact, the report found that parents were usually informed about changes after the decisions had been made. The report concluded that a lack of structure prohibited the inclusion of parents' voices in the decision-making and planning processes. This finding is disappointing. If we are to truly involve parents in the education of their children with ASD, then we need to make the decision-making process transparent, intentional, structured and more inclusive of parents.

Key Signposts: Decision-making

- Involving parents in key educational decisions about their child is something that is really important to parents of children with additional needs.
- Recognizing parents as the experts on their child promotes partnership and allows parents a voice when key decisions have to be made about their child with ASD.
- If we are to truly involve parents in the education of their children with ASD, then we need to make the decision-making process transparent, intentional, structured and more inclusive of parents.

Figure 7.3: Drawing by a Child in a Mainstream Primary Irish-Speaking School

Role of Fathers

Research tells us that when we use the word 'parents', it tends to be equated with mothers (Morgan 2017). Morgan proceeds to tell us that, in addition to mothers, 'fathers play an important role in their children's education' (2017: 62). However, research examining the role of fathers of children with ASD in their children's education is limited (Lashewicz et al. 2007). In fact, these authors go so far as to say that 'experiences of fathers of children with autism have been largely overlooked by researchers' (2017: 1). According to Cheuk and Lashewicz (2016), the voices of fathers have not been listened to and research tends to focus on what mothers have to say. Reasons why fathers in general may not be engaged in their children's education may include work commitments, fathers' perceptions that involvement in their children's education setting is the responsibility of the mothers, lack of acknowledgement of fathers' own sociocultural experiences and, perhaps, fathers who are separated who do not regularly see their children (Morgan 2017). Fabiano (2007) suggests that one reason why fathers are so poorly represented in studies about children with ASD is that fathers may not be interested in taking part in research, or perhaps fathers are not invited to take part. However, the research that does exist acknowledges the unique role that fathers play in their children's lives and the need for all education settings to consider how best to engage fathers in their children's education in order to support best possible outcomes for their children with ASD.

Canadian researchers interviewed twenty-eight fathers of children with ASD to investigate the needs, challenges and successes of fathers of children with ASD (Cheuk and Lashewicz 2016). The findings of this study highlight fathers' willingness to share their experiences of fathering children with ASD and the struggle that exits for them to be heard. The fathers interviewed spoke of universal fathering experiences alongside a sense of loss and the efforts required to come to terms with demands they had not anticipated associated with fathering a child with ASD. This study also highlights that while fathers of children with ASD may not be listened to very often, when they are listened to they have a lot to say. Moreover, what they have to say contributes to our understanding of fathering a child with ASD and consequently provide educators with insights and direction in terms of family-centred approaches to developing relationships and engaging fathers.

Key Signposts: Role of Fathers

- Fathers play an important role in their children's education.
- Experiences of fathers of children with ASD have been largely overlooked by researchers.
- Fathers of children with ASD have a lot to say to provide educators with insights and direction in terms of family-centred approaches to supporting best possible outcomes for children with ASD.

Figure 7.4: Drawing by a Child in a Post-Primary School

Personal Philosophy of Parental Involvement

Our ASD research study highlighted many positive ways in which communication occurred between home and education settings and the findings were positive in almost all cases of parent-satisfaction. As already mentioned, one parent expressed dissatisfaction at the *one-sided* nature of the communication about her child, noting that all of the information was coming from the school (Daly et al. 2016). This draws attention to the challenge often experienced by education settings of how to make the time to ensure communication is two-way and that efforts are made to genuinely listen to parents, to hear what they have to say about their children. Otherwise, we have an incomplete picture or perspective of the child and miss out on valuable knowledge and insights that parents can bring to the table. Perhaps this requires us to question and reflect on how we, as educators, value and regard parents and what we expect of them in terms of relationship and partnership. This provides an opportunity to consider our own personal philosophy of parental involvement.

There are many ways for teachers to go about developing a personal philosophy of parental involvement. It is also important to know that research tells us that parental involvement is most effective when it is linked to children's learning (Webster-Stratton 2012; Goodall and Montgomery 2014). Dardig (2008) offers educators one way of developing their own personal philosophy of parental involvement. It consists of three key components that can be adapted to address how educators in all education settings might go about articulating their own personal philosophy of working with parents of children with ASD. The first component involves outlining an understanding of the role of parents of children with ASD. The second requires teachers to compile an outline of their own beliefs, values and understanding of their role as educators of children with ASD. The final component requires teachers to identify specific parent-involvement strategies that they can use to involve parents of children with ASD in their child's learning. The first component of this personal philosophy of parental involvement is an interesting exercise in considering all of the things a parent has to do and then, in addition, all the extra things a parent of a child with ASD has to do. Reflecting on this provides the teacher with an opportunity to consider the impact of parenting a child with ASD. This exercise, of course, would be considerably enhanced by inviting the parent/s to tell you what it is like for them and their family/ies. The second component requires the teacher to consider the underlying beliefs and values held about their role as teacher and about supporting parents of children with ASD to become involved in their children's learning. The final component involves the teacher identifying 'four to six strategies that you will use with the parents of the students in your class for the current school year' (Dardig 2008: 5). Dardig (2008) suggests teachers complete this activity, which need not be lengthy, and refer to it regularly and update it as necessary.

Key Signposts: Personal Philosophy of Parental Involvement

- Developing a personal philosophy of parental involvement provides educators with an opportunity to reflect on how we value and regard parents.
- Research tells us that parental involvement is most effective when it is linked to children's learning.
- Dardig (2008) offers a three-component strategy for developing our own personal philosophy of parental involvement to support parents of children with ASD.

Figure 7.5: Drawing by a Child in a Special School

A Final Word

Valuing the role of parents in their children's education is essential if educators across all settings are to work in partnership with families with the intention of supporting the best possible outcomes for all children and, in particular, children with ASD. Strengthening the relationship between education settings and parents is one of the Irish government's key themes in the 2017 Action Plan for Education (DES 2017). To do this, early years, primary, post-primary and special school settings need to invite parents to become involved as partners in their children's education. Epstein (2001) demonstrated that beyond all the factors that influence parent-teacher partnership, including parental education, socio-economic status, and family size, the most critical factor to successful teacher-parent partnership is the invitation from teachers to parents to become involved in their children's education. These invitations can take many forms including parent-teacher meetings, classroom volunteering, and helping with homework, all of which were in evidence in our ASD research study (Daly et al. 2016).

As with any relationship, effective communication is key to establishing good relationships with families. Our ASD research study highlighted a range of formal and informal strategies used by schools to effectively communicate with parents, including scheduled parent-teacher meetings, individualized education planning meetings, telephone conversations, and informal conversations when parents dropped off or collected their children. One of the class teachers referred to the 'importance of communicating the positives and the achievements that the child makes rather than always focusing on concerns' (NCSE 2016: 86). This is something for all education settings to reflect on, as it can be so easy to get caught up in a cycle of concern.

Research consistently demonstrates that children have better outcomes when parents and education settings work in partnership (Zablotsky et al. 2012). This is true for all children, including children with ASD (Schultz et al. 2016). However, partnership with parents is never just for the sake of partnership with parents. It must be with a view to providing high-quality education for children. Partnership between early years, primary, post-primary, and special school settings and parents is dependent, in particular, upon effective communication and the evidence is very clear that when education settings and parents communicate effectively, the child with ASD benefits. Our ASD research study clearly 'acknowledged the potential for children's learning and teaching in developing effective communication systems with parents' (Daly et al. 2016: 86). The research findings from the ASD research study also suggest that effective communication between education settings and families contributes to the creation of inclusive environments for children with ASD, while also acknowledging in this context that inclusion is a process which is never complete, but always in process (Clough and Corbett 2000). As we continue the process of inclusion, let us be open to communicating with all stakeholders, particularly parents, who provide unique insights and understandings about their children with ASD. Communication with parents enables education settings and families to work together to develop inclusive cultures to support the best possible outcomes for children with ASD.

Bibliography

Bleach, M. J. (2010). *Parental Involvement in Primary Education in Ireland*. Dublin: The Liffey Press.

Broussard, C. A. (2000). 'Preparing Teachers to Work with Families: A National Survey of Teacher Education Programs', *Equity & Excellence in Education*, 33(2), 41–49.

Cheuk, S., and Lashewicz, B. (2016). 'How are they Doing? Listening as Fathers of Children with Autism Spectrum Disorder compare Themselves to Fathers of Children who are Typically Developing', *Autism*, 20(3), 343–352.

Clough, P., and Corbett, J. (2000). *Theories of Inclusive Education*. London: Sage.

Daly, P., Ring, E., Egan, M., Fitzgerald, J., Griffin, C., Long, S., McCarthy, E., Moloney, M., O'Brien, T., O'Byrne, A., O'Sullivan, S., Ryan, M., Wall, E., Madden, R., and Gibbons, S. (2016). *An Evaluation of Education Provision for Students with Autism Spectrum Disorder in Ireland*. Trim: National Council for Special Education.

Dardig, J. (2008). *Involving Parents of Children with Special Needs*. Thousand Oaks, CA: Corwin Press.

DePape, A., and Lindsay, S. (2015). 'Parents' Experiences of Caring for a Child With Autism Spectrum Disorder', *Qualitative Health Research*, 25(4), 569–583.

Department of Education and Skills (2006). *An Evaluation of Planning in Thirty Primary Schools*. Dublin: Department of Education and Skills.

Department of Education and Skills (2017). *Action Plan for Education 2017*. Dublin: Department of Education and Skills.

Epstein, J. L. (1984). 'School policy and parent involvement: Research results', *Educational Horizons*, 62, 70–72.

Epstein, J. L. (1986). 'Parents' reactions to teacher practices of parent involvement', *The Elementary School Journal*, 86, 277–294.

Epstein, J. L. (2001). *School, Family, and Community Partnerships: Preparing Educators and Improving Schools*. Boulder, CO: Westview Press.

Fabiano, G. A. (2007). 'Father Participation in Behavioral Parent Training for ADHD: Review and Recommendations for Increasing Inclusion and Engagement', *Journal of Family Psychology*, 21(4), 683–693.

Ferguson, D. (2008). 'International Trends in Inclusive Education: The Continuing Challenge to Teach Each One and Everyone', *European Journal of Special Needs Education*, 23(1), 109–120.

Gazi, A., and Mandell, D. S. (2016). 'Concerns of Parents and Teachers of Children with Autism in Elementary School', *Autism*, 20(4), 435–441.

Goodall, J., and Montgomery, C. (2014). 'Parental Involvement to Parental Engagement: A Continuum', *Educational Review*, 66(4), 399–410.

Government of Ireland (1937). *Irish Constitution, 1937*. Dublin: The Stationery Office.

Government of Ireland (1998). *Education Act, 1998*. Dublin: The Stationery Office.

Government of Ireland (2000). *Welfare Act, 2000*. Dublin: The Stationery Office.

Government of Ireland (2004). *Education for Persons with Special Educational Needs (EPSEN) Act (2004)*. Dublin: The Stationery Office.

Green, C., Walker, J., Hoover-Dempsey, K., and Sandler, H. (2011). 'Parents' Motivations for Involvement in Children's Education: An Empirical Test of a Theoretical Model of Parental Involvement', *Journal of Educational Psychology*, 99(3), 532–544.

Griffin, S., and Shevlin, M. (2007). *Responding to Special Educational Needs: An Irish Perspective*. Dublin: Gill and Macmillan.

Henderson, A. T., and Berla, N. (1994). *A New Generation of Evidence: The Family is Critical to Student Achievement*. Columbia, MD: National Committee for Citizens in Education.

Hornby, G. (2011). *Parental Involvement in Childhood Education: Building Effective School-Family Partnerships*. New York: Springer.

Jeynes, W. H. (2005). 'A meta-analysis of the relation of parental involvement to urban elementary school student academic achievement', *Urban Education*, 40(3), 237–269.

King, G., King, S., Law, M., Kertoy, M. Rosenbaum, P., and Hurley, P. (2002). *Family-Centred Service in Ontario: A "Best Practice" Approach for Children with Disabilities and Their Families*. Ontario: CanChild.

Lamb, B. (2009). *Lamb Inquiry: Special Educational Needs and Parental Confidence*. Accessed online on 24 October 2017 at <http://webarchive.national-archives.gov.uk/20130321053358/https://www.education.gov.uk/publications/eOrderingDownload/01143-2009DOM-EN.pdf>.

Lashewiz, B. M., Shipton, L., and Lien, K. (2017). 'Meta-synthesis of Fathers' Experiences raising Children on the Autism Spectrum', *Journal of Intellectual Disabilities*, 20(10) 1–15.

Marjoribanks, K. (1979). *Families and their learning environments: An empirical analysis*. Boston, MA: Routledge & Kegan Paul.

Moore, T. (2010). 'Consultation to early childhood settings: Rationale and role for ECIS providers', *Presentation at Northern Metropolitan Region ECIS Professional Development Day*, Victoria, 14 July 2010. Victoria: Early Childhood Intervention Services.

Morgan, N. S. (2017). *Engaging Families in Schools*. Oxon: Routledge.

Murray, M. M., Ackerman-Spain, K., Williams, E. U., and Ryley, A. T. (2011). 'Knowledge is Power: Empowering the Autism Community through Parent–Professional Training', *The School Community Journal*, 21(1), 19–36.

National Council for Curriculum and Assessment (1999) *Primary School Curriculum*, Dublin: National Council for Curriculum and Assessment.

National Council for Curriculum and Assessment (2008). *Reporting to Parents in Primary School: Communication, Meaning and Learning*. Dublin: National Council for Curriculum and Assessment.

National Council for Curriculum and Assessment (2009). *Aistear: The Early Childhood Curriculum Framework*. Dublin: National Council for Curriculum and Assessment.

National Parents Council (2013). *Supporting Parents Supporting Children: National Parents Council Primary Strategic Plan 2013–2017*. Dublin: National Parents Council.

O'Connor, U. (2008). 'Meeting in the Middle? A study of Parent–Professional Partnerships', *European Journal of Special Needs Education*, 23, 253–268.

Schultz, T. R., Able, H., Sreckovic, M. A., and White, T. (2016). 'Parent-Teacher Collaboration: Teacher Perceptions of What is Needed to Support Students with ASD in the Inclusive Classroom', *Education and Training in Autism and Developmental Disabilities*, 51(4), 344–354.

Sheridan, S. M., Holmes, S. R., Smith, T. E., and Moen, A. L. (2016). 'Complexities in field-based partnership research: Exemplars, challenges, and an agenda for the field', in Sheridan, S. M., and Moorman Kim, E. (eds), *Family-School Partnerships in Context*. Cham, Switzerland: Springer International, 1–23.

Stoner, J. B., and Angell, M. E. (2006). 'Parent Perspectives on Role Engagement: An Investigation of Parents of Children with ASD and Their Self-Reported Roles with Education Professionals', *Focus on Autism and Other Developmental Disabilities*, 21(3), 177–189.

Stoner, J. B., Bock, S. J., Thompson, J. R., Angell, M. E., Heyl, B. S., and Crowley, E. P. (2005). 'Welcome to Our World: Parent Perceptions of Interactions Between Parents of Young Children With ASD and Education Professionals', *Focus on Autism and Other Developmental Disabilities*, 20(1), 39–51.

Syriopoulou-Delli, C. K., Cassimos, D. C., and Polychronopoulou, S. A. (2016). 'Collaboration between Teachers and Parents of Children with ASD on Issues of Education', *Research in Developmental Disabilities*, 55, 330–345.

Walton, E., and Moonsamy, S. (eds) (2015). *Making Education Inclusive*. Newcastle upon Tyne: Cambridge Scholars Publishing.

Webster-Stratton, C. (2012). *Incredible Teachers: Nurturing Children's Social, Emotional, and Academic Competence*. Seattle, WA: Incredible Years, Inc.

Wilder, S. (2014). 'Effects of parental involvement on academic achievement: a meta-synthesis', *Educational Review*, 66(3), 377–397.

Zablotsky, B., Boswell, K., and Smith, C. (2012). 'An Evaluation of School Involvement and Satisfaction of Parents of Children with Autism Spectrum Disorders', *American Journal on Intellectual and Developmental Disabilities*, 117(4), 316–330.

8 Harnessing the Reggio Emilia Concept of the Environment as the 'Third Teacher' for Children with Autism Spectrum Difference

ABSTRACT

The research conducted by Daly and colleagues (Daly et al. 2016) identified a range of positive practice in relation to learning and teaching; management; staff development and the promotion of an inclusive culture for children with ASD. Assessment; planning; the inclusion of the child's voice; curriculum access; the availability of external support services and parental involvement were all identified as areas for further improvement. Participants across early years, primary, post-primary and special school settings in the study consistently referred to the challenges they experienced in managing children's 'behaviour'. In this chapter, the philosophy of early childhood education developed by Loris Malaguzzi in Reggio Emilia in Northern Italy, with particular reference to the concept of the environment as the 'third teacher', is explored (Edwards, Gandini and Forman 2012). The possibility of harnessing this concept as a key principle in mitigating the oft cited 'behaviour' problem for the education of children with autism spectrum difference (ASD) is considered and interrogated.

'Behaviour' and Children with Autism Spectrum Difference

While a positive approach to supporting children's behaviour was evident throughout the research conducted by Daly and colleagues, participants frequently referred to the challenges they experienced in managing children's 'behaviour' as noted by a teacher in a special class who observed that it was necessary to engage in 'a lot of thinking around where the behaviour is coming from' (Daly et al. 2016: 50). Notably, the contribution of special needs assistants (SNAs) in supporting children's care needs through behaviour intervention programmes was acknowledged. However, concern was also articulated by principals and teachers in relation to the challenges involved in enabling children with more complex needs to access the curriculum. A principal in a primary school site noted the challenge in balancing children's curriculum access, preparing children for society and accommodating children's behaviour, concluding that it was 'difficult to get it right' (Daly et al. 2016: 75). Many of the research sites expressed the need for targeted continuing professional development (CPD) in working with what were often referred to as 'challenging behaviours'.

In research conducted by Ring (2010) across early intervention, primary and special school settings in Ireland with forty-two children with ASD, aged from three years and nine months to sixteen years and eight months with a range of additional needs, similar findings in relation to the challenges in managing children's 'behaviour' were articulated by teachers and principals. While the research was focused on investigating the impact of CPD on teachers' practice, findings in relation to the contributing factors that achieve positive behavioural outcomes for children with ASD also emerged.

Data from twenty individual semi-structured interviews with principals and teachers of children with ASDs; ten focus-group interviews with other teachers in the school; photographic classroom data and video-data comprising periods of classroom observation of twenty-six to fifty-four minutes were collected and analysed. Individual children's behavioural outcomes were determined from the video data through a two-minute time-sampling process. All children's behaviour was graphed and the two graphs in Table 8.1 indicate levels of children's on-task behaviour recorded in two different research settings.

In the first setting, high levels of on-task behaviour were recorded for all children, whereas in the second setting, Pupil 1 and Pupil 3 displayed three incidences of off-task behaviour. While it is important to acknowledge that behaviour is a complex and multifaceted construct based on a variety of intrinsic and extrinsic variables, it was evident from the data that contributing factors in achieving positive behavioural outcomes for children were inextricably linked to the physical, temporal and interactional environment of the setting. Children's behavioural outcomes were

Table 8.1: Time-Sampling of Children's On-Task Behaviour

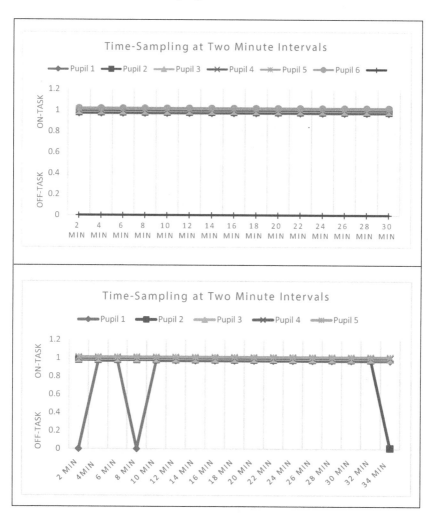

more positive when attention was directed towards the physical layout, organization and environmental stimuli of the classroom; where routine and predictability was a key element of the pedagogical approach adopted and where adult-child interactions were responsive and demonstrated an understanding of the implications of ASD for children's learning and teaching. These findings align with the key principle of the environment as the 'third teacher' embedded in the pedagogy of Reggio Emilia and create an opportunity to shift the 'behaviour' as being a problem for the child to providing a potential solution for educators in the environment (Edwards, Gandini and Forman 2012).

Key Signposts: 'Behaviour' and Children with Autism Spectrum Difference

- Participants in the study conducted by Daly et al. (2016) frequently referred to the challenges they experienced in managing children's 'behaviour'.
- Analysis of the data in research conducted by Ring (2010) suggests that the contributing factors in achieving positive behavioural outcomes for children are inextricably linked to the physical, temporal and interactional environment.
- The key principle of the environment as the 'third teacher' embedded in the pedagogy of Reggio Emilia presents an opportunity to shift the 'behaviour' as being a problem for the child to providing a potential solution for educators in the environment (Edwards et al.).

Education

Following the Second World War, through the vision and combined efforts of parents, teachers and the local community, a pioneering approach to the education of young children was developed in the city of Reggio Emilia in Northern Italy (Edwards et al.). This approach was underpinned by a mosaic of philosophies of education initiated by its visionary founder, Loris Malaguzzi, which were influenced by Friedrich Froebel (1782–1852); John Dewey (1859–1952); Maria Montessori (1870–1952); Lev Vygotsky (18986–1934); Jean Piaget (1896–1980) and Erik Erikson (1902–1994) (Edwards et al.). The key principles of the philosophy of education articulated in the pedagogy of Reggio Emilia focus on the child as having rights and being an active constructor of knowledge, researcher and social being; the teacher as a collaborator, co-learner, guide, facilitator, researcher and reflective practitioner and the concept of knowledge as being socially constructed and including multiple forms of knowing (Mercilliott Hewett 2001, see Figure 8.1).

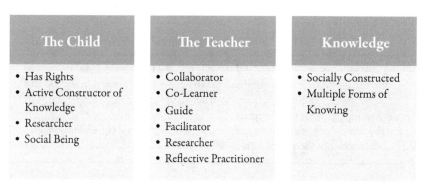

The Child	The Teacher	Knowledge
• Has Rights • Active Constructor of Knowledge • Researcher • Social Being	• Collaborator • Co-Learner • Guide • Facilitator • Researcher • Reflective Practitioner	• Socially Constructed • Multiple Forms of Knowing

Figure 8.1:   Key Elements in the Philosophy of Education at Reggio Emilia

The principles embedded in the philosophy of the Reggio Emilia approach, concerned primarily with cultivating and guiding each child's holistic development, continue to be interrogated, reflected upon, expanded and adapted with reference to emerging theories of child development and pedagogy in the context of the unique cultural milieu of Northern Italy itself (Rinaldi 2012). Unsurprisingly, this philosophy of education has influenced pedagogy and curriculum globally, in particular in the area of early childhood education (Gardner 2012). In Ireland, the core themes of wellbeing; identity and belonging, exploring and thinking and communicating associated with *Aistear: The Early Childhood Curriculum Framework* (National Council for Curriculum and Assessment (NCCA) 2009) are clearly influenced by the principles at the heart of the philosophy of Reggio Emilia. While all of these principles can, and should, be applied to the education of children with ASD, for the purposes of this chapter, the potential of the concept of the environment as the 'third teacher' as a key pedagogical construct in the learning and teaching of children with ASD across early years, primary, post-primary and special school settings is considered.

Key Signposts: The Reggio Emilia Approach to Early Childhood Education

- Following the Second World War, a pioneering approach to the education of young children was developed in the city of Reggio Emilia in Northern Italy (Edwards et al. 2012).
- The key principles of the philosophy of education articulated in the pedagogy of Reggio Emilia focus on the child as having rights and being an active constructor of knowledge, researcher and social being; the teacher as a collaborator, co-learner, guide, facilitator, researcher and reflective practitioner and the concept of knowledge as being socially constructed and including multiple forms of knowing (Mercilliott Hewett 2001).
- This philosophy of education has influenced pedagogy and curriculum globally, in particular in the area of early childhood education (Gardner 2012).

The Environment as the 'Third Teacher'

Based on the concept that environments matter for young children, Loris Malaguzzi suggested that the environment in early years settings should be viewed as the 'third teacher' after the adults and the children themselves (Gandini 2012). Pairman and Terreni (2001) extend this concept further and identify three key aspects to the environment in early childhood education as the physical environment; the temporal environment and the interactional environment. These three key aspects of the environment reflect the findings reported by Ring (2010) in relation to the identifiable elements of the environment that contribute to positive behavioural outcomes for children with ASD. Throughout the research conducted by Daly and colleagues (Daly et al. 2016), it was clear that these three aspects of environments had the potential to enrich or frustrate children's learning and impact positively or negatively on their wellbeing. Physical, temporal or interactional environments, when neglected, had a potentially detrimental impact on children's learning and wellbeing. This was particularly evident in data collected under the Learning Environment and Wellbeing criteria of Middletown Centre for Autism and the National Council for Special Education (MCA/NCSE) Evaluation Framework (MCA/NCSE 2013).

The Learning Environment criterion evaluated the commitment of the education setting to improving the physical environment in order to meet the diverse physical, emotional, social and aesthetic needs of children, and the Wellbeing criterion considered the extent to which the environment was conducive to promoting positive mental health and awareness. Wellbeing was conceptualized as focusing on a child's psychological and physical wellbeing and was concerned with children's need to feel valued, respected, empowered, catered for and included (NCCA 2009). Where the physical, temporal and interactional environments ranged from good to excellent, they were observed to impact positively on children's wellbeing and consequently on their engagement-levels. Good to excellent practice was observed in early intervention classes, mainstream primary schools and special schools with scope for further development identified in post-primary schools and varied practice observed in home-based provision. Based on the data collected during the research project, this chapter examines the potential of these three aspects of the environment to enhance education provision for children with ASD and shift the focus from 'behaviour' to environment.

Key Signposts: The Environment as the 'Third' Teacher

- Based on the concept that environments matter for young children, Loris Malaguzzi suggested that the environment in early years settings should be viewed as the 'third teacher' after the adults and the children themselves (Gandini 2012).
- The physical environment; the temporal environment and the interactional environment have been identified as three key aspects of environment that matter for young children (Pairman and Terreni 2001).
- The physical; temporal and interactional aspects of the environment have been identified as by Ring (2010) in contributing to positive behavioural outcomes for children with ASD at early years, primary and post-primary levels.

The Physical Environment

As noted in Chapter 1, the organization of the physical environment has been identified as a significant factor that impacts on the engagement levels of children with ASD (Schopler, Mesibov and Hearsey 1995; Porter and Ashdown 2002; Ring 2010; Taylor and Preece 2010; Probst and Glen 2011). In the research conducted by Daly and colleagues (Daly et al. 2016), three aspects of the physical environment that were observed to have a particular impact on children's educational experiences were the organization of space, the availability of appropriate resources and aesthetics. Where attention was directed to these three elements and determined by the needs of individual children, a positive impact was evident on children's sense of belonging, the ease with which they navigated their learning environments and their engagement in learning and teaching.

Almost all classroom and school environments were well-structured and children navigated the environment comfortably and confidently. In these environments, clearly delineated areas facilitated individual, small and large-group learning and children had a secure knowledge of how to navigate their environment. These environments supported children in taking movement breaks and were effective in accommodating children's sensory differences. The availability of spacious environments and structured environments ensured there was adequate space for children to self-regulate when necessary and scaffolded children's transitioning within and between activities.

A particularly positive practice was observed in one early intervention site, where a room adjacent to both classes was at children's disposal throughout the school day. The room was furnished with a range of commercial and teacher-devised multi-sensory resources aligned with children's interests and included a ball pool, a trampoline, a swing, sand-corner and plastic bottles filled with coloured water. Children were empowered to initiate movement breaks from their adjoining classrooms and were observed to do so independently. In this site also, different spaces in the classroom were used for different activities such as snack-time, circle-time and story-time. The attention directed towards creating a supportive physical learning environment for children was affirmed by almost all parents as encapsulated by one parent 'it is a very small school and doesn't have much land around it to go out and go for walks, but the layout inside the school is perfect' (Daly et al. 2016: 142).

Excellent sites demonstrated a recognition of the importance of creating an ASD-friendly environment throughout the school, which reflected children's expressed preferences, and were actively responded to. In post-primary sites, it was reported that children with ASD almost always experienced anxiety using the locker area. Through locating lockers in a calm and quieter area of the school, children successfully accessed their lockers, as described by Peter: 'most students have to go to the resource room and they have a shelf there and they have their name and their books there. But I wanted my own locker. I didn't really like being seen going into the room. I was kind of uncomfortable with that and it was embarrassing. They were good enough to let me have my own locker as long as I was organized and that was no problem for me' (p. 109). Where children were included in mainstream classes, these classrooms were typically 'busy' and featured colourful displays of all children's work and curriculum-related materials. Accommodating the needs of children with ASD through seating children in an area of the classroom with least distraction and providing adequate space for the child to self-regulate through building movement breaks into the child's schedule were observed as effective and valuable strategies.

Aesthetics can be defined as the appreciation of a pleasant sensorial experience, which may involve features pleasing to the cognitive faculties such as repetition, pattern, continuity, clarity, contrast, balance and proportion (Dissanayake 1992). In almost all early intervention classes, primary and special schools, curriculum displays were attractively presented and included samples and records of children's work. Through directing attention to the organization of learning spaces, children moved freely between areas and had unobstructed views of all areas in the classroom. When children's work was displayed in the environment and where children demonstrated an awareness and understanding of this work, it was observed to contribute positively to children's sense of belonging and ownership of their environment (Ring 2010; Daly et al. 2016).

Related to aesthetics is the location of ASD-specific classes in the school. In Reggio Emilia, the integration of each classroom with the rest of the school is critical and linked to the concept that the education of young children is a community-based concern and responsibility (Gandini 2012). The architecture reflects the local community and all classrooms open to a center area, modelled on the 'piazza', the Italian word for 'square'. The 'piazza' is a traditional feature of all Italian towns and the area where the community converge in the evenings for the 'passeggiata' to meet with one another. In one mainstream primary school, a particulary excellent practice was observed whereby each corridor was allocated a theme associated with the locality. The benefits of locating special classes in a central position in the school was noted by a principal in a primary school, who described the classroom as 'a very positive thing' for the whole school and how the other children in the school 'loved going in there' (Daly et al. 2016: 86). A kitchen was deliberately included in the special class which was shared with all of the classes in the school as a space for learning life-skills.

The benefits of connecting children with their local community were evident in a primary school located by the sea, where each classroom in the school was represented by a corresponding visual associated with a maritime location, for example, 'octopus' class. In three primary school sites, excellent practice was also observed in the school-yard where specific resources and equipment were available to engage children during unstructured periods of the school day, which can be particularly challenging for children with ASD.

In a responsive physical environment, children, teachers and SNAs were observed to take ownership of the space, as described by a special class teacher in a mainstream primary school, 'the space is ours, it really works for us' (Daly et al. 2016: 60).

Key Signposts: The Physical Environment

- Three aspects of the physical environment that were observed to have a particular impact on children's educational experiences were the organization of space, the availability of appropriate resources and aesthetics.

- Where attention was directed to organization of space, the availability of appropriate resources and aesthetics, a positive impact was evident on children's sense of belonging, the ease with which they navigated their learning environments and their engagement in learning and teaching.
- Spacious and structured environments ensured there was adequate space for children to self-regulate when necessary and scaffolded in transitioning within and between activities.
- Children's engagement was positive where resources were available, which were attractive, stimulating and aligned with children's interests and sensory preferences.

The Temporal Environment

The temporal environment is inextricably linked to the physical environment and refers to the embedding of routines and predictability in the child's day (Pairman and Terreni 2001). A range of supports was provided in almost all schools to assist children's engagement and included providing blu-tac when a child was observed to be becoming agitated; visual schedules; the colour-coding of books and attractive areas for children to take movement breaks and self-regulate.

In line with the discussion in Chapters 1 and 3, particular attention was directed towards visual approaches to learning and accommodating children's sensory differences in almost all sites. The importance of visual schedules for children with ASD was emphasized in all early intervention sites as described by one special class teacher: 'visual schedules reduce their anxiety. [There are] visuals all around the class. [There are] expectations of behaviour and visuals to support that, such as "waiting/stopping", visuals to show "gentle play" or "easy voice"' (Daly et al. 2016: 56). In four of the five primary sites, teachers were well prepared in relation to supporting children with anxiety that can stem from sensory differences and unpredictability in the environment. In these sites, children were provided with sensory toys; mental and physical breaks from learning; direct teaching of self-regulation strategies, such as visualization; the use of calming techniques, such as mindfulness, and promoting structure and predictability in daily routines. It was evident that almost all teachers understood the identifiers for children's anxiety. One teacher noted that the child would get very fidgety, asking to go to the toilet frequently and that she 'would know then that [the child] would need to take a break' (p. 88). While visual schedules continued to be a feature of practice at post-primary level, expectations for independence changed as children got older. As noted by one class teacher, 'I use more verbal approaches and try and reduce the visual supports. We pull back on the individualized work and aim towards more group work' (p. 134).

The benefits of working with parents in relation to the temporal environment were evident. A parent in a primary school site reported that the school worked closely with her to develop strategies to address the child's school refusal. The child's school refusal was partly attributed to the anxiety experienced by the child arriving in school in the morning and leaving in the evening when there was a lot of activity and auditory and visual stimulation at these times. An effective strategy was devised for the child to arrive five minutes later and leave five minutes earlier through a side-exit route.

A mainstream primary class teacher summarized the importance of augmenting the temporal environment for children with ASD through visual prompts and ensuring structure and routine are adhered 'so that he knows when he comes down what is expected of him and what we are doing' (p. 74).

Key Signposts: The Temporal Environment

- The temporal environment is inextricably linked to the physical environment and refers to the embedding of routines and predictability in the child's day.
- A range of supports was provided in almost all schools to assist children's engagement and included providing blu-tac when a child was observed to be becoming agitated; visual schedules; the colour-coding of books and attractive areas for children to take movement breaks and self-regulate.
- Visual schedules were observed to reduce children's anxiety and contribute to their understanding of the sequence and structure of the day.
- The benefits of working with parents in relation to the temporal environment both at home and at school are significant for the child and the family.

The Interactional Environment

The interactional environment refers to the quality of social interactions children experience and, in relation to children with ASD, the extent to which these interactions accommodate the specific differences experienced. Increasingly, research is demonstrating the critical role of interactions in driving children's development from the beginning (O'Sullivan and Ring 2018). The challenges of coping with the stresses associated with ASD create a higher risk of emotional disorders, such as depression and anxiety (Wing, 1981; Sainsbury, 2000; Silberman 2015). It is critical therefore that attention is consistently directed to the interactional environment for children with ASD and that all interactions and responses are underpinned by a knowledge and understanding of the implications of ASD in interacting with children.

In almost all sites, excellent interactional environments were observed and in the words of a principal in a primary school site 'all children are valued' and their 'sense of self-importance and belonging is consistently nurtured' (Daly et al. 2016: 88). Staff were proactive in tuning into individual children's early indicators of difficulties and in responding earlier in order to avoid children experiencing anxiety or exhibiting behaviours that challenge. A mainstream teacher in a primary school described how she identified one child's anxiety, noting that 'his face would tense up' (p. 88) at times of less structure and the importance of being alert to this and intervening with counting/breathing strategies or providing distracters for the child. The support teacher in this site referred to the strong focus on ensuring the child was aware of his own emotional state and tracking his own feelings.

Settings were aware of the importance of children interacting appropriately with their peers and child-protection and anti-bullying policies were widely available. The central role of the interactional environment in relation to children's wellbeing was described by a special class teacher in a primary school as 'if children feel disconnected from the world around them, isn't that what it is really ... mental illness? We need to let them see that the world is for them. You make things predictable in the beginning, you can tell the day when they reach that equilibrium and then you can push them a little'. The teacher concluded that 'once you have invested in the relationship they can open like flowers' (p. 61).

Key Signposts: The Interactional Environment

- The interactional environment refers to the quality of social interactions children experience and, in relation to children with ASD, the extent to which these interactions accommodate the specific differences experienced by children.
- Increasingly, research is demonstrating the critical role of interactions in driving children's development from the beginning. In relation to children with ASD, this involves creating an interactional environment where all interactions and responses are underpinned by a knowledge and understanding of the implications of ASD in interacting with children.
- As educators, we have a responsibility to create an interactional environment where children with ASD are supported in interacting appropriately with their peers.

Conclusion

The research findings reported in this chapter suggest that directing attention to the physical, temporal and interactional environments for children with ASD can significantly enhance the learning experience for children and educators (Ring 2010; Daly et al. 2016). Critically concentrating on the environment presents an opportunity to re-focus the lens through which we view 'behaviour' and presents a potential solution for us as educators to create enriched learning and teaching experiences, which enable each child to reach his/her potential. Communicating these possibilities to parents has the potential to contribute to the twenty-four-hour curriculum required for children with ASD. The negative impact of chaotic environments on the quality of experiences for children with ASD is unquestionable. As demonstrated in Table 8.2, a particularly striking feature of the children's drawings, irrespective of the children's age or the setting in which children were receiving an education, was their own sense of structure and organization.

Table 8.2: Children's Work Included in Classroom Displays

	Child included in a reception class in a mainstream primary school.
	Child at middle-primary level in a special class in a mainstream school.
	Child in second-year in a post-primary mainstream school.
	Child in a senior class in a special school.

The possibility that children are communicating the value they place on the provision of a structured, predictable and ordered environment to us through their drawings should be considered. It is suggested that recruiting the environment as a 'third teacher' has the potential to impact positively on children's level of engagement in activities, while simultaneously reducing the potential for concerns emerging related to children's learning and wellbeing.

Bibliography

Daly, P., Ring, E., Egan, M., Fitzgerald, J., Griffin, C., Long, S., McCarthy, E., Moloney, M., O'Brien, T., O'Byrne, A., O'Sullivan, S., Ryan, M., Wall, E., Madden, R., and Gibbons, S. (2016). *An Evaluation of Education Provision for Students with Autism Spectrum Disorder in Ireland.* Trim: National Council for Special Education.

Dissanayake, E. (1992). *Homo Aestheticus: Where Art Comes From and Why.* New York: The Free Press.

Edwards, C., Gandini, L., and Forman, G. (eds) (2011). *The Hundred Languages of Children: The Reggio Emilia Experience in Transformation* (3rd edn). Oxford: Praeger.

Gandini, L. (2012). 'Connecting through Caring and Learning Spaces'. In C. Edwards, L. Gandini, and G. Forman (eds), *The Hundred Languages of Children; The Reggio Emilia Experience in Transfomation* (3rd edn), pp. 317–341. Oxford: Praeger.

Gardner, H. (2012). 'Foreword'. In C. Edwards, L. Gandini and G. Forman (eds), *The Hundred Languages of Children: The Reggio Emilia Experience in Transformation* (3rd edn), pp. xiii–xvi. Oxford: Praeger.

Mercilliott Hewett, V. (2001). 'Examining the Reggio Emilia Approach to Early Childhood Education', *Early Childhood Education Journal*, 29(2), 95–100.

Middletown Centre for Autism and National Council for Special Education (2013). *Evaluation Framework to Underpin the Evaluation of Educational Provision for Students with ASD.* Trim: National Council for Special Education.

National Council for Curriculum and Assessment (2009). *Aistear: The Early Childhood Curriculum Framework.* Dublin: National Council for Curriculum and Assessment.

O'Sullivan, L., and Ring, E. (2018). 'Play as an Antidote to the "Schoolification Epidemic": Implications for Parents and Educators from Findings of a National Evaluation of School Readiness in Ireland', *International Journal of Play* [in press].

Pairman, A., and Terreni, L. (2001). *If the Environment is the Third Teacher What Language Does She Speak*. Wellington: Ministry of Education.

Porter, J., and Ashdown, R. (2002). *Pupils with Complex Learning Difficulties: Promoting Learning using Visual Materials and Methods*. Tamworth: NASEN.

Probst, P., and Glen, I. (2011). 'TEACCH-based Interventions for Families with Children with Autism Spectrum Disorders: Outcomes of a Parent Group Training Study and a Home-based Child-parent Training Single Case Study', *Life Span and Disability*, 2, 111–138.

Rinaldi, C. (2012). 'The Pedagogy of Listening: The Listening Perspective from Reggio'. In C. Edwards, L. Gandini and G. Forman (eds), *The Hundred Languages of Children: The Reggio Emilia Experience in Transformation* (3rd edn), pp. 233–246. Oxford: Praeger.

Ring, E. (2010). *An Evaluation of the Effects of an Autistic Spectrum Disorder-Specific Post-Graduate Certificate Continuing Professional Development Programme on Practice in Six Schools*, Unpublished Ph.D. Thesis, Dublin: St. Patrick's College, Dublin City University.

Sainsbury, C. (2000). *The Martian in the Playground: Understanding the Schoolchild with Asperger's Syndrome*. Bristol: Lucky Duck Publishing Ltd.

Schopler, E., Mesibov, G. B., and Hearsey, K. (1995). 'Structured teaching in the TEACCH System'. In E. Schopler and G. B. Mesibov (eds), *Learning and Cognition in Autism*, pp. 243–292. New York: Plenum Press.

Silberman, S. (2015) *Neurotribes: The Legacy of Autism*. London: Allen and Unwin.

Taylor, K., and Preece, D. (2010). 'Using Aspects of the TEACCH Structured Teaching Approach with Students with Multiple Disabilities and Visual Impairment: Reflections on Practice', *British Journal of Visual Impairment*, 28:3, 244–259.

Wing, L. (1981). 'Asperger Syndrome: A Clinical Account', *Journal of Psychological Medicine*, 11, 115–129.

PATRICIA DALY

9 Promoting Children's Wellbeing

ABSTRACT

This chapter presents our current interpretations of the concept of wellbeing followed by the evidence gleaned from the study of the evaluation of educational provision for children with autism spectrum difference (ASD) across education settings (Daly et al. 2016). This evidence is framed by theoretical understandings of wellbeing. Implications are then drawn for parents, early childhood, primary and post-primary teachers on ways to support the wellbeing of children with ASD at home and in all educational settings.

What Is Wellbeing?

The concept of wellbeing and therefore how it is evaluated is not universally agreed. The term is often considered synonymous with quality of life and positive mental health. Adult wellbeing is considered to be different to child or youth wellbeing. Child wellbeing is influenced by early years settings, schools and schooling, although child wellbeing is also strongly influenced by experiences outside of school. The actual definition of wellbeing used in any study determines the kinds of data that can count as evidence when reporting on the concept. Before examining ASD and wellbeing, it is instructive to consider how wellbeing is conceptualized in the literature for the general population.

Two broad conceptualizations of wellbeing derived from different philosophical traditions are evident. Danker, Strnadová and Cumming, (2016) describe these traditions as 'hedonic' and 'eudemonic'. The hedonic roots of wellbeing lead to the notion of the child's satisfaction with life in school and the predominance of positive emotions over negative ones. Typically, this form of wellbeing would be evaluated using self-reports of happiness and is considered 'subjective wellbeing' (Moreira et al. 2015: 76). Subjective wellbeing has two components: affect (feelings, mood and emotions) and life satisfaction (work, family and social participation). This approach to wellbeing was espoused in the Positive Psychology of Seligman (2002). The eudemonic conceptualization, on the other hand, is concerned with several domains, including realizing one's potential in school or elsewhere; autonomy; competence; engagement and connectedness (Danker et al. 2016). This is considered psychological wellbeing and may be evaluated both by self-reports and through the perceptions of critical others, including parents, teachers and other school personnel in addition to objective evidence. Many researchers are now combining both approaches to understanding and evaluating wellbeing, as is evidenced in Seligman's later work on happiness which he expanded from a life which is pleasant, good and meaningful to what he now calls the PERMA (positive emotions, engagement, relationships, meaning and accomplishments) model of flourishing (Seligman 2011). As noted previously, the definition of wellbeing in turn determines what counts as evidence of its presence or absence. Any definition of wellbeing may also be affected by the presence of additional needs, especially the extent of those needs, which in turn influences whether the child is aware of and can express states of feeling. Within the broad domain of complex needs, proxy reports from parents, carers and early years and school personnel may be the primary sources of evidence of wellbeing. The use of proxy reports is further described below.

From this brief overview of the concept of wellbeing it is clear that any evaluation of children's wellbeing should include their voice whenever possible as well as a rich supporting body of evidence for their psychological as well as their subjective wellbeing garnered and triangulated from multiple informed sources.

Key Signposts: What Is Wellbeing?

- A universal concept of wellbeing is not clearly identifiable and any definition is affected by the presence of additional needs, and the extent of those needs.
- The 'hedonic' tradition equates wellbeing with the child's satisfaction levels and the predominance of positive emotions over negative ones, typically evaluated by self-reporting and hence considered subjective.

> - The 'eudemonic' conceptualization or psychological wellbeing is concerned with several domains, including realizing one's potential in school or elsewhere; autonomy; competence; engagement and connectedness. It is evaluated both by self-reporting and through the perceptions of others.
> - Any evaluation of wellbeing must include the child's voice.

Wellbeing and Additional Needs

It is generally accepted that children with additional needs express lower levels of wellbeing in studies than their peers without additional needs. In a study which explored the subjective ratings of the lives of 603 participants (between the ages of four and twenty) with additional needs, the type of additional need and the extent to which individuals with different types of additional need depended on social supports had a differential impact on wellbeing ratings (Moreira et al. 2015). All children with additional needs expressed lower scores on overall quality of life at school compared to their peers without additional needs. However, children with attention deficit hyperactivity disorder (ADHD) had the lowest scores with significant difficulties identified in making and keeping friends. Children with sensory impairments (hearing and vision) also reported lower scores.

Wellbeing and Autism Spectrum Difference

Children with ASD may have characteristics that dispose them to having a reduced sense of wellbeing. The core differences associated with ASD generally include difficulty understanding and responding to social cues, information and events, communication difficulties, particularly the development of social reciprocity, and the presence of restricted repetitive behaviours. As described in Chapter 3, most children with ASD also present with sensory differences and hence have unique sensory needs. These characteristics occur across a continuum of severity requiring varying levels of support. Further, the most commonly co-occurring additional need with ASD is a general learning disability, which itself is on a continuum from none to profound (Rodgers, Glod, Connolly, and McConachie 2012). The ability of children with ASD to communicate vocally also varies, with up to 15 per cent never developing this capacity (McCrimmin et al. 2014). Children with ASD are also vulnerable to anxiety, with up to 40 per cent meeting the criteria for an anxiety disorder (Rogers et al. 2012). Rogers also found a correlation between high levels of reported anxiety in children with ASD and concomitant levels of restricted, repetitive behaviours, as well as insistence on sameness.

Since ASD is a broad spectrum, and intellectual capacity is on a continuum, it becomes clear that soliciting input from children in relation to their wellbeing or happiness can present a number of challenges. This is the first caveat that must be explored further. The capacity of the child with ASD to inform any determination of his/her own wellbeing is reliant on the child's awareness of his/her own emotional states and the ability to somehow share that information reliably.

If we consider ASD on a continuum from high to low interacting with the continuum of intellectual capacity from high to low, as in Figure 9.1, the four resulting quadrants mirror the potential relationships that can exist between ASD and intellectual capacity.

The extent to which children in each quadrant are aware of their emotional states and express those states accurately will vary. So too will the need for adult carers and educators to interpret the presence or absence of anxiety, depression and irritability as proxy evidence of wellbeing. Research is equivocal in terms of the agreement between adult interpretations and the children's own views of satisfaction with different aspects of their lives. For example, a study by (Clark, Magill-Evans and Koning 2015) which used self-reports and proxy reports by parents of twenty-two teenage children with ASD on quality of life (QoL) and adaptive skills found high levels of correspondence between proxy and child reports. They used the KIDSCREEN-53 (2006) which has ten domains to collect self-reports and proxy reports from parents (KIDSCREEN-52 Group Europe 2006). The domains were: physical wellbeing, psychological wellbeing, moods and emotions, self-perception,

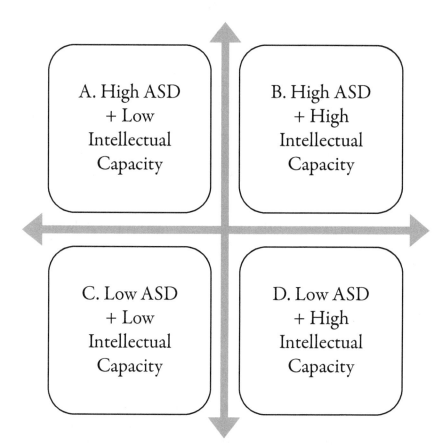

Figure 9.1: The Interrelationships Between ASD and Intellectual Capacity

autonomy, parent relations and home life, social support and peers, school environment, social acceptance (bullying) and financial resources. They found the highest QoL scores for school environment from both sources. Participants who could rate their own QoL more than likely did well at school and considered the support available to them there relatively positively. The lowest QoL scores by both sources were for social acceptance and peers. This is consistent with other literature given the social deficits inherent in autism. They also found a negative correlation between high scores on the Adaptive Behaviour Assessment System-II (2008) and psychological QoL.

This implies that higher levels of adaptive behaviours led to increased awareness of negative perceptions of others and hence lower psychological QoL.

Conversely, in a study which examined the effects of cognitive behavioural group treatment for anxiety in children with high-functioning ASD (Ehrenreich-May et al. 2014), the post-treatment parent ratings of their children's anxiety were significantly lower than the children's own post-treatment ratings indicating low levels of correspondence. Therefore, using proxy ratings of wellbeing without some form of input from the children themselves might not be reflective of the true state of wellbeing of some children with ASD.

The second caveat to note is raised in a philosophical discussion of the nature of wellbeing authored by parents of children with ASD (Rodogno, Krause-Jensen and Ashcroft 2016). Here, the assumptions of what constitutes 'the good life' which leads to happiness, and therefore positive wellbeing, are examined for children with ASD, particularly those with limited capacity to provide direct evidence of their own emotional states. Essentially, the authors recommend that typical evidence of a good life needs to be evaluated in terms of the neurodiversity that is autism. The authors claim that ASD seems to go deeper than language and culture and, if children are so different, it might be advisable to have 'epistemic humility' (p. 403) in approaching what can be equated as good for children with ASD. In their approach to understanding wellbeing, happiness is associated with the fate of people's 'attachments', which are things, events and people of importance to us. They recommend asking the question: what are the things, events and people which could be considered 'attachments' for children with ASD. They also noted that for children with ASD and significantly reduced intellectual capacity, the absence of irritability, depression and anxiety might be considered proxy evidence of wellbeing. Two examples of this type of difference or neurodiversity are evident in studies on friendships by (Calder, Hill and Pellicano 2012) and O'Hagan and Hebron (2016). In psychological models of wellbeing for children above, peer friendships would exemplify the 'connectedness' element (Danker et al. 2016).

The Calder (2012) study focused on primary age children with High Functioning ASD and the children themselves, their parents and their peers served as informants. There was evidence that some children did not know what a friend was and cited family members. Friends for others were peers they did things with and friendships were difficult for the children to establish and maintain. Some parents did explicit teaching of social rules and roles for their children with ASD. Parents were aware that giving them multiple opportunities to access peers in clubs sometimes resulted in higher levels of anxiety than positive outcomes for their children. Parents also noted that sometimes their child wanted to be alone rather than with a friend. Teachers reported peers accepted, tolerated and supported their peers with ASD rather than choosing them as friends. Friendships were noted to be more unidirectional than reciprocal. The status of the child with ASD in the class mattered and if the child was academically excellent then the chances of selection for interaction (if not friendship) were higher.

In the second study (O'Hagan and Hebron 2016), qualities of friendships reported by adolescents with and those without ASD were compared. Friendship was conceptualized to have three qualities: companionship, intimacy and closeness. Companionship essentially meant doing things together with a like-minded person. Intimacy involved sharing private thoughts and feelings, and closeness was related to liking each other. Cognitive ability and Theory of Mind ability were variables measured in the study. For the children with ASD, their concept of a friend was certainly 'less than' that of their peers without ASD and included companionship mostly. Interestingly though, regardless of cognitive ability and Theory of Mind ability, among the children with ASD there was a consistently expressed satisfaction with friendships. In other words, it is conceivable that children with ASD are happy with companionable friends and do not miss intimacy or closeness as elements of their friendships.

Both studies highlight the qualitative differences of peer friendships for children with ASD. Whereas teachers and parents may consider the companionship aspect of friendship to be less 'deep' in terms of quality, Rodogno et al. (2016) would caution us to respect the difference merely as being different and not less.

In summary, evaluations of wellbeing for children with ASD should consider, as evidence, both the presence of school-based systems and supports, the presence, engagement and achievement of children with ASD, their connectedness and autonomy in that environment, as well as the absence of negative emotions, irritability and depression as a balancing act. Sources of this evidence must include the children themselves as well as all other relevant connected stakeholders.

Key Signposts: Wellbeing and Autism Spectrum Difference

- Children with additional needs rate themselves lower on measures of wellbeing than those without additional needs.
- Children with ADHD and those with sensory differences scored particularly low on wellbeing measures.
- Key characteristics of children with ASD dispose them to a reduced sense of wellbeing.
- Communication, social and sensory needs, as well as the presence of anxiety, influence the wellbeing of children with ASD.
- The capacity of children with ASD to inform any evaluation of their own wellbeing varies and proxy evidence from critical adults is needed when children themselves have limited capacity to contribute.
- Children with ASD could be considered so neuro-diverse that common conceptualizations of wellbeing may not apply to the same extent to them.
- Wellbeing must be considered in its broadest sense for children with ASDs and informants should include the children and critical adults.

Wellbeing for Children with Autism Spectrum Difference in Ireland

Child wellbeing was evaluated under the Promotion of Students' Positive Mental Health criterion of Middletown Centre for Autism (MCA)/ National Council for Special Education (NCSE) *Evaluation Framework* (MCA and NCSE 2013) Over sixty children were invited to converse about their school experiences and/or to draw a picture showing some aspect of their life at school thereby representing the children's voices. Also, as described in Chapter 4, Special Needs Assistants (SNAs), teachers, principals and parents were interviewed to provide rich nuanced descriptions. The data from the study provided insight into both subjective and psychological aspects of wellbeing for students with ASD.

First, personnel in all sites were knowledgeable about and aware of the negative influence of anxiety on wellbeing. Teachers monitored children's reactions during the school day, intervened early when signs of anxiety presented, connected with parents and carers to support children, and accessed external professional services depending on their availability. As one teacher noted: 'We need to let them see that the world is for them' (Daly et al. 2016: 61). Sources of stress and anxiety included transitions, sensory sensitivities, sensory overload, lack of predictability in the daily schedule, homework, examinations and interactions with peers. This is reflected in the literature, which also suggests that the amount of work to be completed, meeting deadlines, the speed of teacher speech and the extent to which help from adults is obvious to peers as potential stressors (DePape and Lindsay 2016). One of the children commented on transition from primary to post-primary: 'I was nervous about how I would cope as a lot of things in my life are difficult' (Daly et al. 2016: 115). However, the levels of knowledge and awareness of school staff was much higher when there was an established special class for children with ASD in the school. Personnel new to working with children with ASD were aware of their lack of knowledge and expertise, particularly at post-primary level. Teachers and SNAs felt particularly lacking in expertise when anxiety was related to mental health issues, such as suicidal thoughts, self-injurious behaviour or inappropriate sexual behaviour. The critical importance of early childhood teachers, primary and post-primary teachers having specific expertise in relation to ASD is evident in the literature. Qualified, knowledgeable, flexible teachers, who listened and related to children, and who made difficult content accessible and fun, were critical in terms of increasing positive and reducing negative emotions. Teacher characteristics also related strongly to engagement levels (Danker et al. 2016; Brewin, Renwich and Schormans 2016).

> *Key Signposts: Wellbeing for Children with Autism Spectrum Difference in Ireland*
>
> - SNAs and teachers were tuned in to the negative influence of anxiety on the wellbeing of children with ASD.
> - Sources of anxiety included transitions, predictability of the environment, sensory overload, examinations, peer interactions.
> - Early childhood teachers, primary and post-primary teachers, who were knowledgeable about ASD, were more adept at reducing and managing anxiety levels and increasing positive engagement of children with ASD, than those new to working in the field of ASD.

Strategies for Promoting Wellbeing and Managing Anxiety

Although some interventions were age-specific or targeted for children with complex needs, several approaches to support wellbeing were evident in the research findings (Daly et al., 2016). Many settings established links and strong relationships with external services where possible. This allowed them to acquire professional development opportunities for staff as well as support for difficult individual and challenging situations. In most settings, attention was directed to structuring the environment and supporting instruction with approaches such as the Treatment and Education of Autistic and related Communication-handicapped CHildren (TEACCH) (Schopler 2001) and the Picture Exchange Communication System (PECS) (Bondy and Frost 2002) with visual supports also used to support children's understanding and engagement. Sensory support was provided through the use of sensory rooms; spaces and activities including sensory gardens; the school grounds; the prayer room or the gym, and movement breaks during instruction periods.

Some of these approaches were scheduled to support children and prevent anxiety. Some were used in response to evidence of stress. Schools which lacked additional physical space for children's self-regulation in times of anxiety reported concerns with children's wellbeing. Schools with special classes were able to use those environments as safe spaces or havens for children with ASD who spent much of their day in mainstream classes. Special needs assistants functioned in multiple roles to support children with ASD, including direct support, serving as communication conduits between teachers, as well as being observers and prompters of social communication between children with ASD and their peers. Specific attention was directed to preparing children with ASD to manage key transitions depending on each child's individual response to change, which was systematically monitored. Finally, strong communication channels with parents were established and maintained, and the importance of giving and receiving information frequently was well understood. In general, schools did not have a named person associated with student wellbeing. All schools had anti-bullying policies in operation and some provided specific social skill teaching to both children with ASD and their peers.

There was evidence also that schools with ASD expertise were aware of the need for a range of intensity of supports for children to manage their wellbeing depending on their levels of stress and anxiety, particularly in post-primary environments. The intensity of supports needed tended to be high in first year with adjustment to the new environment, and to increase again with access to senior cycle. Some self-awareness and self-regulation strategies were taught in some schools, such as meditation, mindfulness and breathing techniques. Personnel were aware of the importance of positive relationships between the adults and the children in schools as mediators of anxiety and supports for wellbeing. While they recognized the need for children with ASD to learn about their own emotional states, they rarely asked the children about their wellbeing, levels of happiness and feelings about situations and events.

It is useful to reflect on these findings through the lens of the literature on wellbeing, both subjective and psychological. In terms of subjective wellbeing, as noted above, children were rarely asked directly about their positive thoughts or happiness. Parents interpreted their children's levels of 'happiness', especially when the children were young or nonverbal. Inviting the children's perspectives verbally is dependent on their familiarity with the asker, their awareness of their own emotional states of being, and their ability to express those states accurately. Critically, it is dependent on us as educators to develop innovative and effective ways of capturing children's voices and listening to and responding to children, irrespective of age or ability (Ring and O'Sullivan 2016). For this research study, children were invited to draw pictures of how they perceived their education setting. While it is acknowledged that the analysis of children's drawings is complex, nonetheless the children's drawings were interesting and could be considered to be reflective of how children see their environment and what they focus on in that environment. Subjective wellbeing was also explored through inviting children to engage in a conversation about the school.

Children's happiness and satisfaction with their education setting can be inferred through their willingness to attend: levels of participation in activities; and their self-regulation strategies. The pictures they drew of themselves with others, of family members, of children with smiling faces, and the extent to which they see themselves as belonging could also be considered as evidence of happiness. Consider the two pictures in Figure 9.2 drawn by primary-age children with ASD from the research.

Whereas multiple interpretations of children's art are possible, the children in the research study engaged in this activity in a purposeful manner and described the drawings clearly. In the left drawing, the child noted that he was the left figure in red and was playing soccer, which he referred to as his main interest. He identified the figure in green as his cousin and drew his parents in the background. In the drawing on the right, the child drew himself and his friend looking out a window to the school yard where there is a basketball hoop. They are not out in the yard playing but are standing together as friends. In the first, there is no friend external to the family. This child was in first class. In the second, the child has a school friend and they are both observing, not participating. This child was in fifth class. Both pictures show the companionship element of friendship thus serving as some evidence of wellbeing. Children who participated in discussions around school, articulated clearly what was important for their own wellbeing, what caused anxiety and stress and what helped. It is possible

Figure 9.2: Pictures by Primary-Age Children with ASD

therefore to derive subjective evidence of wellbeing from interacting with children with ASD, which can be supported by parental interpretation and teacher and SNAs' views.

Psychological wellbeing was evidenced through children's success levels at school including belonging; friendships; engagement in co-curricular activities; ability to advocate for self, and success in State examinations or equivalent qualifications. Competence in navigating complex environments was determined by the level of SNA support required and the manner in which this varied in response to need or to increased expectations for independence. This required extensive and insightful observation by critical school personnel working with children and youth with ASD in order to adjust supports to meet needs and generate increasing competence and independence. Much of the evidence in wellbeing in the research relates to psychological wellbeing.

There is significant evidence that if wellbeing is related to reduced levels of debilitating anxiety and management of unique sensory needs associated with ASD, then educational environments can successfully prevent and intervene to support positive wellbeing for these children. This is accomplished by making the environment predictable, supportive and instructive, by developing and using high levels of skilful observation of, and intervention on early signs of anxiety, and by planning with families to manage stress, anxiety and emotional regulation around critical internal and external transitions. It can also be accomplished by direct teaching of the wellbeing curriculum strands from early years to post-primary. Specifically, the wellbeing strand of *Aistear: The Early Childhood Curriculum Framework* provides extensive guidelines in relation children's wellbeing in early years and primary settings (National Council for Curriculum and Assessment (NCCA) 2009). At post-primary, Mannion (2017) recently investigated the effects of direct teaching of emotional regulation, conflict resolution strategies and coping skills to children with additional needs in a special school though the Personal Care and Living in the Community section of the Junior Cycle Guidelines (NCCA 2015). She found that this form of teaching needed to be 'explicit, collaborative, active, accessible and relevant' (Mannion 2017: 134). Finally, it is important to acknowledge that in wellbeing crisis situations, schools and families require timely access to relevant external services.

Key Signposts: Strategies for Promoting Wellbeing and Managing Anxiety

- Key interventions for promoting wellbeing in the Daly et al. 2016 research study were accessing external services; structuring the environment, and sensory and visual supports.
- Special needs assistants played crucial roles in managing transitions reducing anxiety and supporting wellbeing of children with ASD.
- Communication with families was also significant.
- School personnel indicated they rarely asked children with ASD about their own wellbeing.
- Subjective wellbeing was assessed through children's drawings and conversations in this research.
- Psychological wellbeing was determined through intensive interviews with parents of children with ASD and with various early childhood and school personnel.
- Direct support for promoting wellbeing through curriculum initiative such as the *Aistear* Framework and the Junior Cycle Wellbeing Guidelines is strong.

Conclusion

The literature pushes us to consider what counts as evidence of wellbeing in particular for children with ASD in educational settings. In an exhaustive review of the school experiences of children with ASD and their relationship to wellbeing, Danker et al. (2016) suggest that eight domains are useful for collecting evidence of wellbeing (see Table 9.1). These are offered here as a broad, inclusive framework for evaluating whether children with ASD are experiencing positive wellbeing in educational settings. Consider within your own particular, unique environment what would count as evidence for each category for particular children with ASD.

Table 9.1: Evaluating Positive Wellbeing for Children with
ASD in Educational Settings

Domains of student wellbeing from Danker et al. study (2016)		What would count as evidence in your school? Some ideas …
Positive emotions	Joy, contentment, interest, affection – related to interactions AND to the curriculum	Strong interest in history
Absence of negative emotions	Worries about school, complaints and anxiety	Inability to remain in the class for more than thirty minutes
Engagement	Sense of school belonging, time spent on school-related activities, attendance, adherence to school rules, enthusiasm for learning	Participation in the school's hillwalking club
Relationships	With peers, teachers and parents	Eats lunch with a peer regularly
Accomplishment	Meaningful goals and sense of capability in doing everyday tasks	Completes experiment in science class
Mental health	Gloominess, anger, loneliness and misery, depression and suicidal thoughts	Has a 'go to' staff person to consult with when anxious
Intrapersonal	Emotional regulation, self-esteem, resilience	Uses a break card when needs a short break from any class
Access to resources	Technological tools, highly qualified teachers, positive learning environment, affordable and appropriate services and programmes	Uses computer for writing assignments, teachers taking CPD in autism, additional homework support available in resource room

As noted by the National Educational Psychological Service (NEPS) Guidelines for mental health promotion (NEPS 2015), the World Health Organisation in 2001 defined mental health as 'a state of well-being in which the individual realizes his or her own abilities, can cope with the normal stresses of life, can work productively and fruitfully and is able to make a contribution to his or her own community' (p. 10). Hopefully, this chapter has emphasized the likelihood that 'normal stresses of life' may be very different for children with ASD, that these stresses may vary in intensity throughout their educational experiences, and that in the home and at early years, primary and post-primary levels there are excellent opportunities to provide unique and individualized supports for children so they can make their own unique and valued contributions to society.

Bibliography

Bondy, A., and Frost, L. (2002). *A Picture's Worth: PECS and Other Visual Communication Strategies in Autism*. Bethesda: Woodbine House.

Brewin, J., Renwich, R., and Schormans, A. F. (2008). 'Parental Perspectives of the Quality of Life in School Environments for Children with Asperger Syndrome', *Focus on Autism and Other Developmental Disabilities*, 23(4), 242–252.

Calder, L., Hill, V., and Pellicano, E. (2012). 'Sometimes I want to Play by Myself: Understanding what Friendship Means to Children with Autism in Mainstream Primary Schools', *Autism* (17)3, 296–316.

Clark, B. G., Magill-Evans, J. E., and Koning, C. J. (2015). 'Youth with Autism Spectrum Disorders: Self- and Proxy-reported Quality of Life and Adaptive Functioning', *Focus on Autism and Other Developmental Disabilities*, 30(1), 57–64.

Daly, P., Ring, E., Egan, M., Fitzgerald, J., Griffin, C., Long, S., McCarthy, E., Moloney, M., O'Brien, T., O'Byrne, A., O'Sullivan, S., Ryan, M., Wall, E., Madden, R., and Gibbons, S. (2016) *An Evaluation of Education Provision for Students with Autism Spectrum Disorder in Ireland*. Research Report No. 21, National Council for Special Education.

Danker, J., Strnadová, I., and Cumming, T. M. (2016). 'School Experiences of Students with Autism Spectrum Disorder within the Context of Student Wellbeing: A Review and Analysis of the Literature', *Australasian Journal of Special Education*, 40(1), 59–78.

DePape, A. M., and Lindsay, S. (2016). 'Lived Experiences from the Perspective of Individuals with Autism Spectrum Disorder: A Qualitative Meta-Synthesis', *Focus on Autism and Other Developmental Disabilities*, V3(1), 60–71.

Ehrenreich-May, J., Storch, E. A., Queen, A. H., Hernandez Rodriquez, J., Ghilain, C. S., Alessandri, M., Lewin, A. B., Arnold, E. B., Murphy, T. K., Lin, C. E., Fujii, C., Renno, P., Piacentini, J., Laugeson, E., and Wood, J. J. (2014). 'An Open Trial of Cognitive-Behavioural Therapy for Anxiety Disorders in Adolescents with Autism Spectrum Disorders', *Focus on Autism and Other Developmental Disorders*, 29(3), 145–155.

KIDSCREEN Group Europe. (2006). *The KIDSCREEN Questionnaires–Quality of Life Questionnaires for Children and Adolescents*. Lengerich, Germany: Pabst Science Publishers.

McCrimmon, A. W., Altomare, A. A., Smith, A. D., Jitlina, K., Matchullis, R. L., and Sakofske, D. H. (2014). 'Overview of Autism Spectrum Disorder'. In L. A. Wilkinson (ed.), *Autism Spectrum Disorder in Children and Adolescents: Evidence-based Assessment and Intervention in Schools*, pp. 17–36. Washington, DC: American Psychological Association.

Mannion, N. (2017). *What is the Impact of Explicit Teaching of Wellbeing on Students' Behaviour in a Special School Setting?* Unpublished Masters thesis. Limerick: Mary Immaculate College.

Middletown Centre for Autism and National Council for Special Education (2013) *Evaluation Framework to Underpin the Evaluation of Educational Provision for Students with ASD*, Trim: National Council for Special Education.

Moreira, P. A. S., Bilimoria, H., Alvez, P., Santos, M. A., Macedo, A. C., Maia, A., Figueiredo, F., and Miranda, M. J. (2015). 'Subjective wellbeing in students with special educational needs'. *Cognition, Brain & Behavior. An Interdisciplinary Journal*, 19, 75–97.

National Council for Curriculum and Assessment (2009). *Aistear: The Early Childhood Curriculum Framework*, Dublin: The Stationery Office.

National Council for Curriculum and Assessment (2017). *Junior Cycle Wellbeing Guidelines*. Dublin: The Stationery Office.

National Educational Psychological Service (2015). *Well-being in Primary Schools: Guidelines for Mental Health Promotion*. Dublin: The Department of Education and Skills.

O'Hagan, S. and Hebron, J. (2017). 'Perceptions of Friendship among Adolescents with Autism Spectrum Conditions in a Mainstream High School Resource Provision', *European Journal of Special Needs Education*, 32(4), 314–328

Ring, E., and O'Sullivan, L. (2016). 'The Importance of Including the Child's Voice in the Transition Process: Signposts from a National Evaluation of Concepts of School Readiness in Ireland', *Children's Research Digest*, 2(3), 37–44.

Rodgers, J., Glod, M., Connolly, B., and McConachie, H. (2012). 'The Relationship between Anxiety and Repetitive Behaviours in Autism Spectrum Disorder', *Journal of Autism and Developmental Disorders*, 42, 2404–2409.

Rodogno, R., Krause-Jensen, K., and Ashcroft, R. E. (2016). "'Autism and the good life": A New Approach to the Study of Well-Being', *Journal of Medical Ethics*, 42, 401–408.

Schopler, E. (2001). 'TEACCH (Treatment and Education of Autistic and related Communication-handicapped Children. In The National Autistic Society (ed.), *Approaches to Autism*, p. 68. London: The National Autistic Society.

Seligman, M. E. P. (2002). *Authentic Happiness*. New York: Free Press.

Seligman, M. E. P. (2011). *Flourish*. New York: Simon and Schuster.

PART III

Management and Staff Development

STELLA LONG

10　Developing Knowledge and Understanding
　　of Autism Spectrum Difference

ABSTRACT

As has been discussed in previous chapters, the development of inclusive education in Ireland has been guided by national and international policy directives. Across early years, primary, post-primary and special school settings, there have been increased enrolments of children with additional needs, including those with autism spectrum difference (ASD) This has placed additional demands on education communities. The knowledge, skills and attitudes of the educator is central to inclusion. While there have been positive developments in inclusive practices, there are some concerns regarding the level of support provided to education settings to enable them to provide a fully inclusive education. It is recognized that supporting staff development in inclusive practices requires ongoing continuing professional development (CPD) opportunities. The absence of dedicated training for special needs assistants (SNAs) has been noted in the literature. The introduction of the Access and Inclusion Model (AIM) with its focus on CPD for early childhood teachers represents a commitment by government to supporting inclusive practice from the beginning (Inter-Departmental Group (IDG) 2015) The provision of CPD in inclusive practices and in ASD specific approaches by the Special Education Support Service (SESS) has enabled many teachers and principals at primary, post-primary and special school levels to participate in CPD. The provision of CPD across each sector in the inclusive education system is essential for successful inclusive education. A co-ordinated approach to CPD within a framework of professional development would reaffirm learning and contribute positively to inclusive education practices.

Introduction

National and international policy directives have influenced the trend towards inclusive education in Ireland and elsewhere (Department of Children and Youth Affairs (DCYA) 2016; Government of Ireland

2004; United Nations Educational, Scientific and Cultural Organisation (UNESCO) 1994). Inclusive education in an Irish context is defined as a process of 'removing barriers to education through the accommodation and provision of appropriate structures and arrangements, to enable each learner to achieve the maximum benefit from his/her attendance at school' (Winter and O'Raw 2010: 39). The inclusive education process in Ireland has adopted a 'flexible continuum of provision' (Westwood 2013: 2), ranging from inclusion in early years settings, primary and post-primary schools, special classes in mainstream schools and special schools. A particular feature of inclusive education in Ireland has been the specific approaches to educational provision for children with ASDs (a pupil/teacher ratio of six to one, with SNA support) in special classes within mainstream schools or with additional supports in mainstream classes (Parsons, Guldberg, MacLeod, Jones, Prunty, and Balfe 2009; Daly et al. 2016). Researchers agree that inclusion has placed additional demands on all education communities (Greer and Meyen 2009; Ring and Prunty 2012; Ainscow 2014; Rose 2017). Researchers also agree that the knowledge, skills and attitudes of educators are central to inclusion (Shevlin, Winter and Flynn 2013). There are some concerns regarding the level of support provided for education settings to support inclusive education provision (Ring and Travers 2005; Shevlin, Kenny and Loxley 2008; Black-Hawkins 2014). Concerns have been expressed by teachers and SNAs regarding their personal lack of knowledge and skills for supporting children with additional needs (Shevlin et al. 2013; Kerins, Casserly, Deacy, Harvey, McDonagh and Tiernan 2018). It is recognized however, that supporting teacher/staff development of inclusive practices in a process of inclusion requires ongoing professional development (Forlin 2010; Sindelar, Brownell and Billingsley 2010; National Council for Special Education (NCSE) 2015). This chapter will critically review the literature base relating to the knowledge and understanding required to implement inclusive practices with a specific focus on ASD (Middletown Centre for Autism/NCSE 2013; Daly et al. 2016). Key findings from the current research study will be presented. The implications of these findings in the context of the literature will inform future professional development initiatives for educators from early years to post-primary levels.

Key Signposts: Introduction

- National and international policies have influenced the development of an inclusive education system in Ireland.
- The implementation of an inclusive education system requires all education settings to engage in a review of their function, curriculum and pedagogy to accommodate all learners.
- The knowledge, skills and attitudes of educators are central to inclusion.

Opportunities to Develop Knowledge and Understanding of Inclusive Practices

Inclusive practice is generally based on the concept of accommodating all learners within the education setting (Winter and O'Raw 2010; Ainscow 2014). Inclusive practice has however a broader remit than the individual classroom and aims to enable all learners to participate fully in their school community where difference is 'accommodated and celebrated' (Department of Education and Skills '(DES) 2007:38). Common features of inclusive practices in the literature include a whole-school culture or community of practice in relation to inclusive education (Ainscow and Sandill 2010); effective leadership for inclusion, positive teacher attitudes to inclusion (Shevlin et al. 2013) and the provision of CPD for educators and SNAs (Forlin 2010; O'Connor, Hansson and Keating 2012; Daly et al. 2016).

There is international recognition that high-calibre educators, who are afforded opportunities to develop professionally are at the epicentre of education systems (Government of Ireland 1995; Conway, Murphy, Rath and Hall 2009). In Ireland, early childhood education has developed rapidly in recent years and currently there is a welcome focus on developing national guidelines in relation to initial early childhood teacher education (Early Years Education Policy Unit Working Group 2017). At primary and post-primary levels, the continuum of teacher education is the process through which teachers acquire the professional knowledge, attributes and skills essential to their role as teachers (The Teaching Council 2011). Beginning their professional learning and development during their Initial Teacher Education (ITE), newly qualified teachers are supported by whole school approaches to their professional learning during their induction phase (The Teaching Council 2017). The process of life-long teacher learning is referred to as CPD and is guided by *Cosán*, the framework for Teachers' Learning (The Teaching Council 2016). This stage of learning holds a pivotal position in enriching the professional knowledge of teachers so that they can adapt to the changing educational needs of the knowledge society over the duration of their teaching career (Conway et al. 2009; The Teaching Council 2016).

As the literature has indicated, an inclusive education system demands educators skilled in the necessary practices and has implications for teacher education (Brownell, Sindelar, Kiely, and Danielson 2010). The importance of preparing educators to teach in inclusive contexts is firmly noted (Greer and Meyen 2009; Jordan, Schwartz and McGhie-Richmond 2009) as it is recognized that possessing the necessary knowledge and skills base is central to the successful inclusion of children with additional needs including those with ASD (Jordan et al. 2009; Brownell et al. 2010; Shevlin et al. 2013; NCSE 2015). Inclusion has been identified as a core area of learning by The Teaching Council (2016). Within this context, teachers' learning will 'improve their capacity to address and respond to the diversity of students' needs' (The Teaching Council 2016: 18). An input on inclusion during ITE provides the foundation for lifelong learning (European Agency for Development in Special Needs Education (EADSNE) 2010). Inclusion is a compulsory requirement on ITE programmes in Ireland (NCSE 2015). The EADSNE developed a *Profile of Inclusive Teachers* to guide ITE programmes in developing teacher skills for inclusion. Four core values were identified (EADSNE 2012). The area of competence for each core value constitutes attitudes and beliefs, knowledge and understanding, skills and understanding (Hick 2017).[1]

---

1   A certain *attitude* or belief demands certain *knowledge* or level of understanding and then *skills* in order to implement this knowledge in a practical situation (EADSNE 2012: 11).

Table 10.1: Profile of Inclusive Teachers (European Agency for
Development in Special Needs Education 2012)

Core Value	Area of Competence
Valuing Learner Diversity	*Conceptions of inclusive education* *Teacher's view of learner difference*
Supporting All Learners	*Promoting the academic, practical,* *social and emotional learning of all* *learners* *Effective teaching approaches in het-* *erogeneous classes*
Working with Others	*Working with parents and families* *Working with a range of educational* *professionals*
Personal Professional Development	*Teachers as reflective practitioners* *ITE as a foundation for ongoing pro-* *fessional learning and development*

Despite the inputs on inclusive education at the ITE phase, the research acknowledges that newly qualified teachers continue to express their lack of preparedness in inclusive practices (Winter 2006; Ware et al. 2009; Forlin 2012). International evidence suggests that some teachers hold the view that they do not have the knowledge or skills to teach children with additional needs (Rix, Sheehy, Fletcher-Campbell, Crisp and Harper 2013; Black-Hawkins 2014). Following their research into special educational provision in Ireland, Shevlin et al. (2008) reported that class teachers believed they had inadequate knowledge and skills to teach children in inclusive settings. This finding was also noted in the study by (Rose, Shevlin, Winter and O'Raw 2015) on inclusive education. Similarly, a study by Banks, McCoy, Frawley, Kingston, Shevlin and Smyth (2016) found that teachers in special classes expressed similar sentiments. Findings from these studies may be explained by the fact that prior to the development of the reconceptualized Bachelor of Education (B.Ed.) programme in 2012, there was a lack of consistency between colleges of education in terms of the input on special education in teacher education programmes (Kearns and Shevlin 2006). A significant number of teachers in the study of Ware, Butler, Robertson, O'Donnell and Gould (2011) reported that they had received little or no input in special education. However, younger teachers in the same study were 'more likely' to acknowledge that their ITE input in inclusive education had prepared them satisfactorily. Interim findings from the study of Hick (2017) on the role of ITE in preparing teachers for inclusive teaching in Ireland suggests that the education system is currently evolving in this regard. Forlin's (2010) argument and that of others (The Teaching Council 2011) that ITE provide a foundational base for teacher learning furnishes a rationale for the future development of teacher skills and knowledge through the medium of CPD.

The role of CPD in providing educators with the opportunity to enhance their knowledge, skills and understanding of inclusive practices is well recognized and is essential for the future development of inclusive education (DES 1993; Pugach and Blanton 2014; Banks et al. 2016). Professional development in inclusive practices tends to focus on adapting/changing practices and the acquisition of skills and knowledge to enable teachers to become more inclusive in their teaching (Billingsley 2011; Rose et al. 2015). In addition to the competencies required for inclusive educators outlined previously (EADSNE 2012), the research suggests that teachers of learners with ASD require specific expertise in areas related to the characteristics of learners with ASD; the implications for teaching and learning; individualized planning and assessment incorporating the particular interests and motivations of learners with ASD; how to manage transitions; the teaching and learning of social and communication skills and the generalization of skills (Parsons et al. 2011; NCSE 2015). Policy directives recommend that qualified educators may continue to require CPD to acquire the knowledge, skills and competencies necessary to teach in ASD specific settings (NCSE 2015) and in special schools (Ware et al. 2009). The provision of CPD in inclusive education in Ireland has evolved in tandem with CPD in general education settings. Recently, AsIAm, the ASD advocacy group in Ireland, announced the development of a national programme called 'Teach me AsIAm'. This is an early years CPD programme, focused on developing practical skills and tools aimed at supporting early childhood teachers in creating inclusive early years environments for children with ASD (AsIAm 2018). This programme is firmly located within the concepts and principles of the Better Start Access and Inclusion Model, which provides for a new model of government-funded supports aimed at enabling all children with additional needs to participate fully in free preschool mainstream settings alongside their peers (IDG 2015). Level Three of the model refers to the centrality of a qualified and confident workforce, while Level Four includes the provision of expert early years educational advice and policy support, which is provided by the Better Start National Support Service.

Research indicates that qualified teachers perceive that CPD is their route to the acquisition of the specialist knowledge required in inclusive education settings (Ware et al. 2011). Prior to the publication of the Special Education Review Committee (SERC) Report (DES 1993), in-service in remedial education was provided primarily by the Colleges of Education. The formation of the In-Career Development Unit (ICDU)/Teacher Education Section (TES) by the DES in 1992 led to the development of funded professional development accredited programmes for special education teachers. ASD-specific post-graduate programmes as recommended by The Task Force on Autism (DES 2001) are now offered in two Higher Education Institutions (HEI). On the successful completion of post-graduate programmes in special education and/or ASD, there are opportunities for teachers to undertake professional development at Master's level (Ware et al. 2011). However, some of these programmes are limited to teachers working specifically in special education posts and have therefore narrowed access to professional development in special education for mainstream class teachers (O'Gorman 2007; Ware et al. 2011). There is considerable variation in the literature in terms of the number of teachers in special education settings including ASD specific classes who have accessed professional development (Ware et al. 2009; Daly et al. 2016). Some studies suggest that between a quarter and a third of teachers in special schools have post graduate qualifications in special education (Ware et al. 2009). A national study undertaken by O'Gorman and Drudy (2011) to identify the professional development needs of special education teachers noted that one third of the respondents had no specialist qualification in special education Most of the teachers in ASD settings in the study of Daly et al. (2016) had such qualifications in special education and/or ASD.

Similar to the establishment of Better Start referred to previously, the establishment of the Special Education Support Service (SESS) by the In-Career Development Unit (ICDU) in 2003 resulted in a co-ordinated, strategic response to the provision of CPD in special education across all settings (PricewaterhouseCoopers (PwC) 2012). The SESS responded to the professional needs of teachers in special education contexts including ASD specific settings through the provision of seminars and workshops, online courses and onsite support for schools in partnership with other government agencies such as the National Educational Psychological Service (NEPS) and the National Behaviour Support Service (NBSS). The SESS provide ASD specific professional support across a range of areas including input on the Treatment and Education of Autistic and related Communication-handicapped Children (TEACCH) Autism programme, Contemporary Applied Behaviour Analysis (ABA), the Assessment of Basic Language and Learning Skills – Revised (ABLLS-R) and the Verbal Behaviour Milestones Assessment and Placement Programme (VB-MAPP) for example. Additional ASD professional development opportunities are offered by the SESS in association with Middletown Centre for Autism (MCA). Education centres continue to provide professional development for inclusive practice at local level. Teachers in special education settings including ASD specific settings commonly avail of CPD provided by the SESS, MCA and local providers such as Education Centres (Rose et al. 2015; Daly et al. 2016). Increased access to CPD provided by the SESS and other providers has led to higher levels of teacher knowledge and understanding of ASD (Daly et al. 2016; NCSE 2016).

It is interesting to note that the literature base relating to the evaluation of CPD in terms of its' impact on teaching and learning is not well developed either nationally or internationally (Garet et al. 2001; Ware et al. 2009). There are suggestions that the provision of high quality CPD specific to ASD leads to an increase in teacher knowledge and skills (NCSE 2015). The research generally however, focuses on teachers' self-reported changes in terms of their knowledge, skills and practical application in the classroom (Garet, Porter, Desimone, Birman, and Yoon 2001). Teachers who report increased skills and knowledge in inclusive practices through CPD are more positively disposed to change their teaching approaches (Garet et al.

2001). Situated in Level Three of the AIM, The Leadership for INClusion in the Early Years (LINC) programme commenced in September 2016 to provide 900 early childhood teachers each year, for a period of four years, with the requisite knowledge, understanding and skills to lead inclusive culture, practice and pedagogy in their settings. Initial evaluation findings suggest that that the programme has the potential to increase teachers' confidence in leading inclusion in the early years (Ring, Breen and Stapleton 2017). An evaluation of the work of the SESS indicated that the service was meeting its aims to increase teacher knowledge, skills and practice in special education (PwC 2012). This finding was supported by teachers in the study of Rose et al. (2015) who had accessed training provided by the SESS and noted that it was of a high standard. Teachers of learners with ASD valued the level of CPD afforded to them by the SESS (Daly et al. 2016).

The predominant model of CPD in Ireland has been that of the 'one-shot workshop model' '(Conway et al. 2009: xxviii) featuring a transfer of information which focuses on building teacher skills within the context of curriculum change (O'Sullivan, McConnell and McMillan 2012). Shevlin et al. (2008) argue that shorter courses such as in-service days were not sufficient for teachers in special education settings. Although mainstream class teachers in a study by Kenny, Shevlin and Loxeley (2006) agreed that some short courses were of an excellent standard, they also supported the view of the inadequacy of shorter professional development courses in meeting their needs. This traditional format of CPD fails to provide teachers with the conditions necessary for the development of skills and knowledge (Birman, Desimone, Porter and Garet 2000). Continuing professional development which was of longer duration and which occurred on a regular basis was proposed by O'Gorman and Drudy (2011). Conway et al. (2009) suggest that future CPD developments should include models which allow teachers to become interactive in the process, thus enabling the sharing of new practices with teaching colleagues within a community of learners. O'Gorman and Drudy (2011) note also the value of collaboration in inclusive professional development. Some teachers avail of collaborative learning in professional learning communities external to their schools in the form of online supports such as special education forums or blogs (Kershner 2014). Ainscow (2014) meanwhile proposes that changes in practices are more likely to occur when teachers have the opportunity to 'examine teachers' practices and the responsiveness of the students to planned activities' in the context of a collaborative approach to professional development known as *lesson study* (p. 175). Garet et al. (2001) suggest that collaborative CPD involving educators from the same setting has the advantage of supporting sustained change in the setting. Schools who participate in collaborative CPD 'contribute to a shared professional culture' leading to whole school reforms enabling individual changes in practice (Garet et al. 2001: 922).

As detailed further in the next chapter, leadership is a key factor in the provision of an inclusive education (Department of Education and Skills 2007; Ware et al. 2011; Banks et al. 2016). Early years managers and school principals are responsible for developing whole-school inclusive cultures, a task which involves collaborations with a wide range of stakeholders (DES 2007). Education leaders can support the development of knowledge and understanding of ASD in learning community by providing opportunities for staff to access CPD (DES 2007). Professional development for leaders should address their leadership role in inclusion in addition to core content knowledge in special educational needs (Travers et al. 2010). Evidence of the positive impact of CPD for principals on management and administrative approaches in ASD specific settings was noted by Daly et al. (2016) in their recent study. They also noted that principals of special schools tended to have specialist qualifications in special education. This supports the findings of O'Gorman and Drudy (2011) who found that 70 per cent of special education teachers in their study held management positions in their schools.

As noted in Chapter 4, special needs assistants (SNAs) were initially appointed to support children with additional needs in special schools (Stevens and O'Moore 2009). The service rapidly expanded to provide support for the increasing numbers of children with additional needs attending mainstream schools (Griffin and Shevlin 2011; Rose and O'Neill 2009). By 2015 there were just under 12,000 SNAs working in a care role supporting children with specific additional needs in Irish schools (Department of Education and Skills 2014; NCSE 2016). Forty per cent of children supported by SNAs had ASD (NCSE 2015). ASD specific classes are supported by SNAs on a pupil/teacher ratio of 6:1 (Banks et al. 2016). A recent study has found that the SNA scheme of provision is effective in its care remit (Department of Education and Skills 2011). The supporting role of the SNA is welcomed by teachers in inclusive and ASD specific settings including special classes (Logan 2006; Banks et al. 2016; Daly et al. 2016). However, it has been noted that in practice their role has deviated from that of a care role to supporting teaching and learning (Rose and O'Neill 2009; O'Connor et al. 2012; Rose et al. 2015; Long 2017). It appears that misunderstandings exist on the role of the SNA and this has led to a somewhat blurring of their role (DES 2011; O'Connor et al., 2012). The misconceptions have resulted in some operational difficulties for some teachers and SNAs (Banks et al. 2016). The DES has maintained a firm stance on the role of the SNA and continues to highlight to schools that 'responsibility for the learning and teaching of students with SEN is the remit of the teacher' (DES 2011: 13). Although the care role of the SNA involves supporting learners with diverse needs including ASD, SNAs are not required to have a qualification related to their role (Keating and O'Connor 2012; Kerins et al. 2018). Concerns have been expressed about their lack of qualifications and expertise in inclusive practices and in particular in ASD specific settings (Banks et al. 2016; Daly et al. 2016). The literature base strongly advocates for CPD for SNAs that is relevant to their role (DES 2011; O'Connor et al. 2012; Brock and Carter 2015; Kerins et al. 2018) and SNAs themselves have indicated their preference for CPD (Kerins et al. 2018). It is of interest that the DES funded a National Induction Programme for SNAs and a subsequent Certificate Course in SEN for SNAs from 2005 until 2014. Special needs assistants tend to access training provided by external providers or provided internally in their schools (Long 2017; Kerins et al. 2018). The literature suggests that training for SNAs include content on specific additional needs, their care role, working collaboratively, behaviour management and supporting learning (Kerins et al. 2018). Findings from the research by Daly and colleagues suggests that training for SNAs working with learners with ASD should also consider input on their supporting role in the 'application of ASD specific interventions and teaching methodologies' (Daly et al. 2016: 205).

Key Signposts: Opportunities to Develop Knowledge and Understanding of Inclusive Practices

- Currently there is a welcome focus on developing national guidelines in relation to initial early childhood teacher education.
- The Continuum of Teacher Education is the process through which teachers acquire the skills and knowledge to accommodate all learners in their classrooms.
- Some teachers feel that they lack the skills and knowledge to support teaching and learning in inclusive classes.
- The Better Start Access and Inclusion Model provides for a new model of government-funded supports aimed at enabling all children with additional needs to participate fully in free-preschool mainstream settings alongside their peers
- Continuing Professional Development plays a key role in developing teacher knowledge and skills for inclusive practices.
- The development of a national framework for CPD for SNAs would increase their knowledge and skills, enhance their work with teachers and provide positive outcomes for the children they support.

Implications for Practice

Findings from the literature and recent government initiatives in Ireland indicate positive developments in inclusive education for learners with additional needs including those with ASD (Rose et al. 2015; Daly et al. 2016; NCSE 2015). The legislative framework and associated inclusive education policies reflect a commitment to ensuring that children are educated in inclusive settings (Government of Ireland 2004; DES 2005). While there is a general commitment to providing inclusive education, the research has identified a number of areas for development to ensure the provision of a truly inclusive education for all learners including those with ASD (Rose et al. 2015; Banks et al. 2016; Daly et al. 2016; Kerins et al. 2018). Continuing professional development in relation to developing a knowledge and understanding of ASD emerges as a core area of focus.

Researchers agree that highly skilled educators are central to the successful implementation of inclusive practices (NCSE 2013; Shevlin et al. 2013; Ainscow 2014). Positive teacher attitudes to inclusion guide and direct inclusive approaches to teaching and learning (Loreman 2007; Ainscow and Sandill 2010). Although the research indicates that teachers are generally positively disposed to inclusion, they can be challenged in its' implementation (Shevlin et al. 2013). The rapid increase in the numbers of children with ASD in recent years has placed additional demands on educators to acquire the specialist pedagogies required to support them (Parsons et al. 2011). The literature indicates the variation that exists in terms of the perceived ability of teachers to implement inclusive practices – some teachers expressing their lack of knowledge and others appearing to have acquired the necessary skills (Ring and Travers 2005; Travers et al. 2010; Daly et al. 2016). Educators are supported by SNAs and by their managers or principals in their efforts to develop and implement inclusive practices for all learners (DES 2007; Brock and Carter 2015). Training for SNAs is strongly advocated in the literature (Daly et al. 2016). Given the pivotal central role of the manager or principal in enabling inclusive practices, it is imperative that they are provided with CPD relevant to their needs (Ware et al. 2009; Banks et al. 2016).

The provision of CPD across each sector in the inclusive education system is essential for successful inclusive education. The approach to CPD adopted in the context of the AIM could usefully be adapted and extended across primary, post-primary and special school settings. The inequities in the system (for example, the lack of funded, accredited CPD for SNAs by comparison to the funded CPD available to teachers and principals) continue to be problematic for schools (Daly et al. 2016). Accessing CPD relevant to the needs of specific teachers and principals in schools is also problematic. Teachers have varying needs in relation to the CPD they require – ranging from those who require a basic awareness to those requiring accreditation or specialist pedagogies such as ASD specific methods (Brock, Huber, Carter, Juarez and Warren 2014; NCSE 2015). The timing of CPD requires consideration. Should teachers require ASD specific input for example, prior to commencing teaching in ASD classes? When is best for whole-school professional development? During school hours or after? Would the professional needs of SNAs be met by partaking in selected whole-school professional development? (Daly et al. 2016). In addition, the model of CPD provision needs to be considered. Will stand-alone workshops provide teachers and SNAs with the skills and knowledge they require? Would collaborative approaches to professional development such as *lesson study* be effective for inclusion? The absence of specific guidelines and CPD programmes from the DES in relation to the professional requirements for SNAs has resulted in SNAs accessing training from private providers resulting in a disjointed approach to their professional development.

The provision of funded CPD in special education for teachers by the DES is to be applauded as are the supports provided to schools and teachers by the SESS and MCA (Daly et al. 2016). The implementation of a Framework for ASD Professional Development as outlined by the NCSE (2015) is recommended. So doing would provide a coherent framework of knowledge, skills and competencies for teachers of children with ASD ranging from ITE to CPD at graduate levels. A similar Framework of CPD should be developed for all teachers in inclusive settings. Setting these structures of competencies and skills within the *Cosán* Framework for teacher learning (The Teaching Council 2016) would serve to 'affirm the value of teachers' learning and acknowledge the full range of learning activities that teachers undertake for their benefit and that of their students' (p. 27). The development of a quality assurance process as suggested by The Teaching Council (2016) to CPD approaches would reaffirm the 'quality of teachers' learning' (p. 27). In addition, consideration should be given to the evaluation of the impact of CPD on the acquisition of new knowledge and skills of both teachers and SNAs. While the data base on such evaluation processes is scant (Brock and Carter 2015), and challenging to implement, the introduction of an evaluative measure would serve to adapt CPD to meet the specific needs of teachers and SNAs. It would also result in improved outcomes for learners with additional needs including those with ASD.

Key Signposts: Implications for Practice

- The provision of CPD across each sector in the inclusive education system is essential for successful inclusive education.
- The approach to CPD adopted in the context of the AIM could usefully be adapted and extended across primary, post-primary and special school settings.
- Most teachers in ASD specialist settings have availed of CPD provided by the SESS and/or DES.
- A co-ordinated approach to CPD within a framework of professional development would reaffirm learning and contribute positively to inclusive education practices.

Bibliography

Ainscow, M. (2014). 'From Special Education to Effective Schools for All: Widening the Agenda'. In L. Florian (ed.), *The SAGE Handbook of Special Education*, pp. 171–185. London: SAGE Publications Ltd.

Ainscow, M., and Sandill, A. (2010). 'Developing Inclusive Education Systems: The Role of Organisational Cultures and Leadership', *International Journal of Inclusive Education*, 14(4), 401–416.

AsIAm (2018). Teach me ASIAM Early Years Programme. Accessed online on 27 January 2008 at <https://asiam.ie/announcing-teach-early-years-programme>

Banks, J., McCoy, S., Frawley, D., Kingston, G., Shevlin, M., and Smyth, F. (2016). *Special Classes in Irish schools – Phase 2: A Qualitative Study*. Dublin: Economic and Social Research Institute. Accessed online on 2 January 2018 at <http://www.esri.ie/pubs/BKMNEXT308.pdf>.

Billingsley, B. (2011). 'Factors Influencing Special Education Teacher Qualiaty and Effectiveness'. In J. M. Kauffman and D. P. Hallahan (eds), *Handbook of Special Education*, pp. 391–406. New York: Routledge.

Birman, B. F., Desimone, L., Porter, A. C., and Garet, M. S. (2000). 'Designing Professional Development that Works', *Educational Leadership*, 57(8), 28–33.

Black-Hawkins, K. (2014). 'Researching Inclusive Classroom Practices: The Framework for Participation'. In L. Florian (ed.), *The SAGE Handbook of Special Education*, pp. 390–403. London: SAGE Publications Ltd.

Brock, M. E., and Carter, E. W. (2015). 'Effects of a Professional Development Package to Prepare Special Education Paraprofessionals to Implement Evidence-Based Practice', *The Journal of Special Education*, 49(1), 39–51.

Brock, M. E., Huber, H. B., Carter, E. W., Juarez, A. P., and Warren, Z. E. (2014). 'Statewide Assessment of Professional Development Needs Related to Educating Students With Autism Spectrum Disorder', *Focus on Autism and Other Developmental Disabilities*, 29(2), 67–79.

Brownell, M. T., Sindelar, P. T., Kiely, M. T., and Danielson, L. (2010). 'Special Education Teacher Quality and Preparation: Exposing Foundations, Constructing a New Model', *Exceptional Children*, 76(3), 357–377.

Conway, P., Murphy, R., Rath, A., and Hall, K. (2009). *Learning to Teach and its Implications for the Continuum of Teacher Education: A Nine-Country Cross-National Study*. Maynooth, Co. Kildare: The Teaching Council. Accessed online on 21 October 2014 at <http://www.teachingcouncil.ie/en/Publications/Research/Documents/Learning-to-Teach-and-its-Implications-for-the-Continuum-of-Teacher-Education.pdf>.

Daly, P., Ring, E., Egan, M., Fitzgerald, J., Griffin, C., Long, S., McCarthy, E., Moloney, M., O'Brien, T., O'Byrne, A., O'Sullivan, S., Ryan, M., Wall, E., Madden, R., and Gibbons, S. (2016). *An Evaluation of Education Provision for Students with Autism Spectrum Disorder in Ireland*. Trim: National Council for Special Education. Accessed online on 2 January 2018 at <http://ncse.ie/wp-content/uploads/2016/07/5_NCSE-Education-Provision-ASD-Students-No21.pdf>.

Department of Children and Youth Affairs (2016). *Diversity, Equality and Inclusion Charter and Guidelines for Early Childhood Care and Education*. Dublin: Department of Children and Youth Affairs. Accessed online on 2 January 2018 at <http://aim.gov.ie/wp-content/uploads/2016/06/Diversity-Equality-and-Inclusion-Charter-and-Guidelines-for-Early-Childhood-Care-Education.pdf>.

Department of Education and Skills (1993). *Report of the Special Education Review Committee*. Dublin: The Stationery Office.

Department of Education and Skills (2001). *Educational Provision and Support for Persons with Autistic Spectrum Disorders: The Report of the Task Force*. Accessed online on 3 October 2012 at <http://www.sess.ie/sites/default/files/Autism%20Task%20Force%20Report.pdf>.

Department of Education and Skills (2005). *Organisation of Teaching Resources for Pupils who need Additional Support in Mainstream Primary Schools-Circular 02/05*. Athlone, Co. Westmeath: Department of Education and Skills. Accessed online on 3 January 2018 at <https://www.sess.ie/sites/default/files/Docu ments_Publications/Circular_SP_02_05.pdf>.

Department of Education and Skills (2007). *Inclusion of Pupils with Special Educational Needs: Post-Primary Guidelines.* Dublin: The Stationery Office. Accessed online on 13 December 2016 at <http://www.sess.ie/sites/default/files/insp_inclu sion_students_sp_ed_needs_pp_guidelines.pdf>.

Department of Education and Skills (2011). *The Special Needs Assistant Scheme: A Vaule for Money Review of Expenditure on the Special Needs Assistant Scheme.* Dublin: Department of Education and Skills. Accessed online on 3 January 2018 at <https://www.education.ie/en/Publications/Value-For-Money-Reviews/ pub_sna_vfm_june_2011.pdf>.

Department of Education and Skills (2014). *The Special Needs Assistant (SNA) Scheme to Support Teachers in meeting the Care Needs of some Children with Special Edu-cational Needs, arising from a Disability – Circular 30/14.* Dublin: Department of Education and Skills. Accessed online on 4 January 2018 at <http://www. education.ie/en/Circulars-and-Forms/Active-Circulars/cl0030_2014.pdf>.

Early Years Education Policy Unit Working Group (2017). *Professional Award Crite-ria and Guidelines for Initial Professional Education (Level 7 and Level 8) Degree Programmes in Early Childhood Education and Care (ECEC) in Ireland.* Dublin: Early Years Education Policy Unit Working Group.

European Agency for Development in Special Needs Education (2010). *Teacher Education for Inclusion: International Literature Review.* Odense, Denmark: Euro-pean Agency for Development in Special Needs Education. Accessed online on 4 January 2018 at <http://www.europeanagency.org/agency-projects/teacher-education-for-inclusion/teacher-education-web-files/TE4ILiterature-Review. pdf>.

European Agency for Development in Special Needs Education (2012). *Profile of Inclusive Teachers.* Odense, Denmark: European Agency for Development in Special Needs Education. Accessed online on 3 January 2018 at <http://www. european-agency.org/sites/default/files/Profile-of-Inclusive-Teachers.pdf>.

Forlin, C. (2010). 'Reframing Teacher Education for Inclusion', In C. Forlin (ed.), *Teacher Education for Inclusion: Changing Paradigms and Innovative Approaches,* pp. 3–12. Oxon: Routledge.

Forlin, C. (2012). 'Future Directions: What is Needed now for Effective Inclusive Teacher Education?'. In C. Forlin (ed.), *Future Directions for Inclusive teacher Education: An International Perspective,* pp. 173–182. Oxon: Routledge.

Garet, M. S., Porter, A. C., Desimone, L., Birman, B. F., and Yoon, K. S. (2001). 'What makes Professional Development Effective? Results from a National sample of Teachers', *American Educational Research Journal,* 38(4), 915–945.

Government of Ireland (1995). *Charting our Education Future: White Paper on Education*. Dublin: The Stationery Office. Accessed online on 5 January 2018 at <https://www.education.ie/en/Publications/Policy-Reports/Charting-Our-Education-Future-White-Paper-On-Education-Launch-Copy-1995-.pdf>.

Government of Ireland (2004). *Education for Persons with Special Educational Needs (EPSEN) Act (2004)*. Dublin: The Stationery Office.

Greer, D., and Meyen, E. (2009). 'Special Education Teacher Education: A Perspective on Content Knowledge', *Learning Disabilities Research & Practice*, 24(4), 196–203.

Griffin, S., and Shevlin, M. (2011). *Responding to Special Education Needs: An Irish Perspective*. Dublin: Gill and Macmillan.

Hick, P. (2017). *Initial Teacher Education for Inclusion (ITE41) 2015–2018*. Paper presented at the National Council for Special Education Research Conference, Croke Park, Dublin. Accessed online on 3 January 2018 at <http://ncse.ie/wp-content/uploads/2017/11/Peter-Hick-ITE41-NCSE-Research-Conf-2017-FINAL.pdf>.

Inter-Departmental Group (2015). Supporting Access to the Early Childhood Care and Education (ECCE) Programme for Children with a Disability. Accessed online on 11 December 2017 at <http://nda.ie/nda-files/Supporting-Access-to-the-Early-Childhood-Care-and-Education-for-Children-with-a-Disability.pdf>.

Jordan, A., Schwartz, E., and McGhie-Richmond, D. (2009). 'Preparing Teachers for Inclusive Classrooms', *Teaching and Teacher Education*, 25(4), 535–542.

Kearns, H., and Shevlin, M. (2006). 'Initial Teacher Preparation for Special Educational Needs: Policy and Practice in the North and South of Ireland', *Teacher Development*, 10(1), 25–42.

Keating, S., and O'Connor, U. (2012). 'The Shifting Role of the Special Needs Assistant in Irish Classrooms: A Time for Change?', *European Journal of Special Needs Education*, 27(4), 533–544.

Kenny, M., Shevlin, M., and Loxeley, A. (2006). *Special Education Provision for Children with Disabilities in Irish Primary Schools: The Views of Stakeholders*. Dublin: Natioinal Disability Authority. Accessed online on 24 October 2013 at <http://www.nda.ie/cntmgmtnew.nsf/0/5B4CE56E1452B0E18025717E00525CDE?OpenDocument>.

Kerins, P., Casserly, A. M., Deacy, E., Harvey, D., McDonagh, D., and Tiernan, B. (2018). 'The Professional Development Needs of Special Needs Assistants in Irish Post-Primary schools', *European Journal of Special Needs Education*, 33(1), 31–16.

Kershner, R. (2014). 'What do Classroom Teachers need to know about Meeting Special Educational Needs?'. In L. Florian (ed.), *The SAGE Handbook of Special Education*, pp. 841–857). London: SAGE Publications Ltd.

Logan, A. (2006). 'The Role of the Special Needs Assistant Supporting Pupils with Special Educational Needs in Irish Mainstream Primary Schools', *Support for Learning*, 21(2), 92–99.

Long, S. (2017). *Examining Special Education Teacher Learning in Mathematics.* Unpublished PhD Thesis, Dublin: Trinity College Dublin.

Loreman, T. (2007). 'Seven Pillars of Support for Inclusive Education: Moving from "Why?" to "How?"', *International Journal of Whole Schooling*, 3(2), 22–39.

Middletown Centre for Autism and National Council for Special Education (2013). *Evaluation Framework to underpin the Evaluation of Educational Provision for Students with Autistic Spectrum Disorder.* Trim, Co. Meath: National Council for Special Education.

National Council for Special Education (2013). *Supporting Students with Special Educational Needs in Schools.* Trim, Co. Meath: National Council for Special Education. Accessed online 3 January 2018 at <http://ncse.ie/wp-content/uploads/2014/09/Supporting_14_05_13_web.pdf>.

National Council for Special Education (2015). *Supporting Students with Autism Spectrum Disorder in Schools.* Trim, Co. Meath: National Council for Special Education. Accessed online on 3 January 2018 at <http://ncse.ie/wp-content/uploads/2016/07/1_NCSE-Supporting-Students-ASD-Schools.pdf>.

National Council for Special Education (2016). *National Council for Special Education: Annual Report 2015.* Trim, Co. Meath: National Council for Special Education. Accessed online on 4 January 2018 at <http://ncse.ie/wp-content/uploads/2016/08/National-Council-for-Special-Education-Annual-Report-2015.pdf>.

O'Connor, U., Hansson, U., and Keating, S. (2012). *Capacity Building for Inclusion: The Role and Contribution of Special Needs Assistants and Classroom Assistants in Ireland and Northern Ireland.* Londonderry: University of Ulster and National University of Ireland Galway. Accessed online on 2 January 2018 at <http://www.childandfamilyresearch.ie/media/unescochildandfamilyresearchcentre/documentspdf/Capacity-Building-for-Inclusion-Briefing-Paper.pdf>.

O'Gorman, E. (2007). 'Reflections on Teacher Education in Special Educational Needs in Ireland', *LEARN*, 29, 100–110.

O'Gorman, E., and Drudy, S. (2011). *Professional Development for Teachers Working in Special Education/Inclusion in Mainstream Schools: The Views of Teachers and Other Stakeholders.* Dublin: University College Dublin. Accessed online on 3 January 2018 at <http://ncse.ie/wp-content/uploads/2014/10/Professional_Development_of_Teachers.pdf>.

O'Sullivan, H., McConnell, B., and McMillan, D. J. (2012). *Continuous Professional Development and its Impact on Practice: A North-South Comparative study of Irish*

Teachers' Perceptions, Experiences and Motivations. Armagh: Standing Conference on Teacher Education, North and South. Accessed online on 4 January 2018 at <http://scotens.org/wp-content/uploads/Final-Report1.pdf>.

Parsons, S., Guldberg, K., MacLeod, A., Jones, G., Prunty, A., and Balfe, T. (2009). *International Review of the Literature of Evidence of Best Practice Provision in the Education of Persons with Autistic Spectrum Disorders.* Trim, Co. Meath: NCSE. Accessed online 4 January 2018 at <http://www.ncse.ie/uploads/1/2_NCSE_Autism.pdf>.

Parsons, S., Guldberg, K., MacLeod, A., Jones, G., Prunty, A., and Balfe, T. (2011). 'International Review of the Evidence on Best Practice in Educational Provision for Children on the Autism Spectrum', *European Journal of Special Needs Education*, 26(1), 47–63.

Pugach, M. C., and Blanton, L. P. (2014). 'Inquiry and Community: Uncommon Opportunities to Enrich Professional Development for Inclusion'. In L. Florian (ed.), *The SAGE Handbook of Special Education, Vol. 2*, pp. 873–887. London: SAGE Publications Ltd.

PricewaterhouseCoopers (2012). *An Evaluation of the Special Education Support Service.* Dublin: Department of Education and Skills. Accessed online on 23 October 2015 at <https://www.education.ie/en/Publications/Value-For-Money-Reviews/An-Evaluation-of-the-Special-Education-Support-Service-SESS-.pdf>.

Ring, E., Breen, F., and Stapleton, S. (2017). 'Transforming lives through blended learning: Initial findings from the evaluation of the leadership for inclusion in the early years programme', *Shaping and Re-Shaping the Landscape of Teaching and Learning: Perspectives from the Shannon Consortium*, Limerick, 30 May 2017, Limerick: University of Limerick.

Ring, E., and Prunty, A. (2012). 'Adapting the Curriculum to Include Learners with Autistic Spectrum Disorders in Irish Schools'. In T. Day and J. Travers (eds), *Special and Inclusive Education: A Research Perspective*, pp. 289–302. Oxford: Peter Lang.

Ring, E., and Travers, J. (2005). 'Barriers to Inclusion: A Case Study of a Pupil with Severe Learning Difficulties in Ireland', *European Journal of Special Needs Education*, 20(1), 41–56.

Rix, J., Sheehy, K., Fletcher-Campbell, F., Crisp, M., and Harper, A. (2013). *Continuum of Education Provision for Children with Special Educational Needs: Review of International Policies and Practices (Vol. 1).* Trim, Co. Meath: NCSE. Accessed online on 25 September 2015 at <http://ncse.ie/wp-content/uploads/2014/10/Report_13_Continuum_07_08_13.pdf>.

Rose, R. (2017). *Shaping Sustainable Inclusion Policy through Practice.* Oxford Research Encloypedia of Education. Accessed online on 3 January 2018 at <http://

education.oxfordre.com/view/10.1093/acrefore/9780190264093.001.0001/
acrefore-9780190264093-e-149?print=pdf>.

Rose, R., and O'Neill, A. (2009). Classroom Support for Inclusion in England and
Ireland: An Evaluation of Contrasting Models', *Research in Comparative and
International Education*, 4(3), 250–261.

Rose, R., Shevlin, M., Winter, E., and O'Raw, P. (2015). *Project IRIS – Inclusive Research
in Irish schools: A Longitudinal Study of the Experiences of and Outcomes for Pupils
with Special Educational Needs (SEN) in Irish Schools*. Trim, Co. Meath: National
Council for Special Education. Accessed online on 5 January 2018 at <http://
www.pdst.ie/sites/default/files/NCSE-IRIS-Report-No20.pdf>.

Shevlin, M., Kenny, M., and Loxley, A. (2008). 'A Time of Transition: Exploring
Special Educational Provision in the Republic of Ireland', *Journal of Research in
Special Educational Needs*, 8(3), 141–152.

Shevlin, M., Winter, E., and Flynn, P. (2013). 'Developing Inclusive Practice: Teacher
Perceptions of Opportunities and Constraints in the Republic of Ireland', *International Journal of Inclusive Education*, 17(10), 1119–1133.

Sindelar, P. T., Brownell, M. T., and Billingsley, B. (2010). 'Special Education Teacher
Education Research: Current Status and Future Directions', *Teacher Education
and Special Education*, 33(1), 8–24.

Stevens, P., and O'Moore, M. (2009). *Inclusion or Illusion? – Educational Provision
for Primary School Children with Mild General Learning Disabilities*. Dublin:
Blackhall Publishing.

The Teaching Council. (2011). *Policy on the Continuum of Teacher Education*. Maynooth, Co. Kildare: The Teaching Council. Accessed online on 25 October
2013 at <http://www.teachingcouncil.ie/_fileupload/Teacher%20Education/
FINAL%20TC_Policy_Paper_SP.pdf>.

The Teaching Council (2016). *Cosan: Framework for Teachers'Llearning*. Accessed
online on 12 October 2017 at <http://www.teachingcouncil.ie/en/Publications/
Teacher-Education/Cosan-Framework-for-Teachers-Learning.pdf>.

The Teaching Council (2017). *Key Points of Information about Droichead*. Accessed
online on 3 January 2018 at <http://www.teachingcouncil.ie/en/_fileupload/
Droichead-2017/Ten-key-points-with-growth-phase.pdf>.

Travers, J., and Balfe, T. etc (2010). *Addressing the Challenges and Barriers to Inclusion
in Irish Primary Schools*. Dublin: St. Patrick's College.

United Nations Educational, Scientific and Cultural Organisation (1994).
*The Salamanca Statement and Framework for Action on Special Needs
Education*. Paris: United Nations Educational, Scientific and Cultural
Organisation.

Ware, J., Butler, C. etc (2011). *Research Report on the Role of Special Schools and Classes in Ireland*. Trim, Co. Meath: National Council for Special Education.

Ware, J., Butler, C., Robertson, C., O'Donnell, M., and Gould, M. (2011). *Access to the Curriculum for Pupils with a Variety of Special Educational Needs in the Mainstream Classroom*. Trim, Co. Meath: National Council for Special Education.

Westwood, P. S. (2013). *Inclusive and Adaptive Teaching: Meeting the Challenge of Diversity in the Classroom*. London: New York: Routledge.

Winter, E. (2006). 'Preparing New Teachers for Inclusive Schools and Classrooms', *Support for Learning*, 21(2), 85–90.

Winter, E., and O'Raw, P. (2010). *Literature Review of the Principles and Practices Relating to Inclusive Education for Children with Special Educational Needs*. Trim, Co. Meath: National Council for Special Education. Accessed online on 5 January 2018 at <http://ncse.ie/wpcontent/uploads/2014/10/NCSE_Inclusion.pdf>.

JOHANNA FITZGERALD

11 Leading Learning for Children with Autism Spectrum Difference

ABSTRACT

In an era of unrelenting educational policy and curricular reform (Griffin and Shevlin 2011), the centrality of leadership in promoting extensive and collaboratively mediated change across educational environments is profound (Fullan 2005). This chapter argues the necessity for a model of leadership which reconceptualizes the interplay between leadership and learning in efforts to bring about leadership *for* learning, facilitating meaningful engagement for *all* learners in an education community (Rayner 2009; Swaffield and Macbeath 2009). The key principle maintains that learning is for everybody, including teachers and other setting personnel and it is a complex activity which is dynamically linked to leadership in an ongoing cycle of action, participation, reflection, collective and collaborative practice (Swaffield and Macbeath 2009). If a culture of learning and continuous professional growth is cultivated by leaders in early years, primary, post-primary and special school settings, it becomes embedded in practice and facilitates a flexible, setting-wide response to learner diversity (Ainscow and Sandill 2010; Hargreaves and Fullan 2012). This chapter will weave together findings related to effective leadership derived from data collected for the research with current international literature relating to educational leadership. Key insights from the research will be presented which will have implications for leaders in early years, primary, post-primary and special school settings.

Introduction

The educational landscape for children with autism spectrum difference (ASD) has witnessed considerable transformation over the past two decades, with more children with ASD attending mainstream education (Daly et al. 2016). Furthermore, inclusion of children with ASD in mainstream education has been recognized as complex and challenging (Humphrey and

Lewis 2008). In Ireland, inclusive education for children with additional needs, including those with ASDs, recognizes the importance of providing a *continuum of provision* to meet a *continuum of need* (Department of Education and Skills (DES) 2007a; 2010). Various placement options exist for children with ASD, ranging from full-time placement in special schools or classes, to placement in mainstream provision with part-time withdrawal for additional support as required (Rose, Shevlin, Winter and O'Raw 2015). There has been a marked increase in the identification of children with ASD from early years to post-primary level. Statistics relating to provision for children with ASD indicate, for example, that the numbers of special classes for learners with ASD in mainstream post-primary schools increased from zero in 2006 to 152 in 2015. Likewise, special classes at primary level increased from 88 in 2006 to 378 in 2015 (Daly et al. 2016). As a consequence, schools have struggled to keep pace with these developments (Humphrey and Symes 2013). Strong leadership and support from early years managers and school principals are acknowledged as integral to the processes of successful change (Fullan 2005; Leadership for INClusion in the Early Years (LINC) Programme 2016–2018) and inclusion (Rayner 2009).

Key Signposts: Introduction

- The number of children with ASD being identified from early years to post-primary levels has continued to increase.
- Inclusive education can be equated with recognizing the importance of providing a *continuum of provision* to meet a *continuum of need*.
- Strong leadership and support from principals and managers is acknowledged as integral to the processes of successful change and inclusive practice.

Effective Leadership in Turbulent Times

Changes to Ireland's inclusion policy and legislation since the 1990s occurred 'swiftly with little discussion' (Stephens and O'Moore 2009: 4) and delivered significant challenges to education settings. However, readiness to embrace transformation is influenced by the nature and quality of leadership (National Council for Curriculum and Assessment (NCCA) 2010). As learner populations become increasingly diverse, literature identifies three broad tasks leaders need to attend to in their efforts to develop inclusive settings. They need to: promote new meanings about difference and diversity embedded in social models; facilitate and encourage inclusive practice; and develop communities of practice within the setting and with the wider community to continually strengthen inclusive culture (Riehl 2000).

Findings from the research conducted by Daly and colleagues (2016a) indicate that a positive culture was a prominent feature of most sites. Leaders' personal and professional commitment to inclusive education, and the translation of this commitment into practice, were significant in cultivating organizational cultures which were positively disposed to welcoming children with ASD, as illustrated by the principal in one primary site when she said: 'when they transfer into mainstream, they bring all this with them', concluding that 'I think as a result of it ... it gives us a better perspective on the whole child development ... it gives a depth to the soul of us all' (Daly et al. 2016: 91). Leaders influence the culture of the setting through their own attitudes, actions and symbolic gestures which in turn impacts upon setting-wide attitudes towards difference and diversity (Horrocks, White and Roberts 2008). Evidence from the research sites illustrates that most leaders promoted positive meanings about difference and diversity. In addition, they facilitated inclusive practice and committed time and resourcing to develop provision in their settings.

Key Signposts: Effective Leadership in Turbulent Times

In an inclusive environment:

- there is a culture which is accepting and valuing of learner difference;
- school leaders and setting managers influence this culture through their own attitudes, actions and symbolic gestures;
- colleagues share a common set of values and beliefs about inclusive education; and

- shared values and beliefs about inclusive education are clearly articulated in school/ setting policies (i.e. mission statement/ enrolment policies/ special educational/additional needs policies).
- Has a particular person influenced the development of a shared vision? How?
- Do colleagues contribute to discussion about the shared vision? How is this negotiated?

Principles of Effective Leadership

Effective leaders aim to facilitate transformative and transforming influences on learning in attempts to develop provision for all learners, but in particular, the most vulnerable children (Rayner 2009). Transformational leadership approaches provide an ideal bedfellow for leadership of sustainable change in educational environments (Bass and Riggio 2006) and are particularly relevant to the development of ASD provision in the Irish context. Transformational leaders are described as those who can

> stimulate and inspire followers to both achieve extraordinary outcomes and, in the process, develop their own leadership capacity. Transformational leaders help followers grow and develop into leaders by responding to individual followers' needs by empowering them and by aligning the objectives and goals of the individual followers, the leader, the group, and the larger organization. (Bass and Riggio 2006:3)

Such an approach fosters professional growth and development of all staff by engendering openness to new learning and enquiry (Ainscow and Sandill 2010), a characteristic necessary to flexibly respond to the diverse needs of children with ASD. All leaders in the research sites expressed their support for upskilling staff that assume responsibility for educating children with ASD and redirected resources to facilitate staff's professional learning.

Contemporary educational policy in Ireland across early years, primary, post-primary and special schools demands setting-wide collaboration to interpreting and implementing policy. Transformational leadership models are underpinned by collaborative approaches to decision-making and policy implementation and are therefore important to leaders and leadership teams. Leadership from this perspective is developed around relationships with colleagues and involves an understanding of the contexts, shared goals and decision-making processes essential to the learning organization (Fullan 2005). In the research sites where seamless teamwork was observed and staff clearly understood their roles, these specific roles tended to merge and staff did what needed to be done as encapsulated by a special needs assistant (SNA) in one of the early intervention sites when she said: 'it has to be a team approach ... if not, the class won't work, the class won't function properly' (Daly et al. 2016: 63) In these sites the views of all members of the teams were invited and respected while still maintaining clear lines of ultimate responsibility. In larger schools, principals worked to ensure efficient communication structures were in place to support distributed leadership to co-ordinating teachers of educational provision and relied on these teachers as communication conduits in the school.

Special needs assistants formed valued members of these teams in some sites but were less included as team members in other sites where they reported their input was not welcome unless requested. At sites with special classes, principals were aware of the potential isolation of teachers and highlighted the importance of continuing support for the teachers in special classes. Principals deployed personnel in their schools with care for the staff and with a view to sharing the responsibility for educational provision among those willing to undertake it. Principals frequently rotated staff within their schools to support those working in special classes or difficult classes and to grow expertise among all staff. A principal in one of the primary schools noted that 'if you had a teacher in the unit who was going to be left there for the rest of her time, I think the rest of us would sit back and really we wouldn't be that involved at all but we know that this pot is going to be passed around' (Daly et al. 2016: 91).

The closer leadership is to the site of learning, the greater the learning experience is for learners (Harris 2001). Irish education policy (DES 2007b; 2016b; 2016c; 2016d; 2016e; 2017a; 2018) recognizes that leadership should not reside solely with school senior leadership teams or setting managers and promotes a distributed approach (Duignan 2007; Spillane 2006) which is shared across a team (Gronn 2009; DES 2017a; 2018). The most recent *Action Plan for Education* (DES 2016b) is to be welcomed as it promises increased investment in education, more specifically, educational leadership. Emphasis has been placed on building leadership capacity by increasing the number of middle and senior management posts in schools (DES 2017b; 2018). Furthermore, the moratorium on middle-management posts in school settings has been lifted, which, the Minister for Education and Skills insists, 'recognizes the key role school leadership has in promoting a school environment which is welcoming, inclusive, accountable and focused on high quality teaching and learning' (DES 2017a).

Professional growth infers change, and change can lead to growth which can, however, be a deeply unsettling and painful process (Hargreaves 2004; Netolicky 2016). The significance of relationships in learning indicates that professional learning is a situated individual process as well as being an engaged social practice deeply influenced by the environment or context (Lave and Wenger 1991; Hargreaves and Fullan 2012; Forde, McMahon, McPhee and Patrick 2015; DES 2016d; 2016e). Transformational leadership facilitates the change process by developing systems to support and promote collaborative practice, and which recognizes the significance of relationships, which is essential to facilitate a collective response to potential challenges encountered when leading and managing support for children with ASD. Recent policy initiatives to embed collaborative processes of school self-evaluation through the *Looking At Our Schools Framework* in primary and post-primary schools (DES 2016d; 2016e) provide direction and scaffolding for school leaders to build communities engaged in collective cycles of evaluation, planning, action, reflection and learning. In essence, these evidenced-based quality frameworks provide a blueprint for leading learning and change and guide schools to establish systems which support transformation. Key practices associated with high quality leadership for learning conceptualized by Leithwood and Sea-Shore Louis (2011), embedded in current policy (DES 2016d; 2016e) and evidenced in data collected for the research from sites where excellent practice was observed, included leaders' abilities to:

- *Motivate staff:* foster commitment to shared vision and goals; maintain high expectations; communicate direction; develop relationships;

- *Develop people (capacity build):* provide individualized support; model inclusive values and practices; support and resource professional learning;
- *Design collaborative systems:* facilitate collaborative practice within the education setting; build productive relationships with families and communities; link the setting to the wider community; and
- *Improve the teaching and learning environment:* appoint suitably qualified staff; provide instructional support; foster cultures of learning; monitor progress; and align resources.

However, despite evidence of effective leadership, leaders also reported challenges encountered with efforts to include children with ASD. Many spoke about feeling unsupported when they established special provision for children with ASD. They experienced particular additional leadership tasks in order to provide for children with ASD including appointing teachers and arranging appropriate transport for the July Education Provision (JEP), managing SNA deployment, sharing difficult information with parents, and retaining confidentiality of information in very small schools. Leaders also expressed concerns about meeting their duty of care to children whose 'fit' in the setting was difficult to manage due to significant and complex needs or where language difficulties were compounded in Gaeltacht provision. Timetable management was a particular challenge for principals in some post-primary sites and led to a large number of mainstream teachers with little knowledge of ASD with responsibilities for instruction in special classes. This was perceived to adversely affect the quality of education the children received. These timetabling issues created increased stress for co-ordinating teachers and had a cascading effect on teaching and documentation. Principals fully understood the changing developmental needs of children with ASD progressing through schools and flexed supports to meet those changing needs. All principals reported that it was not always possible to recruit staff with appropriate qualifications and/or prior experience in working with children with ASD due to panel arrangements.

Principals also acknowledged difficulties hiring substitutes for specialist teachers in ASD with the principal in one school with an ASD class noting that not every teacher is suited to teaching children with ASD and reporting that 'I can remember some couple of young girls crying in the evening after it' (Daly et al. 2016: 92) Principals went to significant trouble to find staff in-house to replace those moving to teaching in a special class in post-primary schools. Special school principals in particular were aware of the need for hiring teachers and SNAs who would fit well with the children, would have good insight into how children with ASD see the world and who were willing to complete continuing professional development (CPD) to expand and develop their skill sets. Hiring teachers for the JEP was particularly difficult for primary schools and for some special schools when teachers in the schools did not want to continue to teach after the end of the school year. Also, payment for this additional teaching was not prompt.

Research indicates that where leadership is provided by leaders knowledgeable about ASD, education provision may be considered to be of higher quality (Horrocks et al. 2008, White and Roberts 2008; Bond et al. 2015). Furthermore, when leaders understand the importance of flexibility in allowing children to move between special and mainstream settings, provision for learners with ASD is deemed more successful (Bond, Symes, Hebron, Humphrey and Morewood 2015). Findings from the research indicate that principals in special schools tended to have advanced qualifications in special education and ASD whereas principals at other sites considered provision for children with ASD as part of their commitment to overall quality education for all students in the schools. In non-ASD-specific sites principals were frequently torn between attending CPD opportunities around topics of interest to the whole school community versus those of concern to a smaller portion thereof.

The responsibility levelled on leaders and the complexity of the role in a shifting educational landscape subjected to unrelenting policy and curricular reform is evidenced in the research. Furthermore, as leaders are expected to foster distributed approaches to leadership, such *giving away* of power may prove challenging (Stoll and Fink 1996), especially within increasing performativity-driven agendas (Barnett 2008; Sachs 2001). It requires leaders to trust in the skills, knowledge, values and beliefs of their staff (Bottery 2006) when ultimately accountability for progress in the setting rests with the leaders.

Keynote Signposts: Principles of Effective Leadership

- Transformational approaches to leadership in educational contexts facilitate reflective, flexible and collaborative responses to inclusive education.
- Effective leadership recognizes the importance of relationship building to facilitate collaborative and collective approaches to the leadership and management of educational change.
- The closer leadership is to the site of learning, the greater the learning experience is for learners. Distributed leadership approaches are recommended.
- A culture of professional learning exists in education settings committed to developing inclusive practice, and is spearheaded by setting leaders.
- Leadership of inclusive education is complex and challenging.

Leading Collaboratively Mediated Change: Developing Education Settings as Learning Organizations

In education, the organizational environment for personnel is complex, dynamic and multifaceted (Forde et al. 2015). Inclusive education is evident in settings which are flexibly responsive to the needs of their learners, and who are willing to adapt to meet these needs (Booth and Ainscow 2002; Mittler 2009; Norwich 2010; Nutbrown, Clough and Atherton 2013). Education-setting improvement is linked to collective capacity to respond to change (Senge 1990). In settings where organizational structures are developed which 'stimulate and support processes of interrogation and reflection' (Ainscow and Sandill 2010: 405), recognition of the need for reform is facilitated. In research sites, review of provision occurred within the framework of school self-evaluation in some sites but not in most. In the few sites where reflection and self-evaluation were excellent, data-based instructional decisions were made daily and review of children's learning and teaching was a regular feature of practice. Many teachers highlighted the importance of being open to trying new approaches and 'being able to say to yourself ok, I tried this and it didn't work'

(Daly et al. 2016: 64), as reported by one of the teachers in the early inter-vention sites. In post-primary and the other special school sites review was informal and data on progress in individual targets was unacceptably absent.

Teachers and leaders tended to evaluate the effectiveness of provision at the micro rather than macro level with careful attention to the delivery of instruction and the day-to-day learning of children with ASD. Post-primary schools were inclined to rely on examination results in the context of reviewing children's progress and this was unacceptable. Mainstream, special class and co-ordinating teachers were very sensitive to the success-ful participation of individual children during lessons and engaged in continuous review and checking for understanding. Overall, efficient and structured methods of provision review were significantly absent from most settings' documents and practice.

A reconfiguration of education settings as *communities of practice* (Lave and Wenger 1991), or *learning organizations* (Senge 1990) is required if set-tings are to engage in meaningful and effective self-evaluation and reflec-tion (DES 2016d; 2016e; 2017b). Learning organizations are described as

> Organisations where people continually expand their capacity to create results they truly desire, where new and expansive patterns of thinking are nurtured, where col-lective aspiration is set free, and where people are continually learning how to learn together. (Senge 1990:3)

When leaders create collaborative spaces for colleagues to meet, share, problem-pose and problem-solve towards a collective goal it allows all mem-bers of the education community to seek involvement in decision-making processes and contribute to re-shaping practice and provision (Gronn 2009; Rayner 2009). It may also stimulate individual and personal ownership in relation to setting-wide improvement (Ainscow and Sandill 2010). Using the concept of *situated learning* (Lave and Wenger 1991) the philosophy of inclusion can facilitate opportunities for all members of the educational community to learn and flexibly respond within the community, which may be *legitimately peripheral* initially, but which become more involved and meaningful over time (Lave and Wenger 1991). The creation of *communities of practice* (Lave and Wenger 1991) will, it is suggested, bring about change to inclusive *cultures*, which in turn affect inclusive *practices*. In this way, the actions of individuals can be influenced, but moreover, the 'thinking that informs these actions' (Ainscow and Sandill 2010: 403).

A reconfiguration of the learning organization to enable the development of distributed models of leadership, high levels of staff and learner engagement, collaborative planning and a commitment to continual professional learning and reflective practice are essential to the advancement of systematic collaborative practice (Hargreaves, Halász and Pont 2007; Carroll, Levy and Richmond 2008; Ainscow and Sandhill 2010; DES 2016d; 2016e) and ultimately inclusive education. However, achieving balance between collaborative practice and staff or teachers' individuality can prove challenging (Stoll and Fink 1996) but strong leadership can promote equilibrium when staffs' and leaders' perceptions of the setting's ethos and culture are aligned (Sachs 2001).

Capacity building within education settings recognizes that facilitation and provision of professional development to teaching and other staff is 'a critical factor to ensure consistency of inclusive practice' (Shevlin, Winter and Flynn 2013: 24). Moreover, the role of the teacher is perhaps the single most critical factor in the establishment of such environments (European Agency for Development of Special Needs Education (EADSNE) 2012; Rose et al. 2015). However, despite the complexities associated with provision of appropriate education for children with ASD or indeed any other complex educational need, professional development for teachers and principals in primary, post-primary and special schools is not mandated. Encouragingly, in early years settings, the centrality of leadership and understanding of inclusive education underpins the government's recent commitment to developing the role of dedicated inclusion co-ordinators in early years settings through the Access and Inclusion Model (AIM) (Inter-departmental Group 2015). Notwithstanding current policy impetus, principals at all research school sites demonstrated an excellent awareness of the importance of recruiting staff with knowledge, experience, expertise and qualifications related to the learning and teaching of learners with ASD and reported that they made every effort to recruit such staff. Furthermore, schools provided admirable support structures for teachers to pursue CPD which entailed considerable administrative demands. Principals secured substitute teachers for those taking CPD courses and colleagues covered for them frequently.

While professional learning is a highly individualized endeavour (Netolicky 2016), best-practice models are those identified as 'collaborative and grounded, rather than individual or top-down' (Netolicky 2016: 271). The relationship between the individual teacher and the education setting is critical for professional learning. Strong leadership is facilitative of collaborative and collegial practice based on trust and respect (Bottery 2006; Sachs 2001), where members of the education setting community are equally respected and encouraged to share expertise and take risks (Stoll and Fink 1996). Findings from research sites with special classes and special schools considered specialist teachers to be resident experts and had numerous informal and formal systems for sharing information and expertise. These included conversations during breaks and lunch times, short meetings between classes, presentations at staff meetings and subject meetings, explicit delivery of in-service information, sharing of documents and other materials from CPD opportunities and use of the school intranet. Schools considered Croke Park[1] hours both positively and negatively in this regard. Teachers had opportunities to systematically focus on important school issues, but the requirement to attend these reduced teachers' willingness in some instances to do extra school tasks. The demands of teaching children with ASD increased the fatigue factor associated with attending Croke Park hours at the end of the day.

Where there were no special classes, the resource/learning support teacher was considered the expert in the school. Some post-primary schools had functional systems for specialist teachers to communicate with subject teachers on a regular basis. These systems were better embedded in schools with well-established special classes. Principals invested in developing systematic ways for specialist knowledge to be disseminated to reduce the potential isolation of teachers in special classes. Principals and

---

1   Croke Park hours refer to a directive issued under the Public Service Agreement (2011). It requires teachers to work an additional thirty-six and thirty-three hours per school year at primary and post-primary levels respectively.

co-ordinating teachers were keenly aware of the possibility that clusters of special classes could become schools within schools and not be seen as integral to the host school. Schools new to ASD provision struggled to set up these systems and would perhaps benefit from support from more 'expert' schools.

Creating cultures of trust and collaboration can be difficult (Bolam et al. 2005). In Ireland, there is a long tradition of teaching being something that happens by individual teachers in individual classrooms without intrusion from the outside (Drudy 2001). We need to move beyond this, insist Furlong, Barton, Miles, Whiting, and Whitty (2000) who claim that the era of individualism, isolation and autonomy to make decisions about pedagogy and the curriculum has passed and education settings need support to develop systematic approaches to collaboration and expertise sharing. In essence, teachers need to be learning together in *learning-rich* rather than *learning-impoverished* environments (Barth 2001). Leaders in learning-rich organizations collaborate with colleagues in relation to CPD needs. This necessitates *active participation* by all members of the organization (Cordingley 2014). A focus on developing systems within settings creates:

- setting-wide structures to disseminate information about children with additional needs, including those with ASD;
- opportunities to cascade CPD relevant to children with additional needs to all staff;
- specific teams (where possible), where responsibility for decision-making about provision for learners with additional needs, including those with ASD is collectively owned; and
- time at staff meetings for discussion of issues related to provision for children with additional needs.

In learning environments where staff works with a variety of learners with complex needs, facilitating collaborative practice between colleagues is essential and preferential to individual staff members working in isolation with individual learners (Norwich 2010; Senge 1990). The impact of effective leadership on cultivating collaborative cultures, leading and sustaining change is profound (Fullan 2005).

> *Key Signposts: Leading Collaboratively Mediated Change:*
> *Developing Education Settings as Learning Organizations*
>
> - Education-setting improvement is linked to collective capacity to flexibly respond to change. The principal is central to creating cultures of collaboration and embedding systems which promote collaborative and collective decision-making.
> - Communities *of practice* or *learning organizations* can support education-setting personnel to engage in meaningful and effective self-evaluation and reflection which facilitates recognition of the need for reform.
> - Distributed models of leadership; high levels of staff and learner engagement; collaborative planning; a commitment to continual professional learning and reflective practice are essential to the advancement of systematic collaborative practice.

The Future

Provision for children with ASD has developed at a pace which requires a flexible, setting-wide response, spearheaded by a leadership team which recognizes the significance of collaborative and collective ownership of learning for all children and acknowledges the imperative for specialist expertise for those educators working directly with learners with ASD. This chapter advocated a contextually bound model of leadership which could promote effective provision for children with diverse needs, but specifically for those with ASD at early years, primary, post-primary and special school levels. Findings from the research offer insights relating to the challenges and benefits experienced by leaders and education communities in their quest to provide meaningful education for children with ASD.

The pivotal role of the leader in advancing inclusive practice has been emphasized throughout this chapter. Professional learning for leaders related to effective leadership for inclusion is essential. Inclusive leadership in the research sites, for the most part, equated to leaders' capacity to transform practice and was concerned with 'relationality to other people ...

an understanding of the context, tasks, goals and decision-making processes' (Carroll et al. 2008: 346). Furthermore, if education settings are to develop collaborative and collective approaches to provision, harnessing the positive practice evidenced in most research sites – like, for example, rotating teachers and SNAs between mainstream and special classes and articulating a transparent, consistent and clear rationale in documentation – could further support ASD provision and cultivate systematic collaboration.

Despite principals' attempts to appoint specialist teachers and personnel to work directly with learners with ASD, barriers existed. It would advantage principals appointing personnel for special classes to be able to recruit those most suitable without having to manage within the constraints of the panel system.

Education settings need to invest wholesale to inclusion if it is to work. Inclusion cannot depend on the interest and commitment of a minority of individuals in a setting. The importance of systematic collaboration to enable sharing of expertise allows all staff to lead learning for children with ASD. (Ainscow and Sandill 2010; Kugelmass and Ainscow 2004; Norwich 2010; Nutbrown et al. 2013). If systems do not exist, or do exist but are not embedded in setting-wide practice, the minority of specialist teachers/inclusion co-ordinators risk being seen as the *experts* of children with ASD and therefore may become singularly responsible for their learning (Layton, 2005). Without a shift in setting-wide attitude and approach, children with ASD will not be truly included (Barnard, Prior and Potter 2000). It is important therefore, that education settings recognize the benefit of functional systems for engaging in reflection, self-evaluation and timely review of provision in appropriate-sized teams. In particular, post-primary schools would benefit from functional systems to rate the progress of students on their individual targets in addition to their examination performance. Setting review of the strengths and weaknesses of current provision should be documented and consequent changes in practice recorded. Review and reflection of practice is an essential component of planning. Appendix A provides a reflective template which may support leaders and staff to reflect on current provision and guide future action.

To conclude, setting-wide and effective inclusion requires all staff to have a clear and shared understanding of the aims and expectation of inclusion within their settings (Eldar, Talmor and Wolf-Zukerman 2010). Leading such an approach is a complex and difficult task. When transformational leadership styles are truly embedded, there is an understanding that all members of the education setting can actively participate and share in the leadership (and ownership) of flexible approaches to the inclusion of children with wide and diverse strengths and needs. Such an approach requires leaders to move beyond leadership *of* learning and engage all members of the educational community to bring about leadership *for* learning.

Bibliography

Ainscow, M., and Sandill, A. (2010). 'Developing Inclusive Education Systems: The Role of Organisational Cultures and Leadership', *International Journal of Inclusive Education*, 14(4), 401–416.

Barnard, J., Prior, A., and Potter, D. (2000). *Autism and Inclusion: Is It Working?* London: National Autistic Society.

Barnett, R. (2008). 'Critical professionalism in an age of supercomplexity', in B. Cunningham (ed.) *Exploring Professionalism*, pp. 190–208. London: Bedford Way Papers.

Barth, R. (2001). 'Teacher Leader'. *Phi Delta Kappan*, 82(6), 443–449.

Bass, B. M., and Riggio, R. E. (2006). *Transformational Leadership* (2nd edn). New Jersey: Lawrence Erlbaum Associates.

Bolam, R., McMahon, A., Stoll, L., Thomas, S., Wallace, M., Greenwood, A., Hawkey, K., Ingram, M., Atkinson, A., and Smith, M. (2005). *Creating and Sustaining Effective Professional Learning Communities*. Nottingham: DfES Publications (Report no. RB637).

Bond, C., Symes, W., Hebron, J., Humphrey, N., and Morewood, G. (2015). *Educating Persons with Autistic Spectrum Disorder – A Systematic Literature Review: NCSE Research Report No. 20*. Trim: Co. Meath: NCSE. Accessed online on 26 January 2018 at <http://ncse.ie/wp-content/uploads/2016/07/4_NCSE-Educating-Persons-with-ASD-No20.pdf>.

Booth, T., and Ainscow, M. (2002). *Index for Inclusion: developing learning and participation in schools*. Bristol: CSIE.

Bottery, M. (2006). 'Educational Leaders in a Globalising World: A New Set of Priorities?', *School Leadership & Management*, 26(1), 5–22.

Carroll, B., Levy, L., and Richmond, D. (2008) 'Leadership as Practice: Challenging the Competency Paradigm', *Leadership*, 4 (4), 363–379.

Cordingley, P. (2014). 'Teacher licensing and collaboration: a model for developing the confidence of the profession as a whole'. In: J. Hallgarten, L. Bamfield, and K. McCarthy (eds), *Licensed to Create: Ten essays on improving teacher quality*, pp. 43–48. London: RSA Action and Research Centre.

Daly, P., Ring, E., Egan, M., Fitzgerald, J., Griffin, C., Long, S., McCarthy, E., Moloney, M., O'Brien, T., O'Byrne, A., O'Sullivan, S., Ryan, M., Wall, E., Madden, R. and Gibbons, S. (2016). *An Evaluation of Education Provision for Students with Autism Spectrum Disorder in Ireland.* Trim: National Council for Special Education.

Department of Education and Science (2007a). *A Continuum of Support for Primary Schools: Guidelines for Teachers.* Accessed online on 26 January 2018 at <https://www.education.ie/en/Schools-Colleges/Services/National-Educational-Psychological-Service-NEPS-/neps_special_needs_guidelines.pdf>.

Department of Education and Science (DES) (2007b). *Inclusion of Students with Special Educational Needs: Post-primary Guidelines.* Dublin: The Stationery Office.

Department of Education and Skills (2010). *A Continuum of Support for Post-Primary Schools: Guidelines for Teachers.* Accessed online on 26 January 2018 at <https://www.education.ie/en/Schools-Colleges/Services/National-Educational-Psychological-Service-NEPS-/neps_post_primary_continuum_teacher_guide.pdf>.

Department of Education and Skills (2016b). *Action Plan for Education 2017.* Accessed online on 26 January 2018 at <https://www.education.ie/en/Publications/Corporate-Reports/Strategy-Statement/Action-Plan-for-Education-2017.pdf>.

Department of Education and Skills Inspectorate (2016c). *A Guide to Early-Years Education-Focused Inspection (EYEI) in Early-Years Settings Participating in the Early Childhood Care and Education (ECCE) Programme.* Dublin: Department of Education and Skills.

Department of Education and Skills Inspectorate (2016d). *Looking at Our Schools 2016: A Quality Framework for Post-Primary Schools.* Dublin: Department of Education and Skills.

Department of Education and Skills Inspectorate (2016e). *Looking at Our Schools 2016: A Quality Framework for Primary Schools.* Dublin: Department of Education and Skills.

Department of Education and Skills (2017a) *Press Release by Minister for Education and Skills Richard Bruton: Better Outcomes for Children with Special Educational Needs is the Key Goal of New Model.* Accessed online on 26 January 2018 at <http://www.education.ie/en/Press-Events/Press-Releases/2017-Press-Releases/PR2017-01-18.html>.

Department of Education and Skills (2017b). Leadership and Management in Primary Schools. Dublin: Department of Education and Skills. *Circular Letter 0063/2017.*

Department of Education and Skills (2018). Leadership and Management in Post Primary Schools. Dublin: Department of Education and Skills. *Circular Letter 0003/2018.*

Drudy, S. (2001). 'The Teaching Profession in Ireland: It's Role and Current Challenges', *Studies: An Irish Quarterly Review*, 90(360), 363–375.

Duignan, P. (2007). *Ethical Leadership: Key Challenges and Tensions.* Melbourne: Cambridge University Press.

Eldar, E., Talmor, R., and Wolf-Zukerman, T. (2010). 'Success and Difficulties in the Individual Inclusion of Children with Autism Spectrum Disorder in the Eyes of their Coordinators', *International Journal of Inclusive Education*, 14, 97–114.

European Agency for Development of Special Needs Education (EADSNE) (2012). *Profile of Inclusive Teachers.* Odense: EADSNE.

Forde, C., McMahon, M., McPhee, A., and Patrick, F. (2006). *Professional Development, Reflection and Enquiry.* London: Paul Chapman Publishing.

Fullan, M. (2005). *Leadership and Sustainability.* Thousand Oaks, CA: Corwin Press.

Furlong, J., Barton, L., Miles, S., Whiting, C., and Whitty, G. (2000). *Teacher Education in Transition: re-forming professionalism?* Buckingham: Open University Press.

Griffin, S., and Shevlin, M. (2011). *Responding to Special Educational Needs: An Irish Perspective* (2nd edn). Dublin: Gill and MacMillan.

Gronn, P. (2009). 'From distributed to hybrid leadership practice', in A. Harris (ed.), *Distributed Leadership: different perspectives*, pp. 197–217. London: Springer.

Hargreaves, A. (2004). 'Inclusive and Exclusive Educational Change: Emotional Responses of Teachers and Implications for Leadership', *School Leadership & Management*, 24(3), 287–309.

Hargreaves, A., Halász, G., and Pont, B. (2007). *School Leadership for Systemic Improvement in Finland; A Case Study Report for the OECD Activity Improving School Leadership.* Paris: OECD. Accessed online on 26 January 2018 at <http://www.oecd.org/education/school/39928629.pdf>.

Hargreaves, A., and Fullan, M. (2012). *Professional Capital: Transforming Teaching in Every School.* Moorabbin: Hawker Brownlow Education.

Harris, A. (2001). 'Reflections on Distributed Leadership', *Management in Education*, 19(2), 10–12.

Horrocks, J. L., White, G., and Roberts, L. (2008). 'Principals' Attitudes regarding Inclusion of Children with Autism in Pennsylvania Public Schools', *Journal of Autism and Developmental Disorders*, 38(8) 1462–1473.

Humphrey, N., and Lewis S. (2008). '"Make me Normal": The Views and Experiences of Pupils on the Autistic Spectrum in Mainstream Secondary Schools', *Autism: An International Journal of Research and Practice*, 12(1), 23–47.

Humphrey, N., and Symes, W. (2013). 'Inclusive Education for Pupils with Autistic Spectrum Disorders in Secondary Mainstream Schools: Teacher Attitudes,

Experience and Knowledge', *International Journal of Inclusive Education*, 17(1), 32–46.

Inter-Departmental Group (IDG) (2015). *Supporting Access to the Early Childhood Care and Education Programme for Children with a Disability*. Accessed online on 26 January 2018 at <http://nda.ie/nda-files/Supporting-Access-to-the-Early-Childhood-Care-and-Education-for-Children-with-a-Disability.pdf>.

Kugelmass, J., and Ainscow, M. (2004). 'Leadership for Inclusion: A Comparison of International Perspectives'. *Journal of Research in Special Educational Needs*, 4 (3), 133–141.

Lave, J., and Wenger, E. (1991). *Situated Learning: Legitimate Peripheral Participation*. Cambridge: Cambridge University Press.

Layton, L. (2005). 'Special Educational Needs Co-ordinators and Leadership: A Role Too Far?', *Support For Learning*, 20(2), 53–60.

Leadership for INClusion in the Early Years Programme (2016–2018). *Reflections on Inclusion*, Leadership for INClusion in the Early Years Consortium: Mary Immaculate College, Limerick. Accessed online on 27 July 2018 at https://www.youtube.com/watch?v=AWlsokaaKQ4&feature=youtu.be

Leithwood, K., and Seashore-Louis, K. (2011). *Linking Leadership to Student Learning: Empirical Insights*. San Francisco: Jossey Bass.

Mittler, P. (2009). 'The global context of inclusive education: the role of the United Nations' in D. Mitchell, *Contextualising Inclusive Education*, pp. 22–36. London: Routledge.

National Council for Curriculum and Assessment (NCCA) (2010). *Leading and Supporting Change in Schools: Discussion Paper*. Accessed online on 26 January 2018 at <http://www.sdpi.ie/NCCA_Materials/Leading_and_Supporting_Change_in_Schools_NCCA.pdf>.

Netolicky, D. M. (2016). 'Rethinking Professional Learning for Teachers and School Leaders', *Journal of Professional Capital and Community*, 1(4), 270–285.

Norwich, B. (2010). 'What implications do changing practices and concepts have for the role of SEN coordinator?' In Hallett, F., and Hallett, G. (eds), *Transforming the Role of the SENCO: Achieving the National Award of SEN Coordination*, pp. 37–50. Berkshire: McGraw-Hill/Open University Press.

Nutbrown, C., Clough, P., and Atherton, F. (2013). *Inclusion in the Early Years* (2nd edn). London: SAGE.

Rayner, S. (2009). 'Educational diversity and learning leadership: a proposition, some principles and a model of inclusive leadership?', *Educational Review*, 61(4), 433–447.

Riehl, C. J. (2000). 'The Principal's Role in Creating Inclusive Schools for Diverse Learners: A review of Normative, Empirical and Critical Literature on the Practices of Educational Administration', *Review of Educational Research*, 70(1), 55–81.

Rose, R., Shevlin, M., Winter, E., and O'Rawe, P. (2015). *Project IRIS – Inclusive Research in Irish Schools: A Longitudinal Study of the Experiences of and Outcomes for Pupils with Special Educational Needs (SEN) in Irish Schools.* Trim: National Council for Special Education.

Sachs, J. (2001). 'Teacher professional identity: competing discourses, competing outcomes', *Journal of Education Policy*, 16(2), 149–161.

Senge, P. M. (1990). *The Fifth Discipline: The Art and Practice of the Learning Organisation.* London: Century.

Shevlin, M., Winter, E., and Flynn, P. (2013). 'Developing Inclusive Practice: Teacher Perceptions of Opportunities and Constraints in the Republic of Ireland', *International Journal of Inclusive Education* 17(10), 1119–1133.

Spillane, J. P. (2006). *Distributed Leadership.* San Francisco, CA: Jossey-Bass.

Stephens, P., and O'Moore, M. (2009). *Inclusion or Illusion? Educational Provision for Primary School Children with Mild General Learning Difficulties.* Dublin: Blackhall Publishing.

Stoll, L., and Fink, D. (1996). *Changing Our Schools.* Buckingham: Open University Press.

Swaffield, S. and Macbeath, J. (2009). 'Leadership for Learning' in J. Macbeath and N. Dempster (eds), *Connecting leadership and learning: principles for practice,* pp. 32–52. London: Routledge.

Appendix A: Reflection Facilitates Action

Action Planning

Think about key issues arising from your reflections on leadership for inclusive education that may have developed having read this chapter. In your setting how can you:

- Work with others to evaluate existing leadership practices and approaches?
- Effectively embed the principles of collaborative learning?

Identify three key actions for future development of practices for either yourself or for your setting.

1. _____

   _____

2. _____

   _____

3. _____

   _____

FIONNUALA TYNAN

12 Self-Evaluation: The Way Forward

ABSTRACT

This chapter presents self-evaluation as a key process for ongoing improvement of the educational provision for children with autistic spectrum difference (ASD) across early years, primary and post-primary settings. In this chapter, three aspects of self-evaluation are presented: teacher; education setting and learner. Teacher self-evaluation from early years to post-primary, particularly through the lens of reflective practice, is critical for enhancing teaching and learning for *all* children (Pollard 2014). The self-evaluation agenda has grown in recent years to complement external evaluation processes and to empower education communities to identify their own needs, thus promoting evidence-based improvement (Antoniou, Myburgh-Louw and Gronn 2016). Self-evaluation also encompasses the learner as evaluator. The inclusion of the voice of the learner in matters affecting his/her life is necessary (United Nations (UN) 1989), and has become a feature of informal assessment procedures, as well as of formal data gathering, in education settings.

Contextualizing Self-evaluation within the Inclusion Debate

It is not possible to discuss self-evaluation without linking it to the development of inclusive education practices. Educational inclusion has been shaped by key ideologies from a much-criticized psycho-medical legacy to a more holistic bio-psycho-social response. The 'routes to inclusion' described by Clough (2000) trace the development of inclusive education since the 1950s. They portray the concept of school improvement strategies, most prominent in the 1980s, where schools examined their policy and practice in terms of education for *all* learners. This was, in essence, a self-evaluation process, which was closely linked to the literature on effective education. Many of the indicators of inclusive practice were connected to the practices of 'effective schools' and a focus was maintained on children identified as requiring additional support. Thus, the inclusion debate turned to identifying and remediating barriers to inclusion, within mainstream education, through school development planning processes (see Booth and Ainscow 2002), thereby linking inclusion to classroom practice and school improvement strategies (Clough 2000).

International literature consistently reports specific barriers to the inclusion of children with additional needs in mainstream education, most frequently related to education settings and teachers. The barriers identified encompass poor leadership (Forlin 2010a; Watkins and Meijer 2010); inadequate whole-school approaches (Howley and Kime 2003; Westwood 2011) and closed cultures (Koutrouba, Vamvakari and Steliou 2006; Ainscow 2007). Teacher barriers include negative attitudes (Forlin 2010b; Kaikkonen 2010); lack of knowledge/experience (Forbes 2007; Rose and Shevlin 2010); inadequate professional development (Westwood 2011; Forlin 2010a); insufficient focus on learning (Hornby, Atkinson and Howard 1997; Mowat 2009); inappropriate methodologies including differentiation (Rix, Hall, Nind, Sheehy and Wearmouth 2009; Deng 2010) and low expectations (Rose and Shevlin 2010).

Inclusion is understood to be a process (Barton 1998) and many self-evaluation tools have been developed to enable education settings to formally evaluate and improve their inclusive practices. However, such a notion of self-evaluation can be limiting, particularly if it is assumed that all self-evaluation is carried out at whole-school level, or that it is necessarily a formal process. Education settings in the study conducted by Daly and colleagues described a culture of reflection and review regarding their provision for children with ASD (Daly et al. 2016). However, they communicated that it was more often through a process of on-going reflection and review during daily activities and less likely to be done through formal documentation of evidence. This chapter looks at how self-evaluation can pave a way forward for the ongoing enhancement of educational experiences for children with ASD.

Key Signposts: Introduction

- Self-evaluation as a concept can be traced to the emergence of inclusive education and the concern to examine policy and practice with reference to providing effectively for *all* learners.
- Barriers to inclusive practice from early years to post-primary settings include poor leadership; inadequate whole-school approaches and closed cultures.
- Negative attitudes; lack of knowledge/experience; inadequate professional development; insufficient focus on learning/differentiation; and low expectations have been identified as barriers to inclusion for teachers.
- Self-evaluation presents an opportunity to interrogate barriers to inclusion and develop inclusive educational experiences for children with ASD.

Understanding Self-Evaluation

As seen in Figure 12.1, the 'self' of self-evaluation can be interpreted as an education community, an individual educator or an individual learner. Each element can be practised in its own right, yet all elements are interconnected.

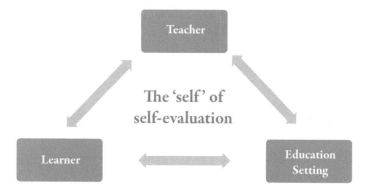

Figure 12.1: The 'Self' of Self-Evaluation

Each element complements the others and, when combined, greatly enhances the possibility for improvement (Department of Education and Skills (DES) 2016). The schools in the research indicated that self-evaluation took place through the school self-evaluation process and through individual teacher reflection on practice, but learner self-evaluation was rarely promoted.

Teacher Self-Evaluation

Early years teachers, primary and post-primary teachers self-evaluate in both informal and formal ways. Teacher self-evaluation focuses on the teacher as practitioner and can be referred to as reflective practice.

> By reflecting, we mean interrogating formative moments that occurred in your learning and teaching experiences through the lens of your current knowledge of educational theory, with a view to deepening your awareness and improving your practice. A reflective approach to teaching will help you to become flexible, self-analytical and responsive to the complex dynamics of classroom interaction. (Bonfield and Horgan 2016: 27)

The idea of teachers as reflective practitioners is not new. In 1910, John Dewey proposed distinct steps to train the mind to think reflectively. It continues to be linked to best professional practice due to the opportunity it creates for professional growth and development (Osterman and Kottkamp 1993). Bassot (2016: 2–4) highlights several reasons why professionals should engage in reflection:

- It provides a space for deep thinking.
- It promotes the evaluation and development of practice.
- It prevents stagnation.
- It allows for the achievement of excellence.
- It can make practice creative.
- It promotes self-awareness.
- It provides an opportunity to challenge one's assumptions.
- It provides a means for constructing professional knowledge.

While reflection on practice can be done formally, many teachers reflect on aspects of their practice in an informal way, as emerged from the findings of the study. Indeed, informal review of learning and teaching was a common feature of practice by teachers. All teachers highlighted the importance of being open to trying new approaches and 'being able to say to yourself ok, I tried this and it didn't work' (Daly et al. 2016: 64). Self-evaluation, in this instance, impacts on daily practice and is important in selecting appropriate approaches to meet the needs of individual learners. However, such self-evaluation is not always written down and therefore, may never be accessed by others. This is not uncommon in the Irish educational landscape. The Chief Inspector's Report (2010–2012) showed that 22 per cent of English lessons observed by the Inspectorate in unannounced (incidental) inspections were not supported by written plans (DES Inspectorate 2013). Long-term and short-term schemes of work can document changes in content, approaches and resources for supporting the learner with ASD and can subsequently provide evidence for the learner's individual education plan, for parent-teacher meetings and, more formally, for data for discussions at whole-school level. Regular reflection on individual practice can support ongoing development as it unifies the dichotomy of theory and practice (Bonfield and Horgan 2016). Teachers can move from the informal self-evaluation to a more formal self-evaluation by recording their observations and adjusting their planning and preparation accordingly. Teachers can reflect on any aspect of classroom life, such as:

- The learning environment
- The quality of learning
- Classroom management
- Planning and preparation
- Differentiation
- Learning needs
- Interventions
- English reading
- Problem-solving in mathematics
- Learner engagement
- A particular incident with a child

- A particular lesson
- A particular teaching approach
- A particular child

There are a number of tools to support teachers to engage in formal self-evaluation. One of the simplest tools for reflection, which suits a person who likes lists, bullet points and key messages, is the SWOT/SCOT analysis. This can also be used at whole-setting level to carry out a review, but its use for individual reflection should not be overlooked.
A SWOT/SCOT analysis stands for

- Strengths
- Weaknesses/Challenges
- Opportunities
- Threats

If we take Harry, a teacher of a child with ASD, who is reflecting on his own capacity at the beginning of the school year, his SCOT analysis may look like Table 12.1:

Table 12.1: Sample SCOT Analysis as Teacher Self-Evaluation

Strengths	Challenges
<ul><li>Four years' teaching experience</li><li>College school placement experience in a class with a learner with ASD</li><li>Previous IEPs to look through</li><li>Experienced SNAs in the school</li><li>I've worked with two SNAs before and it was very positive</li><li>Experienced support teachers</li><li>The child's previous teachers are open to sharing their practice</li><li>The child has performed well academically in subjects of interest to this point</li><li>The child engages in class activities</li><li>The child has an excellent attendance record</li><li>The child knows me from yard duty</li><li>Very supportive parents</li><li>I'm a hard worker and want to support this child</li></ul>	<ul><li>Never taught a child with ASD for a school year</li><li>Never used visual schedules before</li><li>Feel I don't know enough about ASD</li><li>I am aware that the child has displayed some behaviours that were difficult to manage</li><li>The child has some self-injurious behaviours</li><li>I don't like paperwork and detailed records are requested by the school</li><li>I don't know how to motivate this child</li></ul>

Opportunities	Threats
• Staff meeting before the children come back to school • Parents are prepared to come into school to show me how the child uses visual schedule • Class teacher from last year has agreed to spend time with me organizing the classroom and reviewing the child's file • Support teacher will co-ordinate the child's IEP • Professional development available on TEACCH approach, ABA and Social Stories which has been approved by board of management • Support teacher is open to providing in-class support	• Classroom is small, where to put child's individual work station?? • Hand dryer is very loud in adjoining toilets which the child doesn't like • There are many other children in the class with needs

Once this is completed a teacher can action plan around areas that can be improved or developed. A blank SWOT/SCOT can be found in Appendix A for your use.

For teachers who prefer to write in a more narrative style, the 'What Model' is useful. This approach to experiential learning was developed by Driscoll (2007) from the ideas of Borton (1970). This is a three-step reflective process, as can be seen in Figure 12.2.

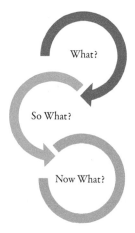

Figure 12.2: 'What' Model of Reflection

Let us now examine what should be done at each stage of this process. The 'What' stage is concerned with the facts of the situation from the perspective of the reflective practitioner. You could ask yourself the following trigger questions:

1. What happened?
2. What is the purpose of reflecting on this?
3. What did I do? What did I not do?
4. What was my initial reaction to this?

The 'so what' stage relates to the emotional response. Again, here are some trigger questions you can reflect upon:

1. How do I feel about the incident/event now?
2. What has 'unsettled' me or caused an emotional response?
3. What do I think triggered these feelings?
4. What does my education/school practice/theory/ current policy say about this?

At the 'now what' stage the practitioner responds with a plan of action.

1. What have I learned?
2. What would I do differently if I were in that situation again?
3. What should I do to improve my practice based on this interaction/ event?
4. What is my view on policy/practice/theory based on this?

You can use the template in Appendix B to reflect using the 'What Model'.

Teaching is an emotional activity (Pollard 2014) and one which is heavily dependent on relationships (Muijs and Reynolds 2011). Considering the emotional component to teaching it is important to also have a way to process the emotion of teaching and the events that elicit strong emotions. It can be useful to talk this through with a mentor, a colleague or a friend. You can simply talk or write about the experience, although this is typically an informal process. A more formal process is to go through established steps to work through the issue or event. One example of a reflective process is Gibb's Reflective Cycle (1988). Gibb's Reflective Cycle (see Figure 12.3) facilitates reflection while giving cognizance to the emotions which is absent from many reflective cycles. It is similar in many ways to the 'What Model' of reflection.

Similar to the 'What Model' of reflection, this cycle promotes reflection through a series of prompt questions.

Step 1: Description

• What happened?
• What was the lead up to this event?
• Who said what?

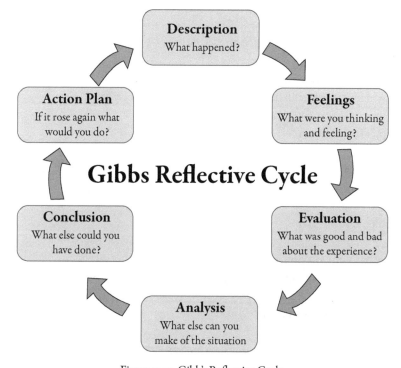

Figure 12.3: Gibb's Reflective Cycle

Step 2: Feelings

- What were you thinking and feeling at the time?
- Did this impact on your reaction/interaction?
- Were you in control of your feelings?

Step 3: Evaluation

- What was good about the experience?
- What did you do well?
- What was the positive outcome?
- What was not so good about the experience?
- Are there any negative consequences?

Step 4: Analysis

- What else can you make of the situation?
- What does policy/literature say?
- What have your colleagues/students/friends said?
- What was it like from the other person's perspective?

Step 5: Conclusion

- What else could you have done?
- What would you do differently if it happened again?

Step 6: Action Plan

- What will you do to transfer this learning to other situations?
- How can you ensure this happens again? (for a positive experience)
- What will you do differently next time? (for a negative experience)
- What supports should you access?

Evaluating your practice is an important aspect of your professional practice and critical for the successful teaching of children with ASD who may have difficulty explaining their learning needs or challenges.

Self-Evaluation in Educational Settings

There are number of ways in which educational settings can formally or informally evaluate their practice. Nowadays, it is agreed that all educational settings from early years settings to post-primary schools are complex organizations and, through increased investment in education, public accountability and marketization of education, are justly subjected to public demands for effectiveness and quality (Kyriakides and Campbell 2004; Klenowski and Wyatt-Smith 2014).

Key Signposts: Teacher Self-evaluation

- Teacher self-evaluation can be of an informal or a formal nature.
- It is strongly linked to reflection and, consequently, reflective practice, which supports professional growth and development.
- Teachers tend to self-evaluate in an informal manner more often than in a formal manner. You can formalize your self-evaluation by engaging in different reflective processes such as a SCOT/SWOT analysis, the 'What Model' of reflection, Gibb's Reflective Cycle (blank templates for each can be found in the appendices of this chapter).
- What aspect of classroom practice have you been reflecting on recently or do you feel you need to reflect on?

Many primary and post-primary schools in the research indicated that they evaluated their practice through the School Self-Evaluation (SSE) process. This is where a school community identifies and affirms good practice and makes decisions on how to improve certain aspects of school life based on evidence. This is one avenue of self-evaluation for a school.

The SSE process complements external evaluations and is primarily about 'schools taking ownership of their own development and improvement' (DES Inspectorate 2016: 6). School Self-Evaluation is also a change management tool and can aid school communities to manage changes to curriculum and to teaching and learning. It is a feature of the educational system in many countries although there tends to be differences in the balance between school improvement and accountability. This is dependent on the alignment of SSE to the external evaluation process by the country's Inspectorate (Janssens and van Amlsvoort 2008). Successful SSE is dependent on a climate of openness, collaboration, transparency and trust (MacBeath 1999) and it is appreciated that it is not an easy task (Antoniou et al. 2016). One model of the SSE process, currently used in the Republic of Ireland, is presented in Figure 12.4, which contains six steps.

Step 1: Identify Focus

In deciding where to start, it can be useful for a staff to conduct a SCOT/SWOT analysis as presented under teacher self-evaluation. It is important to list the strengths and celebrate improvements and developments rather than rushing to identify problems.

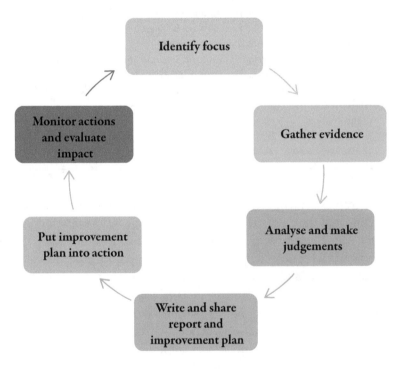

Figure 12.4: The School Self-Evaluation Six-Step Process

Step 2: Gather Evidence

Evidence can be gathered on any aspect of teaching or learning through observation, questionnaires, interviews or focus group discussions. The review of provision for children with ASD was reported to occur in the context of school self-evaluation, although comprehensive detailing of the robust review processes evidenced was rarely documented. One of the reasons for this may be due to the emphasis placed on the use of standardized test results to monitor improvement in literacy and numeracy. Some learners with ASD may not participate in standardized testing due to cognitive or emotional/behavioural difficulties, so how can progress be measured in curriculum areas? Learner progress can be measured effectively through the individual education plan (IEP). Where SMART targets are used, they can be the benchmark against which to measure progress for individual students. At a whole-school level, an analysis of IEP targets can be undertaken to examine the types of targets that tend to be achieved and those that don't. See the example under Step 3.

Step 3: Analyse the Evidence

It may be useful to illustrate how IEP targets can be used as a source of evidence and how this evidence can be analysed. The example here is from a school where no student took a standardized test. The staff decided that each teacher would count the number of targets they had devised for each student, categorize them and indicate which ones had/had not been achieved. The total number of targets for 32 students with learning needs is 160, broken into specific categories as seen in Table 12.2.

Table 12.2: Sample Analysis of IEP Targets as Evidence in the School Self-Evaluation Process

Target area	Social	Emotional	Behavioural	Self-help	Literacy	Numeracy	Other
No. of targets	54	10	13	26	25	12	20
No. of targets achieved	50	7	10	20	7	11	13

Reflect on this information. What does it tell you?

It shows that a high proportion of targets were achieved in each area, particularly in numeracy, but the area in which targets were least likely to be attained were in literacy. There is now a need to examine why this was the case. A deeper analysis of the 25 literacy targets is required. This can be seen in Table 12.3.

Table 12.3: Sample Analysis of IEP Targets in Literacy as Evidence
in the School Self-Evaluation Process

Target area	Listening	Speaking	Reading/ Comprehension	Writing	Other
No. of targets	3	10	7	4	1
No. of targets achieved	3	3	6	4	1

Reflect on this information. What does it tell you?

The information here is, of course, context based, however, we can make some observations. Targets around listening and writing tended to be achieved more than any other literacy targets are, but targets around speaking are least likely to be achieved. Why might this be the case? It may be that the targets were not adequately specific, realistic or achievable. It may also be because the approaches used were not appropriate or that inadequate time was spent on these activities. What else could impact on the achievement of these targets?

Once it is clear why something is happening it is possible to work on a solution to the issue. The information shows that a majority of students with IEPs achieve their targets in an instructional period but literacy targets, and particularly those around speaking, are more difficult to achieve.

Putting this back into the SSE context, it is important that when we look at this evidence, we look at overall literacy results and avoid focusing exclusively on standardized test results. When the results are reflected on, each teacher has a responsibility to discuss why the issue may exist from their perspective and context. This is where an open culture and trusting relationships are critical. Making decisions on the implementation of whole-school approaches may then be agreed when everyone has described their current practice.

Furthermore, it is also recommended, as part of the SSE process, to access the voices of both parents and learners. Feedback from parents can be very encouraging for staff. In the report, all parents expressed satisfaction with the understanding and knowledge of staff in relation to ASD; one parent noted that the teachers use 'excellent teaching methods' and that the staff was 'absolutely brilliant' (Daly et al. 2016: 65).

Step 4: Write and Share Report and Improvement Plan

This should be agreed by all staff members and not written by one person. It should also be shared with the school community. The improvement plan is similar in many ways to an IEP, in that targets are agreed and actions to achieve these targets are decided upon. Targets should be SMART and should enable the setting to measure future improvements. Templates for the SSE report and the improvement plan can be accessed on <http://www.schoolself-evaluation.ie>.

Step 5: Put the Improvement Plan into Action

In many ways this is the difficult step as it requires a concerted effort by each member of staff in their own classroom. It usually requires a change in practice, which is difficult within a busy classroom.

Step 6: Monitor Actions and Evaluate Impact

Due to the complexity of implementing changes, it is essential that one person co-ordinates the actions from the improvement plan and encourages everyone to commit to them. After an agreed period of time the improvement plan should be evaluated and all successes should be celebrated.

A number of self-evaluation tools for the development of inclusive educational practice have also been developed, which may be useful for your educational context when reflecting on practice. These include the Index for Inclusion (Booth and Ainscow 2002), the Inclusive Education Framework (National Council for Special Education (NSCE) 2011) and Reflections on Inclusion (Leadership for INClusion in the Early Years (LINC) Programme 2016–2018), the latter can be found in Appendix D. If we examine the Inclusive Education Framework (NCSE 2011), it is a SSE tool which 'provides guidance to schools on what constitutes good practice for including pupils with special educational needs and is designed to provide clear signposts to schools on their journey towards inclusion' (NCSE 2011: 11). The framework is based around themes rather than settings making it relevant for early years settings, primary schools and post-primary schools. It is envisaged that staff examine the criteria under each of the following themes:

1.   Leadership and management
2.   Whole-school development planning (this is now called SSE)
3.   Whole-school environment
4.   Communication
5.   Pupil and staff wellbeing
6.   Curriculum planning for inclusion
7.   Individualized education planning
8.   Teaching and learning strategies
9.   Classroom management
10. Support for and recognition for learning

The document has a range of self-reflection templates to be used by staff to aid them in the process.

The research indicated a need to devise and implement specific review-systems related to provision for children with ASD based on Middletown Centre for Autism (MCA) and NCSE Evaluation Framework.

Key Signposts: Self-Evaluation in Educational Settings

- Educational settings can reflect on their practice and self-evaluate formally or informally to ensure accountability, manage change, enhance practice and maximize outcomes for learners.
- A formal process of self-evaluation involves settings gathering evidence to identify and affirm good practice and select areas for development.
- Settings can use a range of tools to reflect on current practice including a SCOT/SWOT analysis, Index for Inclusion (Booth and Ainscow 2002), the Inclusive Education Framework (NCSE 2011) the School Self-Evaluation Six-Step Process (DES 2016) or Reflections on Inclusion (Leadership for INClusion in the Early Years (LINC Programme 2016–2018)).
- Self-evaluation in any educational setting requires commitment by all staff to be honest in their discussions, to commit to the agreed actions and to be open to change.

Learner Self-Evaluation/Self-Assessment

Learner self-evaluation can, and should, contribute to the self-evaluation process being conducted in the educational setting (DES 2016) but it should also be used as a method of enhancing learner self-efficacy (Westwood 2011), where learners 'look at their own work in a reflective way, identify aspects of it that are good and that could be improved, and then set personal targets for themselves' (National Council for Curriculum and Assessment (NCCA) 2007: 14). Where this is practised regularly, learners are enabled to play a more central role in the IEP process.

According to Klenowski and Wyatt-Smith (2014: 62) 'student learning and achievement can improve when students are given a role in assessment'. Self-assessment is very useful for getting learners to reflect on their own work rather than waiting for approval from an adult. One of the areas identified for development in the research was extending children's involvement in their own learning, through implementing explicit learner self-assessment strategies. What do you believe to be the benefits of learner self-assessment?

The benefits of learner self-assessment are manifold:

- It gives responsibility in learning.
- It promotes learners' decision-making.
- It facilitates learners in making choices.
- It develops a language of assessment for learners.
- It enhances the learner-teacher relationship.
- It allows learners to grow in confidence.
- It promotes intrinsic motivation.
- It helps learners to understand their learning profile.
- It enables learners to set learning targets.
- It develops meta-cognition.
- It supports self-regulation.

There are many ways in which self-assessment can be promoted. It is often necessary for learners with ASD to have processes modelled explicitly with teachers 'thinking aloud' or explaining the processes step by step until the learner can engage in the process confidently.

1. Use of learning objectives. At the beginning of a lesson a teacher can outline the learning expectations or intentions. This is linked to beneficial learning (Black and Wiliam 1998). This can be done in the form of a WALT chart (we are learning to ...) or a WILF chart (what I'm looking for) or can simply be a list of learning outcomes. This can be done in conjunction with explaining why this learning is necessary. It is essential that this is done in a learner-friendly way, for example, 'we are learning to add two sets', 'we are learning to play a board game' etc. At the end of the lesson, the learning objectives can be examined to see if learners have attained the learning outcomes. This can be done by the learners putting thumbs up or down to show their understanding,

through the use of symbols, for example, red/green cards or through class discussion.

2. Muijs and Reynolds (2011) recommend a plenary session at the end of a lesson to get the whole class to reflect on learning from the lesson. This gives the opportunity for modelling of appropriate language around self-assessment. This should be written on the board and displayed throughout the lesson. Learning intentions that are stated generically allow learners of all abilities to participate and achieve. The tasks can be differentiated as necessary to enable all learners to succeed (Bonfield and Horgan 2016).

3. Identification of likes and dislikes: Learners can indicate from a port-folio their favourite piece of work or a piece of work of which they are particularly proud. This works very well for learners who have difficulty with verbal communication. They can choose work to be displayed or work to be shown to others, which gives them a sense of empowerment.

4. Reflective prompts can be presented to learners as sentence stems rather than as questions as some learners have difficulty with question words. Some reflective prompts could be:

   a. I was able to ...
   b. The part I found difficult was ...
   c. I liked ...
   d. I didn't like ...
   e. I needed help with ...
   f. I am proud of ...
   g. I would like to learn more about ...
   h. I would like to do better in ...

5. Rubrics: According to Muijs and Reynolds (2011: 277), 'getting pupils to judge their own work on the basis of clear criteria can help them to reflect on their own performance, and develop their metacognitive skills ... this requires very clear and pupil-friendly criteria, and some training to help them to do this'. Rubrics describe levels of quality in a piece of work. Rubrics need to be carefully developed to enable learners to make judgements on their work.

6. Two stars, one wish: here learners can identify two areas of their work that they are proud of and a wish for what they can improve on. This can be modelled by the teacher until the learner is able to do it appropriately. This idea of a 'wish' or what the learner would like to be able to do better is also a strategy that can be used to engage the learner in their IEP process to enable their participation.

7. 'I can ...': Bonfield and Horgan (2016) describe the potential for learners to use 'I can' statements at the end of a lesson to self-assess their knowledge or skills. This can be developed into an assessment grid by the teacher to record the learner's self-assessment as shown in Table 12.4:

Table 12.4: Sample 'I Can' Self-Assessment Grid

I can	Ben	Oisín	Sarah	Áine	Maeve	Oscar	Najada	James
Hold my pencil correctly								
Start on the correct side of my copy								
Separate my words with a space								
Write my name on my worksheets								

Whichever approach is used, it is essential that the learner is given time and support to self-assess, as this skill forms the basis of many life skills.

Key Signposts: Learner Self-Evaluation/Self-Assessment

- Learner self-assessment is associated with greater self-efficacy, enhanced learning and outcomes and increased self-awareness.
- It supports learners to set personal targets in their learning and can, therefore, enable the learner to take a more central role in his/her IEP process.
- Learners require the implementation of specific learner self-assessment strategies such as use of learning objectives, identification of likes and dislikes, reflective sentence stems, rubrics, 'two stars and one wish' and/or 'I can' statements.

Conclusion

This chapter presented self-evaluation as a three-pronged concept encompassing teacher self-evaluation, education setting self-evaluation and learner self-evaluation. Self-evaluation was linked to both reflective practice and self-assessment. The benefits of each of the three prongs of self-evaluation were identified, thereby linking the concept with the ongoing improvement of the educational provision for children with ASD. If you are focused on improving the quality of teaching and learning of your students with ASD, as an individual teacher or as an education setting staff, then self-evaluation is certainly the way forward.

Bibliography

Ainscow, M. (2007). 'Taking an Inclusive Turn', *Journal of Research in Special Educational Needs*, 7(1), 3–7.

Antoniou, P., Myburgh-Louw, J., and Gronn, P. (2016). 'School Self-evaluation for School Improvement: Examining the measuring properties of the LEAD surveys', *Australian Journal of Education*, 60(3), 191–210.

Barton, L. (1998). *The Politics of Special Educational Needs*. Lewes: Falmer Press.

Bassot, B. (2016). *The Reflective Journal* (2nd edn). London: Palgrave Macmillan.

Black, P. J., and Wiliam, D. (1998). 'Inside the Black Box: Raising Standards through Classroom Assessment', *Phi Delta Kappan*, 80, 139–148.

Bonfield, T., and Horgan, K. (2016). *Learning to Teach, Teaching to Learn*. Dublin: Gill Education.

Booth, T., and Ainscow, M. (2002). *Index for Inclusion: Developing Learning and Participation in Schools*. Bristol: Centre for Studies on Inclusive Education.

Borton, T. (1970). *Reach Touch and Teach*. London: Hutchinson.

Clough, P. (2000). 'Routes to Inclusion'. In P. Clough and J. Corbett (eds), *Theories of Inclusive Education: A Student's Guide*, pp. 1–33. London: Sage.

Daly, P., Ring, E., Egan, M., Fitzgerald, J., Griffin, C., Long, S., McCarthy, E., Moloney, M., O'Brien, T., O'Byrne, A., O'Sullivan, S., Ryan, M., Wall, E., Madden, R. and Gibbons, S. (2016). *An Evaluation of Education Provision for Students with Autism Spectrum Disorder in Ireland.* Trim: National Council for Special Education.

Department of Education and Skills Inspectorate (2013). *Chief Inspector's Report 2010–2012.* Dublin: Department of Education and Skills Inspectorate.

Department of Education and Skills Inspectorate (2016). *School Self-Evaluation Guidelines 2016–2020: Primary.* Dublin: Department of Education and Skills Inspectorate.

Deng, M. (2010). 'Developing Inclusive Approaches to Teaching and Learning'. In R. Rose (ed.), *Confronting Obstacles to Inclusion,* pp. 204–212. Oxon: Routledge.

Driscoll, J. (2007). *Practising Clinical Supervision: A Reflective Approach for Healthcare Professionals.* (2nd edn). Edinburgh: Bailliere Tindall Elsevier.

Forbes, F. (2007). 'Towards Inclusion: An Australian perspective', *Support for Learning,* 22(2), 66–71.

Forlin, C. (2010a). 'Developing and Implementing Quality Inclusive Education in Hong Kong: Implications for teacher education', *Journal of Research in Special Educational Needs,* 10(1), 177–184.

Forlin, C. (2010b). 'Teacher Education for Inclusion'. In R. Rose (ed.), *Confronting Obstacles to Inclusion: International Responses to Developing Inclusive Education,* pp. 155–170, Oxon: Routledge.

Gibbs, G. (1988). *Learning by Doing: A Guide to Teaching and Learning Methods.* Oxford: Further Education Unit, Oxford Polytechnic.

Hornby, G., Atkinson, M., and Howard, J. (1997). *Controversial Issues in Special Education.* London: David Fulton Publishers.

Howley, M., and Kime, S. (2003). 'Policies and Practice for the Management of Individual Learning Needs'. In C. Tilstone, and R. Rose (eds), *Strategies to Promote Inclusive Practice,* pp. 18–33, London: RoutledgeFalmer.

Janssen, F. J. G., and van Amelsvoort, G. H. W. C. H. (2008). 'School Self-evaluation and School Inspections in Europe: An exploratory study', *Studies in Educational Evaluation,* 34, 15–23.

Kaikkonen, L. (2010). 'Promoting Teacher Development for Diversity'. In R. Rose (ed.), *Confronting Obstacles to Inclusion,* pp. 171–184. Oxon: Routledge.

Klenowski, V., and Wyatt-Smith, C. (2014). *Assessment for Education: Standards, Judgements and Moderation.* London: Sage Publications.

Koutrouba, K., Vamvakari, M., and Steliou, M. (2006). 'Factors Correlated with Teachers' Attitudes towards the Inclusion of Students with Special Educational Needs in Cyprus', *European Journal of Special Needs Education,* 21(4), 381–394.

Kyriakides, L., and Campbell, R. J. (2004). 'School Self-evaluation and School Improvement: A Critique of Values and Procedures', *Studies in Educational Evaluation,* 30, 23–36.

Leadership for INClusion in the Early Years Programme (2016-2018). *Reflections on Inclusion*, Leadership for INClusion in the Early Years Consortium: Mary Immaculate College, Limerick. Accessed online on 27 July 2018 at https://www.youtube.com/watch?v=AWlsokaaKQ4&feature=youtu.be

MacBeath, J. (1999). *Schools Must Speak for Themselves: The Case for School Self-evaluation*. London: Routledge.

Middletown Centre for Autism and National Council for Special Education (2013) *Evaluation Framework to underpin the Evaluation of Educational Provision for Students with ASD*, Trim: National Council for Special Education.

Mowat, J. (2009). 'The Inclusion of Pupils Perceived as Having Social and Emotional Behavioural Difficulties in Mainstream School: A focus upon learning', *Support for Learning*, 24(4), 159–169.

Muijs, D., and Reynolds, D. (2014). *Effective Teaching: Evidence and practice* (3rd edn). London: Sage.

National Council for Curriculum and Assessment (NCCA) (2007) *Assessment in the Primary School: Guidelines for Schools*. Dublin: Author.

National Council for Special Education (NCSE) (2011). *Inclusive Education Framework: A Guide for Schools on the Inclusion of Pupils with Special Educational Needs*. Trim: Author.

Osterman, K. F. and Kottkamp, R. B. (1993). *Reflective Practice for Educators: Professional development to improve student learning*. London: Sage Publications Ltd.

Pollard, A. (2014). *Reflective Teaching in Schools* (4th edn). London: Bloomsbury.

Rix, J., Hall, K., Nind, M., Sheehy, K., and Wearmouth, J. (2009). 'What Pedagogical Approaches Can Effectively Include Children with Special Educational Needs in Mainstream Classrooms? A systematic literature review', *Support for Learning*, 24(2), 86–94.

Rose, R., and Shevlin, M. (2010). *Count Me In!: Ideas for Actively Engaging Students in Inclusive Classrooms*. London: Jessica Kingsley.

United Nations (1989). *United Nations Convention on the Rights of the Child*. General Assembly Resolution 44/25, UN Doc. A/RES/44/25. Accessed online on 27 January 2018 at <http://www.childrensrights.ie/sites/default/files/UNCRCEnglish.pdf>.

Watkins, A., and Meijer, C. (2010). 'The Development of Inclusive Teaching and Learning'. In R. Rose (ed.), *Confronting Obstacles to Inclusion*, pp. 227–244. Oxon: Routledge.

Westwood, P. (2011). *Common Sense Methods for Children with Special Educational Needs* (6th edn). London: Routledge.

Appendix A: Blank SCOT Analysis Template

Area for Self-Evaluation:	
Strengths	Challenges
Opportunities	Threats

Appendix B: Blank 'What' Model of Reflection Template

What?
So What?
Now What?

Appendix C: Gibb's Reflective Cycle in Steps (Blank Template)

What happened?	
What were you thinking?	What were you feeling?
What was good about the experience/event?	What was bad about the experience/event?
What else can you make of the situation?	
What else could you have done?	
If it happened again what would you do?	

Appendix D: Reflections on Inclusion (Leadership for INClusion in the Early Years (LINC) Programme 2016–2018)

Reflections on Inclusion			

A. An Inclusive Culture

A	Reflections	Agree	Disagree	Unsure
1	All children are welcome.			
2	All children are valued.			
3	A focus is placed on promoting respectful interactions.			
4	There are high expectations for all children.			
5	Partnership with parents/carers is actively promoted.			
6	Difference is acknowledged and celebrated.			
7	The environment accommodates the needs of all children.			
8	All policies are inclusive policies.			

A. Inclusive Practice

B	Reflections	Agree	Disagree	Unsure
1	Transitioning to and from the setting is a positive experience for children, families and staff.			
2	Support for children with additional needs is co-ordinated.			
3	Staff members are encouraged to avail of continuing professional development opportunities.			

(Countinued)

Appendix D: (Continued)

B	Reflections	Agree	Disagree	Unsure
4	All staff are aware of their roles and responsibilities in relation to the promotion of inclusive practice.			
5	The expertise of staff is acknowledged and utilized.			

A. An Inclusive Pedagogy

C	Reflections	Agree	Disagree	Unsure
1	Children's experiences are planned with the needs of all children in mind.			
2	Strategies are in place to promote the participation of all children in learning.			
3	A range of appropriate pedagogical approaches is used to support the holistic development of all children.			
4	Play and playful learning are key features of practice for all children.			
5	All children's communication and interaction are promoted.			
6	All children's views are valued and responded to.			
7	Early identification of children who require additional support is central to practice.			
8	A variety of approaches to observation, recording and assessment is in place.			

C	Reflections	Agree	Disagree	Unsure
9	Early years educators plan, implement and evaluate children's learning in partnership with children, parents/carers and relevant others.			
10	Positive relationships are understood and nurtured.			
11	Children's specific assessed needs are understood as 'signposts' that support children's learning and development.			
12	External assistance is elicited where required to support the setting in meeting children's additional needs.			

Notes on Contributors

PATRICIA DALY is Head of the Department of Educational Psychology, Inclusive and Special Education at Mary Immaculate College (MIC), Limerick. She lectures on the Bachelor of Education programmes and also supervises students' research at undergraduate and postgraduate levels. She was Joint-Principal Investigator for the national evaluation of education provision for children with autism commissioned and recently published by the National Council for Special Education in Ireland. She has significant experience and expertise in the area of special education both in the US and in Ireland. She has specific expertise in the area of positively promoting children's engagement and is a qualified applied behaviour analyst.

MICHELE DUNLEAVY-LAVIN has a number of years' experience teaching in mainstream primary, special class and special school settings. She was seconded as an advisor to the Special Education Support Service (SESS) where she worked with teachers in primary, post-primary, special classes and special schools. In addition, she has worked as a part-time and guest lecturer in a number of colleges including NUI Galway, University College Cork and Trinity College Dublin. She also supervises undergraduate dissertations and Masters and doctoral theses. Her research interests lie in the area of autism spectrum difference (ASD) and inclusion, and she completed her Masters and PhD in these areas. She has presented at many conferences on the topic of ASD and inclusion, as well as publishing a number of journal articles in this area, and continues to conduct research in the area of special education. She is currently chairperson of the Irish Learning Support Association (ILSA).

MARGARET EGAN is a member of the Department of Educational Psychology, Inclusive and Special Education at Mary Immaculate College (MIC), Limerick. She was Deputy Principal and Special Educational Needs Co-ordinator in an all-boys' primary school before joining MIC in 2006.

Her Masters in Special Education researched Positive Behaviour Support (PBS), which included an examination of an emotional literacy programme at a school-wide level, and her PhD, on inclusive education policy and practice in primary schools, specifically examined models of support. Her research interests and teaching at undergraduate and postgraduate level include inclusion policy and practice, the language curriculum for students with special educational needs and social and emotional learning for all students, including those with autistic spectrum difference (ASD). She is currently supervising a number of Masters and PhD students in these fields.

SARAH FEENEY is a teacher in Scoil Chormaic Special School in Cashel, Co. Tipperary, which caters for the largest cohort nationwide of students with autism spectrum difference (ASD). She completed a Postgraduate Diploma in Special Educational Needs at Mary Immaculate College (MIC), Limerick, followed by a Masters in Special Education at St Patrick's College, Drumcondra, Dublin. She has worked as a part-time lecturer with the Department of Educational Psychology, Inclusive and Special Education at MIC, lecturing in the area of special and inclusive education for pre-primary, primary and post-primary teachers. She is currently undertaking a research PhD studentship at MIC, funded by Middletown Centre for Autism and entitled 'Structured and Effective Sensory Activities for Children with Autism Spectrum Differences', under the guidance of Dr Patricia Daly and Dr Emer Ring.

JOHANNA FITZGERALD is a lecturer in the Department of Educational Psychology, Inclusive and Special Education at Mary Immaculate College (MIC), Limerick. She teaches across a broad range of programmes including the Bachelor of Education in Primary Teaching, Postgraduate Diploma in Special Educational Needs and the Doctorate in Educational and Child Psychology. Her background is in post-primary education and teacher professional development. Her current research interests include leadership in education, with a particular emphasis on the role of Special Educational Needs Coordinators (SENCOs), teacher professional learning, and inclusive and special education.

CLAIRE GRIFFIN is an educational psychologist and lecturer in educational and developmental psychology at Mary Immaculate College (MIC),

Limerick. She originally worked within primary and special education settings, as well as in residential care centres for children and adults with physical and intellectual disabilities. Following postgraduate training in special education and educational psychology, she undertook PhD studies through University College London under the supervision of Professor Peter Blatchford. Her research pertains to the preparedness and deployment of 'Special Needs Assistants' when supporting children's behavioural care needs and independence development in mainstream primary school settings. She has also worked on a number of national projects in Ireland related to inclusive education. Her additional research interests include educational assessment, Precision Teaching, student engagement and child-centred teaching/learning approaches.

SHIRLEY HEANEY was awarded a BA in Early Childhood Care and Education from Mary Immaculate College (MIC), Limerick in 2008 and an MSc in Applied Behaviour Analysis from the National University of Ireland, Galway (NUIG) in 2010. She has ten years' experience of teaching children with additional needs in the field of early childhood education. She is currently working as a co-developer and tutor with the award-winning Leadership for Inclusion (LINC) in the Early Years Programme, and as a lecturer in the Department of Reflective Pedagogy and Early Childhood Studies in MIC. She is also completing her PhD on the wellbeing of children with additional needs in the early childhood setting under the guidance of Dr. Emer Ring, Dr. Lisha O'Sullivan and Dr. Jennifer Pope.

STELLA LONG is a lecturer in inclusive and special education at Mary Immaculate College (MIC), Limerick. Prior to joining the Faculty of Education at MIC, she taught at primary level, both in mainstream and in special education contexts. Graduating from MIC with a Masters in Special Education, she then completed her PhD at Trinity College Dublin. Her research focused on special education teacher learning in mathematics. Shea lectures on a number of undergraduate and postgraduate programmes at MIC and has a particular interest and expertise in the teaching and learning of mathematics to pupils with special educational needs/learning difficulties.

ANNE O'BYRNE began her career as a primary school teacher in special classes for children with additional needs. Having spent fourteen years teaching in primary schools, she joined Mary Immaculate College (MIC), Limerick, and she has worked in the areas of early childhood care and education, inclusive and special education for the last twenty years. From 2011 to 2014 she was a member of the National Co-ordinating Group for Progressing Disability Services for Children and Young People and two of its subcommittees, namely, the National Health and Education Working Group (2011–2013) and the National Standards and Performance Reporting Working Group (2012). In 2015 she was a member of the team who evaluated education provision for students with ASD in Ireland. Currently, she is a member of the National Outcomes for Children and Families Framework Implementation Group. She is also a parent of a child with additional needs and has first-hand experience of the importance of positive communication between home and school to create inclusive school cultures at pre-school, primary school and post-primary school levels.

LISHA O'SULLIVAN is currently Acting Head of the Department of Reflective Pedagogy and Early Childhood Studies at Mary Immaculate College (MIC), Limerick. She lectures on the Bachelor of Arts in Early Childhood Care and Education Programme programme and the Bachelor of Education programmes at MIC and also supervises students' research at undergraduate, Masters and PhD levels. A qualified play therapist, she has extensive experience in the area of early childhood education and her research interests include developmentally appropriate pedagogy and curricula in the early years, self-regulation and play. She has published widely in these areas.

EMER RING is Head of the Department of Reflective Pedagogy and Early Childhood Studies at Mary Immaculate College (MIC), Limerick. She is also Course Leader for the Bachelor of Arts in Early Childhood Care and Education Programme programme at MIC. She lectures on the BAECCE and the Bachelor of Education programmes and also supervises students' research at undergraduate and postgraduate levels. Emer is consultant placement supervisor for students during practicum experiences. She was Joint-Principal Investigator for the national evaluation of education provision for children with autism commissioned and recently published by the National Council for Special Education in Ireland. She is also a member of the steering committee for the multi-award-winning Leadership for INClusion in the Early Years (LINC) programme. Her research interests include policy and practice in early childhood and primary education, inclusion and autism, and she has published and presented widely in these areas.

MARIE RYAN is an educational psychologist and lectures on developmental and educational psychology at Mary Immaculate College (MIC), Limerick, where she is a member of the Department of Reflective Pedagogy and Early Childhood Studies. She lectures on the Bachelor of Arts in Early Childhood Care and Education programme and the Bachelor of Education programmes at MIC. She has extensive experience in the area of early childhood education and her research interests include developmental and educational psychology, assessment, inclusion and the concept of the teacher as researcher. She has published widely in these areas.

SHARON SKEHILL has worked in the field of early years' education and care for twelve years, as Room Leader and Manager of a full day care facility in Galway, and has led her staff team through the Síolta Quality Assurance Process under Early Childhood Ireland. She began her academic studies by completing a BA in NUI Galway, followed by a Masters of Philosophy in Irish Studies. Following on from her work as a resource teacher for Travellers, she returned to education to complete a Diploma in Community Development and a Diploma in Adult Teaching and Learning with NUI Galway. She has spent several years teaching the QQI Level 5 and 6 ECCE course with Galway Roscommon ETB and Early Childhood Ireland, and completed a Masters in Childhood and Adolescent Studies in 2014. She is currently pursuing a PhD in Education with Mary Immaculate College, Limerick under the guidance of Dr. Emer Ring, Dr. Lisha O'Sullivan and Dr. Kathleen Horgan. She is also working as a co-developer and tutor with the award-winning Leadership for Inclusion (LINC) in the Early Years Programme.

FIONNUALA TYNAN worked as a primary teacher, a facilitator for the School Development Planning Service (Primary) and as an inspector with the Department of Education and Skills prior to joining Mary Immaculate College, Limerick in September 2015. She is a member of the Department of

Reflective Pedagogy and Early Childhood Studies. She lectures across a wide range of programmes and is the co-ordinator of the Graduate Certificate in Autism Studies, a programme which is run jointly by MIC and Middletown Centre for Autism. Her research interests include Williams Syndrome, inclusive and special educational methodologies, anxiety, individual education planning, learner voice, self-perception of learners with SEN and wellbeing.

EUGENE WALL is President of Mary Immaculate College (MIC), Limerick. He is an educational psychologist and lectures on developmental and educational psychology at MIC. He served for twenty-one years on the Council of the National Council for Curriculum and Assessment (NCCA). He has a wide range of experience nationally and internationally in initial teacher education policy and practice and is co-author of the MICRA-T and the SIGMA-T, two of the most widely used standardized assessment and measurement tests used in Irish primary schools.

Index